HIDDEN ®

Kauai

HIDDEN ®

Kauai

Including Hanalei, Princeville and Poipu

Ray Riegert

THIRD EDITION

Ulysses Press®

BERKELEY, CALIFORNIA

Published by:
ULYSSES PRESS
P.O. Box 3440
Berkeley, CA 94703
www.ulyssespress.com

ISSN 1535-8380
ISBN 1-56975-502-7

Printed in Canada by Transcontinental Printing

10 9 8 7 6 5

UPDATE AUTHOR: Joan Conrow
EDITORIAL DIRECTOR: Leslie Henriques
MANAGING EDITOR: Claire Chun
COPY EDITOR: Barbara Schultz
EDITORIAL ASSOCIATES: Kate Allen, Kathryn Brooks, Lily Chou, Nicholas Denton-Brown
PRODUCTION: Lisa Kester, Matt Orendorff
CARTOGRAPHY: Pease Press
COVER DESIGN: Sarah Levin, Leslie Henriques
INDEXER: Sayre Van Young
COVER PHOTOGRAPHY: Douglas Peebles (Wailua Falls)
ILLUSTRATOR: Doug McCarthy

Distributed in the United States by Publishers Group West

To Mignon,
the Great Mamu—with Aloha

What's Hidden?

At different points throughout this book, you'll find special listings marked with this symbol:

◀ HIDDEN

This means that you have come upon a place off the beaten tourist track, a spot that will carry you a step closer to the local people and natural environment of Kauai.

The goal of this guide is to lead you beyond the realm of everyday tourist facilities. While we include traditional sightseeing listings and popular attractions, we also offer alternative sights and adventure activities. Instead of filling this guide with reviews of standard hotels and chain restaurants, we concentrate on one-of-a-kind places and locally owned establishments.

Our authors seek out locales that are popular with residents but usually overlooked by visitors. Some are more hidden than others (and are marked accordingly), but all the listings in this book are intended to help you discover the true nature of Kauai and put you on the path of adventure.

Write to us!

If in your travels you discover a spot that captures the spirit of Kauai, or if you live in the region and have a favorite place to share, or if you just feel like expressing your views, write to us and we'll pass your note along to the author.

We can't guarantee that the author will add your personal find to the next edition, but if the writer does use the suggestion, we'll acknowledge you in the credits and send you a free copy of the new edition.

ULYSSES PRESS
P.O. Box 3440
Berkeley, CA 94703
E-mail: readermail@ulyssespress.com

Contents

Maps

Kauai

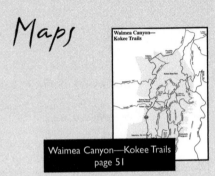

Waimea Canyon—
Kokee Trails

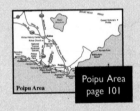

Poipu Area

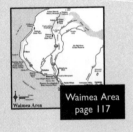

Waimea Area

Wailua–Kapaa Area

North Shore

OUTDOOR ADVENTURE SYMBOLS

The following symbols accompany national, state and regional park listings, as well as beach descriptions throughout the text.

▲	Camping		Windsurfing
	Swimming		Canoeing or Kayaking
	Snorkeling or Scuba Diving		Boating
	Surfing		Boat Ramps
	Waterskiing		Fishing

ONE

The Garden Isle

Seventy miles northwest of Oahu, across a rough, treacherous channel that long protected against invaders, lies Kauai. If ever an island deserved to be called a jewel of the sea, this "Garden Isle" is the one. Across Kauai's brief 33-mile expanse lies a spectacular and wildly varied landscape.

Along the north shore is the Hanalei Valley, a lush patchwork of tropical agriculture, and the rugged Na Pali Coast, with cliffs almost 3000 feet above the boiling surf. Spanning 14 miles of pristine coastline, the narrow valleys and sheer walls of Na Pali are so impenetrable that a road entirely encircling the island has never been built. Here, among razor-edged spires and flower-choked gorges, the producers of the movie *South Pacific* found their Bali Hai. To the east flows the fabled Wailua River, a sacred area to Hawaiians that today supports a sizable population in the blue-collar towns of Wailua and Kapaa.

Along the south coast stretch the matchless beaches of Poipu, with white sands and an emerald sea that seem drawn from a South Seas vision. It was here in November 1982 that Hurricane Iwa, packing 110-mile-an-hour winds and carrying devastating storm surf, overwhelmed the island. Ironically, it was also this area that sustained some of the most severe damage when Hurricane Iniki struck on September 11, 1992.

The tourist enclave of Poipu gives way to rustic Hanapepe, an agricultural town asleep since the turn of the 20th century, and Waimea, where in 1778 Captain James Cook became the first Westerner to tread Hawaiian soil. In Kauai's arid southwestern corner, where palm trees surrender to cactus plants, snow-white beaches sweep for miles along Barking Sands and Polihale.

In the island's center, Mount Waialeale rises 5148 feet (Mount Kawaikini at 5243 feet is the island's tallest peak) to trap a continuous stream of dark-bellied clouds that spill more than 480 inches of rain annually, making this gloomy peak the wettest spot on Earth and creating the headwaters for the richest river system in all Hawaii—the Hanapepe, Hanalei, Wailua and Waimea rivers. Also draining Waialeale is the Alakai Swamp, a wilderness bog that covers 30 square miles of the island's interior. Yet to the west, just a thunderstorm away, lies a barren landscape seemingly borrowed from Arizona and featuring the 2857-foot-deep Waimea Canyon, the "Grand Canyon" of the Pacific.

The island of Kauai boasts one of the wettest spots on earth, but its southwestern flank resembles the Arizona desert!

From Lihue, Kauai's county seat and most important city, Route 50 (Kaumualii Highway) travels to the south while Route 56 (Kuhio Highway) heads along the north shore. Another highway climbs past Waimea Canyon into the mountainous interior.

Papayas, taro, coffee and bananas flourish in lush profusion along these roads and marijuana is grown deep in the hills and narrow valleys, but sugar is still a significant crop. Tourism, however, has overtaken agriculture in the Kauai economy and is becoming increasingly vital to the island's 58,450 population.

It's sad to see the decline of the sugar industry, which is intensifying demands to replace agricultural income with tourist dollars. But the Garden Isle still offers hidden beaches and remote valleys to any traveler possessing a native's sensibility. And even though sugar is in retreat, some cane fields are still evident across the western side of the island. A number of years ago, Kauai provided a window on 19th-century life, when sugar was king. Deep-green stalks covered the landscape in every direction, edging from the lip of the ocean to the foot of the mountains. But foreign competition and a waning industry have led to many cane fields being left fallow or converted to asparagus, papaya and various truck crops and gentlemen's estates.

Nevertheless, one sugar mill is still redolent with the cloyingly sweet smell of cane, and on the westside mammoth cane trucks, sugar stalks protruding like bristles from a wild boar, continue to charge down dusty roads. Depending on the phase of the growing cycle, visitors pass fields crowded with mature cane, tall as Midwest corn, or deep-red earth planted with rows of seedlings. In the evening, when harvested cane is set afire, black smoke billows from deep within the fields.

Historically, Kauai is Hawaii's premier island—the first to be created geologically and the first "discovered" by white men. It was here that Madame Pele, goddess of volcanos, initially tried to make her home. Perhaps because of the island's moist, tropical climate, she failed to find a place dry enough to start her fire and left in frustration for the islands to the southeast.

Formed by a single volcano that became extinct about five million years ago, Kauai is believed by some anthropologists to be the original Hawaiian island populated by Polynesians. After Captain Cook arrived in 1778, explorers continued to visit the island periodically. Ten years later, settlers began to arrive, and in 1820 the first missionaries landed in the company of Prince George, son of Kauai's King Kaumualii. By 1835, the Koloa sugar plantation was founded, becoming the first successful sugar mill on Kauai.

Kauai was the site not only of the original but the anomalous, as well. In 1817, George Scheffer, a Prussian adventurer representing Czar Nicholas of Russia, built a fort in Waimea. He soon lost the support of both the Czar and Kauai's King Kaumualii, but left as his legacy the stone ruins of Russia's imperialist effort.

Kauai was the only island not conquered by Kamehameha the Great when he established the Hawaiian kingdom. Thwarted twice in his attempts to land an attack force—once in 1796 when high seas prevented an invasion from Oahu and again in 1802 when his battle-ready army was suddenly ravaged by disease—he finally won over Kaumualii by diplomacy in 1810.

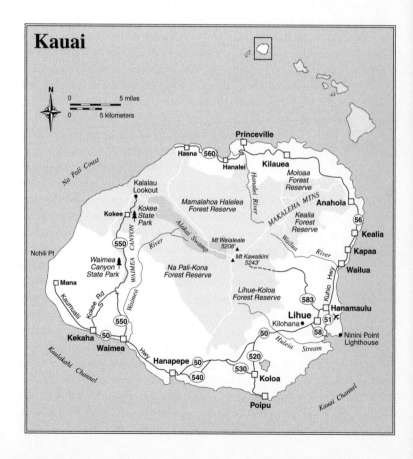

But Kauai's most fascinating history is told by mythmakers recounting tales of the *Menehune*, the Hobbits of the Pacific. These miniature forest people and fishermen labored like giants to create awesome structures. Mysterious ruins such as the Menehune Fishpond outside Lihue reputedly date back before the Polynesians and are attributed by the mythically inclined to an earlier, unknown race. Supernaturally strong and very industrious, the *Menehune* worked only at night, completing each project by dawn or else leaving it forever unfinished. Several times they made so much noise in their strenuous laboring that they frightened birds as far away as Oahu.

According to legend, they were a merry, gentle people with ugly red faces and big eyes set beneath long eyebrows. Two to three feet tall, each practiced a trade in which he was a master. They inhabited caves, hollow logs and banana-leaf huts, and eventually grew to a population of 50,000 adults.

Some say the *Menehune* came from the lost continent of Mu, which stretched across Polynesia to Fiji before it was swallowed by floods. Where they finally traveled to is less certain. After the Polynesians settled Kauai, the *Menehune* king, concerned that his people were intermarrying with an alien race, ordered the *Menehune* to leave the island. But many, unwilling to depart so luxurious a home, hid in the forests. There, near hiking trails and remote campsites, you may see them even today.

When to Go

SEASONS

There are two types of seasons in Kauai, one keyed to tourists and the other to the climate. The peak tourist seasons run from mid-December until Easter, then again from mid-June through Labor Day. Particularly around the Christmas holidays and in August, the visitors centers are crowded. Prices increase, hotel rooms and rental cars become harder to reserve, and everything moves a bit more rapidly. Shop around, however; package deals that include discounts on published rates are available.

If you plan to explore Kauai during these seasons, make reservations several months in advance; actually, it's a good idea to make advance reservations whenever you visit. Without doubt, the off-season is the best time to hit the island. Not only are hotels more readily available, but campsites and hiking trails are also less crowded.

Climatologically, the ancient Hawaiians distinguished between two seasons—*kau*, or summer, and *hooilo*, or winter. Summer extends from May to October, when the sun is overhead and the temperatures are slightly higher. Winter brings more variable winds and cooler weather.

Hawaiian Getaway

Three-day Itinerary

Day 1
- Arrive at the airport in Lihue and drive to the Poipu area. Check in to your condominium or hotel and spend the afternoon relaxing on the beach.

- Have dinner in one of Poipu's many restaurants or venture up to Koloa Town to dine.

Day 2
- Drive out Route 50, stopping in **Hanapepe** (page 116) to peruse the local art galleries (page 125).

- Continue on Route 50, turning right on Route 550 out to what is called the Pacific's "Grand Canyon"—**Waimea Canyon** (page 119). Make sure to continue out to the end of the road to visit the **Kalalau Lookout**, which gives you an extraordinary view of the Kalalau Valley.

- If you want to continue out along Route 50 to the two-mile stretch of white sand at **Polihale State Park** (page 118)—you won't be disappointed.

Day 3
- This is the day to head up to the **North Shore** (assuming it's not raining there). First stop in Lihue at **Ma's Family Restaurant** (page 92) for a local-style breakfast.

- Drive on up to **Hanalei** (page 155) for a look around and to stock up on ice-cold water and other provisions. If you're adventurous, hike the first two miles of the **Kalalau Trail** (page 53) at the end of Route 560. If you're in a lazier mood, join the others relaxing at **Kee Beach** (page 157) and snorkeling along the reef.

- Plan to have dinner in Hanalei or Kapaa before returning to Poipu.

The important rule to remember about Kauai's beautiful weather is that it changes very little from season to season but varies dramatically from place to place. The average yearly temperature is about 78°, and during the coldest weather in January and the warmest in August, the thermometer rarely moves more than 5° or 6° in either direction. Similarly, sea water temperatures range comfortably between 74° and 80° year-round.

Ua mau ke ea o ka aina i ka pono, the state motto, means "The life of the land is perpetuated in righteousness."

Crucial to this luxurious semitropical environment is the trade wind that blows with welcome regularity from the northeast, providing a natural form of air conditioning. When the trades stop blowing, they are sometimes replaced by *kona* winds carrying rain and humid weather from the southwest. These are most frequent in the winter, when the island receives its heaviest rainfall.

While summer showers are less frequent and shorter in duration, winter storms are sometimes quite nasty. I've seen it pour for five consecutive days, until hiking trails disappeared and streets were awash. If you visit in winter, particularly from December to March, you're risking the chance of rain.

A wonderful factor to remember through this wet weather is that if it's raining where you are, you can often simply go someplace else. And I don't mean another part of the world, or even a different island. Since the rains generally batter the northeastern section of the island, you can usually head over to the south or west coast for warm, sunny weather.

CALENDAR OF EVENTS

Something else to consider in planning a visit to Kauai is the lineup of annual cultural events. For a thumbnail idea of what's happening, check the calendar below. You might just find that special occasion to climax an already dynamic vacation. For a comprehensive listing with current updates, check the Hawaii Visitors & Convention Bureau website: www.calendar.gohawaii.com/kauai. Another useful site is www.kauaifestivals.com.

JANUARY   There are no events scheduled in January.

FEBRUARY   **Lihue Area**   Thousands of new-to-you titles await at the **Kauai Community College Annual Used Book Sale.**

Waimea Area   Lei making and ukulele contests, entertainment, food booths and a canoe race are all part of the **Waimea Town Celebration.**

Throughout Kauai   Major festivities on Kauai mark the **Prince Kuhio Festival,** commemorating the birthdate of Prince Jonah Kuhio Kalanianaole, Hawaii's first delegate to the U.S. Congress. Athletes compete in the **Prince Kuhio Ironman/Ironwoman Canoe Race.**
North Shore   Bring the kids to Kilauea Point National Wildlife Refuge's **Family Ocean Fair,** where you'll find live entertainment, food and interactive exhibits on Hawaii's marine life.

MARCH

Throughout Kauai   Buddhist temples mark **Buddha Day,** the luminary's birthday, with special services. Included among the events are pageants, dances and flower festivals.

APRIL

Throughout Kauai   Lei Day (May 1) is enjoyed by people wearing flower leis and colorful Hawaiian garb. This island-wide festival features lei-making contests and entertainment.
Lihue Area   Competitions in Samoan, Tahitian and Maori dance draw spectators to the **Kauai Polynesian Festival,** held over Memorial Day weekend at Kukui Grove Park.
North Shore   The **Kilauea Point Lighthouse** celebrates its anniversary by allowing the public into its lantern room, where the 360-degree view pales beside the four-and-a-half-ton lantern. Classical musicians and Hawaiian performers team up to entertain at the **Prince Albert Music Festival** in Princeville. Children's hula, lei-making contests and artisan demonstrations round out the festivities.

MAY

Throughout Kauai   King Kamehameha Day (June 11), honoring Hawaii's first king, is commemorated with parades, chants, hula dances and exhibits.
Lihue Area   Performers of all ages entertain the crowd with Hawaiian, Tahitian, Maori and Samoan dances at Lihue's **Hula Exhibition of Polynesian Dance.**
Waimea Area   A barbecue and jam session gets things rolling at the **Kauai Cowboy Round-up** in Waimea; this week-long celebration of cowboy culture culminates with the Paniolo Challenge and Mule Races.

JUNE

Wailua–Kapaa Area   Top chefs from around the state whip up culinary tidbits for 2500 ticketholders at the **Taste of Hawaii,** set among the gardens of Smith's Tropical Paradise.

JULY

Throughout Kauai   Folk music and traditional dances are central to the Japanese **Obon** season, which honors the spirits of the deceased; festivities take place in Buddhist temples across the island.

Lihue Area   The **Concert in the Sky,** Kauai Hospice's annual Fourth of July fundraiser, attracts more than 8000 revelers who enjoy live entertainment, games, food and a firework display.

Poipu Area   Poipu celebrates its sugar heritage with **Koloa Plantation Days,** a week-long event featuring a sunset block party, ethnic cooking demonstrations, a rodeo, nature walks, a Polynesian revue and a parade through old Koloa Town.

AUGUST

Throughout Kauai   Local residents celebrate **Admission Day** (August 21), the date in 1959 when Hawaii became the 50th state.

Lihue Area   The **Kauai County Farm Bureau Fair,** held in Lihue's Vidinha Stadium, offers floral exhibits, a petting zoo, a livestock show, entertainment and food.

SEPTEMBER

Throughout Kauai   Participants vie in hula, song-writing and slack-key guitar competitions during the week-long **Kauai Mokihana Festival.**

OCTOBER

Throughout Kauai   The highlight of Kauai's cultural season is the **Aloha Festival,** a week-long celebration featuring parades, street parties and pageants.

Waimea   The **Emalani Festival** commemorates Queen Emma's historic trek up Waimea Canyon and into the Alakai Swamp with a royal procession, authentic hula, traditional Hawaiian music and exhibits at Kokee State Park.

Wailua–Kapaa Area   If coconut bowling sounds intriguing, head over to the **Coconut Festival** at Kapaa Beach Park, where food, games, crafts and contests pay homage to this tropical nut.

NOVEMBER

Lihue Area   The **Hawaii International Film Festival** screens feature films, documentaries and videos with an emphasis on Pacific Rim themes; the lineup includes movies from every corner of the world.

Poipu Area   Watch the pros drive and putt their way to Poipu
Bay Golf Course's 18th hole at the PGA **Grand Slam of Golf.**

Throughout Kauai   Buddha's enlightenment is commemorated   **DECEMBER**
with **Bodhi Day** ceremonies and religious services.

Lihue Area   Lihue's Rice Street radiates with Christmas spirit
during the **Festival of Lights,** when a parade of illuminated vehi-
cles and a craft fair usher in the holiday season.

Waimea Area   The **Waimea Town Parade of Lights** snakes
through the streets of this beachside town.

The **Hawaii Visitors & Convention Bureau,** a state-run   ▼▼▼▼▼▼▼▼▼▼
agency, is a valuable resource from which to obtain free   **Before You Go**
information on Kauai and the rest of Hawaii. With
branches on each of the four largest islands, the Bureau can help   **VISITORS**
plan your trip and then offer advice once you reach Kauai. The   **CENTERS**
Garden Isle office is called the **Kauai Visitors Bureau.** ~ 4334 Rice
Street, Suite 101, Lihue; 808-245-3971, 800-262-1400, fax 808-
246-9235; www.kauaivisitorsbureau.com. You can also contact
the main Hawaii Visitors & Convention Bureau office in Honolulu. ~ 2270 Kalakaua Avenue, Suite 801, Honolulu, HI 96815;
808-923-1811, 800-464-2924; www.gohawaii.com.

Another excellent resource is the **Hawaii State Public Library
System.** With branches in Hanapepe, Kapaa, Koloa, Lihue, Princeville and Waimea, this government agency provides facilities for
residents and non-residents alike. The libraries are good places

◆◆

A CIRCLE OF ALOHA

The lei—a symbol of Hawaii, along with grass skirts and palm trees. If you're
fortunate enough to be met at the airport by someone you know, chances
are you'll be wreathed in fragrant blossoms and kissed on both cheeks. But
if you come to the island as a stranger, give yourself this aromatic gift. Lei-
giving is a tradition that dates back to ancient times, when they were
used as head wreaths as well as flower necklaces in religious ceremonies
and were presented to the *alii.* The craft of lei-making continues to
thrive today. You can still find leis that incorporate ferns, *pukiawe* (red
berries), *lehua* blossoms and *maile* leaves into intricate works of art,
some having hundreds of blossoms and all made with *aloha.*

to find light beach-reading material as well as books on Hawaii. Visitors can check out books by simply applying for a library card (fee for nonresidents) with a valid identification card. ~ www.librarieshawaii.org.

PACKING

When I get ready to pack for a trip, I sit down and make a list of everything I'll need. It's a very slow, exact procedure: I look in closets, drawers and shelves, and run through in my mind the activities in which I'll participate, determining which items are required for each. After all the planning is complete and when I have the entire inventory collected in one long list, I sit for a minute or two, basking in my wisdom and forethought.

Since Hawaii does not practice daylight-saving, their time difference becomes one hour greater during the summer months.

Then I tear the hell out of the list, cut out the ridiculous items I'll never use, halve the number of spares among the necessary items, and reduce the entire contents of my suitcase to the bare essentials.

Before I developed this packing technique, I once traveled overland from London to New Delhi carrying two suitcases and a knapsack. I lugged those damned bundles onto trains, buses, jitneys, taxis and rickshaws. When I reached Turkey, I started shipping things home, but by then I was buying so many market goods that it was all I could do to keep even.

I ended up carrying so much crap that one day, when I was sardined in a crowd pushing its way onto an Indian train, someone managed to pick my pocket. When I felt the wallet slipping out, not only was I unable to chase the culprit—I was so weighted down with baggage that I couldn't even turn around to see who was robbing me!

I'll never travel that way again, and neither should you. Particularly when visiting Kauai, where the weather is mild, you should pack very light. The airlines permit two suitcases and a carry-on bag; try to take one suitcase and maybe an accessory bag that can double as a beach bag. Dress styles are very informal in the islands, and laundromats are ubiquitous, so you don't need a broad range of clothing items, and you'll require very few extras among the essential items.

Remember, you're packing for a semitropical climate. Take along a sweater or light jacket for the mountains, and a poncho to protect against rain. But otherwise, all that travelers on Kauai require are shorts, bathing suits, lightweight slacks, short-sleeved shirts and blouses, and summer dresses or muumuus. Rarely do visitors require sports jackets or formal dresses. Wash-and-wear fabrics are the most convenient.

For footwear, I suggest soft, comfortable shoes. Low-cut hiking boots or tennis shoes are preferable for hiking; for beachgoing, there's nothing as good as sandals.

There are several other items to squeeze in the corners of your suitcase—sunscreen, sunglasses, a towel and, of course, your copy of *Hidden Kauai*. You might also consider packing a mask, fins and snorkel, and possibly a camera.

If you plan on camping, you'll need most of the equipment required for mainland overnighting. You can get along quite comfortably with a lightweight tent and sleeping bag. You'll also need a knapsack, canteen, camp stove and fuel, mess kit, first-aid kit (with insect repellent, water purification tablets and Chapstick), toilet kit, hat, waterproof matches, flashlight and ground cloth.

Accommodations on Kauai range from funky cottages to bed-and-breakfast inns to highrise condos. You will find inexpensive family-run hotels, middle-class tourist facilities and world-class resorts.

LODGING

Whichever you choose, there are a few guidelines to help save money. Try to visit during the off-season, avoiding the high-rate periods during the summer and from Christmas to Easter. Rooms with mountain views are less expensive than oceanview accommodations. Another way to economize is by reserving a room with a kitchen. In any case, try to reserve far in advance.

To help you decide on a place to stay, I've described the accommodations not only by area but also according to price (prices listed are for double occupancy during the high season; prices may decrease in low season). *Budget* hotels are generally less than $60 per night for two people; the rooms are clean and comfortable, but lack luxury. The *moderately* priced hotels run $60 to $120, and provide larger rooms, plusher furniture and more attractive surroundings. At *deluxe*-priced accommodations you can expect to spend between $120 and $180 for a double in a hotel or resort. You'll check into a spacious, well-appointed room with all modern facilities; downstairs the lobby will be a fashionable affair, and you'll usually see a restaurant, lounge and a cluster of shops. If you want to spend your time (and money) in the island's very finest hotels, try an *ultra-deluxe* facility, which will include all the amenities and price well above $180.

Bed-and-Breakfast Inns   The bed-and-breakfast business in Kauai becomes more diverse and sophisticated every year. Today there are several referral services that can find you lodging on any of the islands. Claiming to be the biggest clearinghouse in the state, **Bed and Breakfast Honolulu (Statewide)** represents over 400 properties. ~ 3242 Kaohinani Drive, Honolulu, HI 96817; 808-595-7533, 800-288-4666, fax 808-595-2030; www.hawaiibnb.com.

The original association, **Bed and Breakfast Hawaii**, claims more than 200 locations. This Kauai-based service was founded in 1979 and is well-known throughout Hawaii. ~ P.O. Box 449, Kapaa, HI 96746; 808-822-7771, 800-733-1632, fax 808-822-2723; www.bandb-hawaii.com. For other possibilities, contact **Hawaiian Islands Bed & Breakfast**. ~ 808-261-7895, 800-258-7895, fax 808-262-2181; www.lanikaibeachrentals.com.

You can also try the Maui-based **Affordable Accommodations,** which offers help finding all types of lodging. ~ 2825 Kauhale Street, Kihei, HI 96753; 808-879-7865, 888-333-9747, fax 808-874-0831; www.affordablemaui.com. Or call **All Islands Bed & Breakfast**, an Oahu-based reservation service that represents over 700 bed and breakfasts. ~ 463 Iliwahi Loop, Kailua, HI 96734; 808-263-2342, 800-542-0344, fax 808-263-0308; www.all-islands.com.

While the properties represented by these agencies range widely in price, **Hawaii's Best Bed & Breakfasts** specializes in small, upscale accommodations on all the islands. With about 100 establishments to choose from, it places guests in a variety of privately owned facilities; most are deluxe priced. ~ P.O. Box 563, Kamuela, HI 96743; 808-885-4550, 800-262-9912, fax 808-885-0559; www.bestbnb.com.

Condos   Many people visiting Kauai, especially those traveling with families, find that condominiums are often cheaper than hotels. While some hotel rooms come with kitchenettes, few provide all the amenities of condominiums. A condo, in essence, is an apartment away from home. Designed as studio, one-, two- or three-bedroom apartments, they come equipped with full kitchen facilities and complete kitchenware collections. Many also feature

Vacation Rentals on Kauai

Aloha Rental Hanalei Vacations 800-487-9833; www.800hawaii.com

Castle Resorts & Hotels 800-367-5004; www.castleresorts.com

Century 21 All Islands 808-242-2421; www.pacparadise.com

Grantham Resorts 800-325-5701; www.grantham-resorts.com

Hanalei North Shore Properties 800-488-3336; www.rentalson kauai.com

Hanalei Vacations 808-826-7288, 800-487-9833; www.hanalei-vacations.com

Harrington's Paradise Properties 808-826-9655, 888-826-9655; www.oceanfrontkauai.com

Kauai Vacation Rentals 800-367-5025; www.kauaivacationrentals.com

Marc Resorts Hawaii 800-535-0085; www.marcresorts.com

Na Pali Properties 800-715-7273; www.napaliprop.com

Oceanfront Realty 808-826-6585, 800-222-5541; www.oceanfront realty.com

Outrigger Hotels & Resorts 800-688-7444; www.outrigger.com

Pleasant Hawaiian Holidays 800-742-9244; www.pleasant holidays.net

Poipu Beach Resort Association 808-742-7444; www.poipu-beach.org

Poipu Connection 800-742-2260; www.poipuconnection.com

Premier Resorts 800-225-2683; www.premier-resorts.com

Prosser Realty 800-767-4707; www.prosser-realty.com

R & R Realty & Rentals 808-742-7555, 800-367-8022; www.r7r.com

Regency Pacific Realty 800-826-7782; www.regencypacificrealty.com

ResortQuest Hawaii 877-997-6667; www.resortquesthawaii.com

Suite Paradise 800-367-8020; www.suite-paradise.com

washer/dryers, dishwashers, air conditioning, color televisions, telephones, lanais and community swimming pools.

Utilizing the kitchen will save considerably on your food bill; by sharing the accommodations among several people, you'll also cut your lodging bill.

DINING   A few guidelines will help you chart a course through Kauai's countless dining places. Each restaurant entry is described as budget, moderate, deluxe or ultra-deluxe in price.

To establish a pattern for Kauai's parade of dining places, I've described not only the cuisine but also the ambience of each establishment. Restaurants listed offer lunch and dinner unless otherwise noted.

Dinner entrées at *budget* restaurants usually cost $8 or less. The ambience is informal café style and the crowd is often a local one. *Moderately* priced restaurants range between $8 and $16 at dinner and offer pleasant surroundings, a more varied menu and a slower pace. *Deluxe* establishments tab their entrées above $16, featuring sophisticated cuisines, plush decor and more personalized service. *Ultra-deluxe* restaurants generally price above $24.

Breakfast and lunch menus vary less in price from restaurant to restaurant. Even deluxe-priced kitchens usually offer light breakfasts and lunch sandwiches, which place them within a few dollars of their budget-minded competitors. These early meals can be a good time to test expensive restaurants.

Be sure to check Kauai's newspapers for listings of local luaus. These fundraisers are a great way to mingle with locals while dining on island food at bargain prices.

TRAVELING   Kauai is an ideal vacation spot for family holidays. The pace is slow,
WITH   the atmosphere casual. A few guidelines will help ensure that
CHILDREN   your trip to the islands brings out the joys rather than the strains of parenting, allowing everyone to get into the *aloha* spirit.

Use a travel agent to help with arrangements; they can reserve spacious bulkhead seats on airlines and determine which flights are least crowded. They can also seek out the best deals on inexpensive condominiums, saving you money on both room and board. Some resorts and hotels have daily programs for kids during the summer and holiday seasons. Hula lessons, lei making, storytelling, sandcastle building and various sports activities keep *keiki* (kids) over six happy while also giving Mom and Dad

Camps for Kids

When parents need a break and kids want some pint-sized action, it's worthwhile to check out the *keiki* camps sponsored by the major resorts. These programs offer a range of supervised craft and play activities, and they generally emphasize some aspect of the Hawaiian culture. Half- and full-day sessions are the norm, with some also providing night camps. Many resorts also feature special packages, services and activities for families, so inquire when making travel plans.

The **Hyatt Regency Kauai Beach Resort** serves kids 3½ to 12 at Camp Hyatt. Both day and night programs are offered year-round, with activities that highlight Hawaiian culture, history and environment. These include nature walks, water games, arts and crafts, snorkeling, designing sand paintings and lei making. ~ 1571 Poipu Road; 808-742-1234; www.kauai-hyatt.com.

The **Sheraton Kauai Resort** caters to those ages 3 to 12 with its Keiki Aloha Children's Program. Year-round activities include various Hawaiian arts and crafts, lei making, kite flying, ukulele lessons and supervised outdoor games. ~ 2440 Hoonani Road; 808-742-4016; www.sheraton-hawaii.com.

At the **Kauai Marriott Resort and Beach Club**, the Kalapaki Kids Club offers activities like learning hula, ukulele, Hawaiian songs, lei making and lauhala weaving. Offered year-round Tuesday through Saturday for kids 5 to 12 years. ~ 3610 Rice Street; 808-245-5050; www.marriott.com.

A summertime Keiki Aloha program is among the guest services at the **Princeville Hotel**. Children 5 to 12 years can learn Hawaiian crafts, build sandcastles and play beach and pool games during the day, and watch movies in the evening. Offered Monday through Saturday from June 1 to August 31, Wednesday and Friday the rest of the year. ~ 5520 Ka Haku Road; 808-826-9644; www.princeville.com.

a break (see "Camps for Kids" feature). As an added bonus, these resorts offer family plans, providing discounts for extra rooms or permitting children to share a room with their parents at no extra charge. Check with your travel agent.

When traveling around Christmas, Easter and during the summer high season, it's wise to book reservations as far in advance as possible.

Planning the trip with your kids stimulates their imagination. Books about travel, airplane rides, beaches, whales, volcanos and Hawaiiana help prepare even a two-year-old for an adventure. This preparation makes the "getting there" part of the trip more exciting for children of all ages.

And "getting there" means a long-distance flight. Plan to bring everything you need on board the plane—diapers, food, books, toys and extra clothing for kids and parents alike. I found it helpful to carry a few new toys and books as treats to distract my son and daughter when they got bored. When they were young children, I also packed extra snacks.

Allow extra time to get places. Book reservations in advance and make sure that the hotel or condominium has the extra crib, cot or bed you require. It's smart to ask for a room at the end of the hall to cut down on noise. And when reserving a rental car, inquire to see if they provide car seats and if there is an added charge. Hawaii has a strictly enforced car-seat law.

Besides the car seat you may have to bring along, also pack shorts and T-shirts, a sweater, sun hat, sundresses and waterproof sandals. A stroller with sunshade for little ones helps on sightseeing sojourns; a shovel and pail are essential for sandcastle building. Most importantly, remember to bring a good sunscreen. The quickest way to ruin a family vacation is with a bad sunburn. Also plan to bring indoor activities such as books and games for evenings and rainy days.

Most towns have stores that carry diapers, food and other essentials. However, prices are much higher in Kauai. To economize, some people take along an extra suitcase filled with diapers and wipes, baby food, peanut butter and jelly, etc.

A first-aid kit is always a good idea. Also check with your pediatrician for special medicines and dosages for colds and diarrhea. If your child does become sick or injured on Kauai, contact **Wilcox Memorial Hospital and Health Center.** ~ 808-245-1100. There's also a **Hawaii Poison Center** in Honolulu. ~ 808-941-4411.

Hotels often provide access to babysitters for a fee. The Banyan Harbor Resort in Lihue; Hyatt Regency Kauai Resort & Spa in Poipu; Kauai Sands Hotel in Wailua; and the Princeville Resort in Princeville all provide these referrals.

WOMEN TRAVELING ALONE

Traveling solo grants an independence and freedom different from that of traveling with a partner, but single travelers are more vulnerable to crime and should take additional precautions. An option for those who are alone but prefer not to be is to join a tour group.

It's unwise to hitchhike and probably best to avoid camping alone; the money saved does not outweigh the risk. Bed and breakfasts, youth hostels and YWCAs are generally your safest bet for lodging, and they also foster an environment ideal for bonding with fellow travelers.

Keep all valuables well-hidden and hold on to cameras and purses. Avoid late-night treks or strolls along beaches, or walks through undesirable parts of town, but if you find yourself in this situation, continue walking with a confident air until you reach a safe haven. A fierce scowl never hurts.

These hints should by no means deter you from seeking out adventure. Wherever you go, stay alert, use your common sense and trust your instincts.

On Kauai, the YWCA **Sexual Assault Crisis Line** can help you in case of emergency; representatives offer counseling support and medical advocacy. ~ 808-245-4144 (24-hour crisis response), 808-245-5959 (office).

For more helpful hints, get a copy of *Safety and Security for Women Who Travel* (Traveler's Tales).

GAY & LESBIAN TRAVELERS

The *Pocket Guide to Hawaii,* published by **Pacific Ocean Holidays,** is helpful for gay travelers. It comes out three times a year and lists the best and hottest establishments and beaches that Hawaii has to offer. Send $5 per copy (via mail only) if ordering from the mainland; otherwise, it's distributed free by local gay businesses. This outfit can also help book vacation packages. ~ P.O. Box 88245, Honolulu, HI 96830; 808-923-2400, 800-735-6600 reservations only; www.gayhawaii.com.

Spanning the entire Hawaiian chain, the Big Island–based **Black Bamboo Guest Services** unearths the best cottages and houses for gay and straight travelers. This service also arranges car rentals, hiking tours, birdwatching trips and other sporting activities for its guests. ~ P.O. Box 211, Kealakekua, HI; 808-328-9607, 800-527-7789; e-mail bbamboo@aloha.net.

For further information, be sure to look under "Gay-friendly travel" in the index at the end of the book.

SENIOR TRAVELERS Kauai is a hospitable place for senior citizens to visit. Countless museums, historic sights and even restaurants and hotels offer senior discounts that can cut a substantial chunk off vacation costs.

The **American Association of Retired Persons** (AARP) offers membership to anyone over 50. AARP's benefits include travel discounts with a number of firms. ~ 601 E Street NW, Washington, DC 20049; 800-424-3410; www.aarp.org.

Elderhostel offers reasonably priced, all-inclusive educational programs in a variety of locations throughout the year. One such program explores the culture and environmental history of Hanalei. Contact Elderhostel for more information. ~ 11 Avenue de Lafayette, Boston, MA 02111; 877-426-8056, fax 617-426-0701; www.elderhostel.org.

Be extra careful about health matters. Consider carrying a medical record with you—including your medical history and current medical status as well as your doctor's name, phone number and address. Make sure your insurance covers you while you are away from home. It is wise to have your doctor write out extra prescriptions in case you lose your medication. Always carry your medications on board your flight, not in your luggage.

MADE IN KAUAI

You know you have to bring Aunt Sarah a present from the islands. And *you* have to have something special to remind you of your days (and nights) on the island. *Hele* on down to the local Kauai souvenir shop and bring home some Kauai-made products like island papaya salsa, taro chips, Kauai coffee and *The Kauai Movie Book.* For inexpensive used island wear, check out the local thrift shops such as the Salvation Army and the Kauai Humane Society. And if you're in the area just before take-off, buy a lei at bargain prices from the Blue Orchid in Koloa or the People's Market in Puhi.

The **Commission on Persons with Disabilities** publishes a survey of the city, county, state and federal parks in Hawaii that are accessible to travelers with disabilities. They also provide "Aloha Guides to Accessibility," which cover Kauai as well as the other islands, and give information on various hotels, shopping centers, and restaurants that are accessible. ~ 919 Ala Moana Boulevard, Room 101, Honolulu, HI 96814; 808-586-8121, fax 808-586-8129; e-mail accesshi@aloha.net.

DISABLED TRAVELERS

The **Society for Accessible Travel & Hospitality** (SATH) offers information for travelers with disabilities. ~ 347 5th Avenue, Suite 610, New York, NY 10016; 212-447-7284, fax 212-725-8253; www.sath.org. **Travelin' Talk**, a network of people and organizations, also provides assistance. ~ P.O. Box 1796, Wheatridge, CO 80034; 303-232-2979; www.travelintalk.net. **Access-Able Travel Source** has worldwide information online. ~ 303-232-2979; www.access-able.com.

Be sure to check in advance when making room reservations. Some hotels feature facilities for those in wheelchairs.

Passports and Visas   Most foreign visitors are required to obtain a passport and tourist visa to enter the United States. Contact your nearest United States Embassy or Consulate well in advance to obtain a visa and to check on any other entry requirements.

FOREIGN TRAVELERS

Customs Requirements   Foreign travelers are allowed to carry in the following: 200 cigarettes (1 carton), 50 cigars or 2 kilograms (4.4 pounds) of smoking tobacco; one liter of alcohol for personal use only (you must be 21 years of age to bring in alcohol); and US$100 worth of duty-free gifts that include an additional quantity of 100 cigars. You may bring in any amount of currency, but must fill out a form if you bring in over US$10,000. Carry any prescription drugs in clearly marked containers. (You may have to produce a written prescription or doctor's statement for the customs officer.) Meat or meat products, seeds, plants, fruits and narcotics are not allowed to be brought into the United States. Contact the **United States Customs Service** for further information. ~ 1301 Constitution Avenue NW, Washington, DC 20229; 202-927-6724; www.customs.treas.gov.

Driving   If you plan to rent a car, an international driver's license should be obtained prior to arrival. Some rental car companies require both a foreign license and an international driver's license. Many car rental agencies require that the lessee be at least 25 years of age; all require a major credit card. Seat belts are mandatory for the driver and all passengers. Children under the age of 5 or weighing less than 40 pounds should be in the back seat in approved child safety restraints.

Currency   United States money is based on the dollar. Bills come in seven denominations: $1, $2, $5, $10, $20, $50 and $100. Every dollar is divided into 100 cents. Coins are the penny (1 cent), nickel (5 cents), dime (10 cents), quarter (25 cents), half-dollar (50 cents) and dollar (100 cents).

You may not use foreign currency to purchase goods and services in the United States. Consider buying traveler's checks in dollar amounts. You may also use credit cards affiliated with an American company such as Interbank, Barclay Card, VISA, MasterCard and American Express.

Electricity and Electronics   Electric outlets use currents of 110 volts, 60 cycles. For appliances made for other electrical systems, you need a transformer or adapter. Travelers who use laptop computers for telecommunication should be aware that modem configurations for U.S. telephone systems may be different from their European counterparts. Similarly, the U.S. format for video-tapes is different from that in Europe; U.S. Park Service visitors centers and other stores that sell souvenir videos often have them available in European format.

Weights and Measurements   The United States uses the English system of weights and measures. American units and their metric equivalents are as follows: 1 inch = 2.5 centimeters; 1 foot (12 inches) = 0.3 meter; 1 yard (3 feet) = 0.9 meter; 1 mile (5280 feet) = 1.6 kilometers; 1 ounce = 28 grams; 1 pound (16 ounces) = 0.45 kilogram; 1 quart (liquid) = 0.9 liter.

Transportation

GETTING TO THE ISLANDS

During the 19th century, sleek clipper ships sailed from the West Coast to Hawaii in about 11 days. Today, you'll be traveling by a less romantic but far swifter conveyance—the jet plane. Rather than days at sea, it will be about five hours in the air from California, nine hours from Chicago, or around 11 hours if you're coming from New York.

Chances are you'll be flying through Honolulu on your way into Kauai. **Honolulu International Airport** is served by Air Canada,

Air New Zealand, Aloha Airlines, American Airlines, China Airlines, Continental Airlines, Delta Airlines, Hawaiian Air, Korean Air, Northwest Airlines, Quantas, Philippines Airlines and United.

Visiting Kauai means flying to the centrally located **Lihue Airport**. ~ 808-246-1448. Aloha Airlines, Hawaiian Air, American Airlines, North American, Air Trans Air and United Airlines operate here.

The Lihue Airport has a restaurant, a cocktail lounge, lockers, a newsstand, a gift shop and a flower shop. What you won't find are buses, far more useful to most travelers than cocktails and flowers. Transportation (it's two miles into town) requires reserving a seat on a shuttle, renting a car, hailing a cab, hitching or hoofing. Cabs generally charge about $8 to Lihue.

Kauai's environment is fragile. Part of its natural beauty comes from its geographic isolation from alien ecosystems. Bringing in plants, produce or animals can introduce pests and non-endemic species that could eventually undermine the ecosystem.

Whichever carrier you choose, ask for the economy or excursion fare, and try to fly during the week; weekend flights are generally higher in price. To qualify for the lower fares, it is sometimes necessary to book your flight two weeks in advance and to stay in the islands at least one week. Generally, however, the restrictions are minimal. Children under two years of age can fly for free, but they will not have a seat of their own. Each passenger is permitted two large pieces of luggage plus a carry-on bag. Shipping a bike or surfboard will cost extra. (Be sure to check on the size restrictions.)

In planning a Hawaiian sojourn, one potential moneysaver is the package tour, which combines air transportation with a hotel room and other amenities. Generally, it is a style of travel that I avoid. However, if you can find a package that provides air transportation, a hotel or condominium accommodation and a rental car, all at one low price—it might be worth considering. Just try to avoid the packages that preplan your entire visit, dragging you around on air-conditioned tour buses. Look for the package that provides only the bare necessities, while allowing you the greatest freedom. Two experienced Hawaii packagers are **Suntrips** (800-786-8747; www.suntrips.com) and **Pleasant Hawaiian Holidays** (866-867-4567; www.hawaii-hawaii.com).

Getting between islands usually means hopping on a plane. There are ferries available between Maui, Molokai and Lanai, but the only commercial transportation to and from Kauai is by

**GETTING
BETWEEN
ISLANDS**

air. Aloha Airlines and Hawaiian Airlines, the state's major carriers, provide frequent inter-island jet service. If you're looking for smooth, rapid, comfortable service, this is certainly it. You'll be buckled into your seat, offered a low-cost cocktail and whisked to your destination within 20 to 40 minutes.

CAR RENTALS

Renting a car is as easy on Kauai as anywhere. The island supports several rental agencies, which compete fiercely with one another in price and quality of service. So before renting, shop around: check the listings in this book, and also look for special temporary offers that many rental companies sometimes feature.

There are several facts to remember when renting a car. First of all, a major credit card is essential. Also, many agencies don't rent at all to people under 25. Regardless of your age, many companies charge several dollars a day extra for insurance. The insurance is optional and expensive, and in many cases, unnecessary (many credit cards provide the same coverage when a rental is charged to the card). Find out if you credit card company offers this coverage. Your personal insurance policy may also provide for rental cars and, if necessary, have a clause added that will include rental car protection. Check on this before you leave home. But remember, whether you have insurance or not, you are liable for the first several thousand dollars in accident damage.

You might want to add some of the upscale resorts to your sightseeing itinerary. Several of them (Princeville Resort, Kauai Marriott, Hyatt Regency Kauai and the Sheraton) display excellent examples of Hawaiiana throughout their facilities.

Rates fluctuate with the season; slack tourist seasons are great times for good deals. Also, three-day, weekly and monthly rates are almost always cheaper than daily rentals. However, be sure to reserve in advance during holiday season—agencies can sell out.

I don't recommend renting a jeep. They're more expensive and less comfortable than cars, and won't get you to very many more interesting spots. In addition, the rental car collision insurance provided by most credit cards does not cover jeeps. Except in extremely wet weather when roads are muddy, all the places mentioned in this book, including the hidden locales, can be reached by car.

Across the street from the terminal at Lihue Airport you'll find a series of booths containing car-rental firms. These include **Alamo Rent A Car** (808-246-0645, 800-327-9633), **Avis Rent A**

Car (808-245-3512, 800-331-1212), **Budget Rent A Car** (808-245-9031), **Dollar Rent A Car** (866-434-2226, 800-800-4000) and **National Car Rental** (808-245-5636, 800-227-7368).

Budget Rent A Car has four-wheel drives. However, most Kauai roads, including cane roads, are accessible by car so you probably won't need a jeep. ~ Lihue Airport; 866-434-2226, 800-527-0700.

JEEP RENTALS

Kauai Bus is a shuttle that travels between Lihue and Hanalei seven times a day from 6:45 a.m. to 6 p.m. It stops at about a dozen places, including two major shopping centers. ~ 808-241-6410.

PUBLIC TRANSIT

Aloha Kauai Tours has half- and full-day, off-road four-wheel-drive tours into the mountains of Kokee State Park and other areas of the island. Bring comfortable walking shoes and binoculars, as the tours often include a hike. Lunch is included. ~ 808-452-1113; www.alohakauaitours.com.

JEEP TOURS

Whether you choose a whirlybird's-eye view from a helicopter or prefer the serenity of a glider, aerial sightseeing is one of Kauai's great thrills. From simple flyovers to thrilling acrobatic flights, you'll gain a unique perspective on the island's canyons and rainforests, hidden beaches and tropical retreats.

AERIAL TOURS

Island Helicopters offers a one-hour tour of all the major scenic areas of the island, from the Na Pali Coast to the Mount Waialeale Crater. ~ Lihue Airport; 808-245-8588, 800-829-5999.

Ohana Helicopter Tours provides a 50-minute Makihana tour that hits all the major sights of Kauai—Waimea Canyon, Sleeping Giant, and the Na Pali Coast. The 65-minute Maile Tour offers a more extensive view of the Na Pali Coast, Alakai Swamp and Kaapoko. Shuttle service is available from southern resorts. ~ Lihue Airport; 808-245-3996, 800-222-6989.

Heli USA, based in Princeville Airport, features unique glimpses of scenic treasures like Waialeale, the Na Pali Coast and Waimea Canyon. ~ 808-826-6591, 800-994-9099.

If you want an airplane tour, **Fly Kauai Tropical Bi-planes** will take you up in a bi-plane for a thrilling tour of the island. ~ Lihue Airport; 808-246-9123.

Niihau Helicopters specializes in trips to the Forbidden Isle. Bring your own snorkeling equipment because the twin-engine helicopter will land on one of the island's remote beaches, ideal for exploring its pristine underwater environment. Closed Sunday. ~ Kaumualii Highway; 808-335-3500.

WALKING TOURS Tours on the Hawaiian islands usually focus on outdoor adventures, but to limit your excursions to snorkeling and kayaking is to limit your appreciation of other aspects of Kauai. The **National Tropical Botanical Garden** administers a series of walking tours that concentrates on the beautiful landscaped gardens of the island. The McBryde Garden tour includes the natural history of the McBryde garden, and leads you through the Bamboo Bridge area, which features a fascinating collection of plants. The Allerton Garden tour narrows in on the beautiful retreat of Queen Emma, complete with sculpture and nearly extinct plants. Hint: Wear long pants and bring insect repellent. Reservations required. ~ 808-742-2623; www.ntbg.org.

Sugar plantation tours are available from **Gay & Robinson Tours, Inc.** Learn about the history of sugar on Kauai and catch behind-the-scenes glimpses of how family-owned Gay & Robinson, the last plantation surviving on Kauai, functions. Some tours focus primarily on factory operations while others venture into the fields to see where it all begins. At the **Waimea Sugar Mill Camp Museum,** you can join a tour that takes you through the paces of plantation life. You'll visit the residential community of the plantation workers and hear stories of their values, culture and community. ~ 808-335-2824; www.gandrtours-kauai.com, e-mail toursgandr@hawaiian.net.

TWO

The Land
and Outdoor Adventures

Kauai is part of the Hawaiian archipelago that stretches more than 1500 miles across the North Pacific Ocean. Composed of 132 islands, Hawaii has eight major islands, including Kauai, clustered at the southeastern end of the chain. Together these larger islands are about the size of Connecticut and Rhode Island combined. Only seven are inhabited: the eighth, Kahoolawe, served until recently as a bombing range for the U.S. Navy. Another island, Niihau, is privately owned and is primarily off-limits to the public.

Located 2500 miles southwest of Los Angeles, Kauai is on the same 20th latitude as Hong Kong and Mexico City. It's two hours earlier in Kauai than in Los Angeles, four hours earlier than Chicago and five hours earlier than New York. Since Hawaii does not practice daylight-saving, this time difference becomes one hour greater during the summer months.

Kauai, in a sense, is a small continent. Volcanic mountains rise in the interior, while the coastline is fringed with coral reefs and white-sand beaches. The northeastern face, buffeted by trade winds, is the wet side. The contrast between this side and the island's southwestern sector is sometimes startling. Dense rainforests in the northeast teem with exotic tropical plants, while across the island you'll see cactus growing in a barren landscape!

Although sugar is in decline, it is still a significant part of the island's agricultural economy along with coffee farms, taro farms, guava plantations and other produce venues. Statewide, and on Kauai, tourism is number one. About four million Americans and almost seven million travelers worldwide visit the state of Hawaii every year. It's now a $10.9 billion business that expanded exponentially during the 1970s and 1980s, leveled off in the 1990s and was on the rise until September 11, 2001, and the slow-down in air travel. It has since rebounded on Kauai.

GEOLOGY   More than 25 million years ago a fissure opened along the Pacific floor. Beneath tons of sea water molten lava poured from the rift. This liquid basalt, oozing from a hot spot in the earth's center, created a crater along the ocean bottom. As the tectonic plate that comprises the ocean floor drifted over the earth's hot spot, numerous other craters appeared. Slowly, in the seemingly endless procession of geologic time, a chain of volcanic islands, now stretching almost 2000 miles, has emerged from the sea.

On the continents it was also a period of terrible upheaval. The Himalayas, Alps and Andes were rising, but these great chains would reach their peaks long before the Pacific mountains even touched sea level. Not until about 25 million years ago did the first of these underwater volcanos, today's Kure and Midway atolls, break the surface and become islands. It was not until about five million years ago that the first of the main islands of the archipelago, Niihau and Kauai, broke the surface to become high islands.

For many millennia, the mountains continued to grow. The forces of erosion cut into them, creating knife-edged cliffs and deep valleys. Then plants began germinating: mosses and ferns, springing from windblown spores, were probably first, followed by seed plants carried by migrating birds and on ocean currents. The steep-walled valleys provided natural greenhouses in which unique species evolved, while transoceanic winds swept insects and other life from the continents.

Some islands never survived this birth process: the ocean simply washed them away. The first islands that did endure, at the northwestern end of the Hawaiian chain, proved to be the smallest. Today these islands, with the exception of Midway, are barren uninhabited atolls. The volcanos of Kauai and its sister islands, far to the southeast, became the mountainous archipelago generally known as the Hawaiian Islands.

RED HOT STUFF

Hawaii's two kinds of lava—*aa*, the rough basalt version, and *pahoehoe*, the rope-like rock—both have the same chemical composition. *Pahoehoe* usually flows in a series of small lobes and toes that constantly break out from the cooled crust while *aa* consists of spiny surfaces called clinkers.

Most of the plants you'll see on Kauai are not endemic, or native. In fact, much of the lush vegetation
of this tropical island found its way here from locations all over the world. Sea winds, birds and seafaring settlers
brought many of the seeds, plants, flowers and trees from the islands of the South Pacific, as well as from other, more distant regions. Over time, some plants adapted to Kauai's unique ecosystem and climate, creating strange new lineages and evolving into
a completely new ecosystem. This process has long interested scientists, who call the Hawaiian Islands one of the best natural labs
for studies of plant evolution. Unfortunately, other new arrivals
have become pests and invasive weeds.

Flora and Fauna

FLORA

Sugar cane arrived in Kauai with the first Polynesian settlers,
who appreciated its sweet juices. By the late 1800s, it was well
established as a lucrative crop. Burning sugar cane fields before
harvest increases the stalks' sugar content and gets rid of most of
the vermin in the fields. The pineapple was first planted during
the same century. A member of the bromeliad family, this spiky
plant is actually a collection of beautiful pink, blue and purple
flowers, each of which develops into a fruitlet. The pineapple is a
collection of these fruitlets, grown together into a single fruit that
takes 14 to 17 months to mature. Sugar cane and pineapple are
still the main crops in Hawaii, although competition from other
countries and environmental problems caused by pesticides have
taken their toll.

Visitors to Kauai will find the island a perpetual flower show.
Sweetly scented plumeria, deep red, shiny anthurium, exotic ginger, showy birds of paradise, small lavender crown flowers, highly
fragrant gardenias and the brightly hued hibiscus run riot on the
island and add color and fragrance to the surrounding area. Scarlet
and purple bougainvillea vines as well as the aromatic lantana,
with its dense clusters of flowers, are also found in abundance.

The beautiful, delicate orchid thrives in Kauai's tropical heat
and humidity. The most popular orchids are the *dendrobium*,
which can come in white, purple, lavender or yellow; the *vanda*
(bamboo orchid), which is fuschia and white and often used for
making leis; and the popcorn, which has small, yellow flowers.
The wild *vanda*, with its white and lavender petals, can be spotted along the side of the road year-round.

Each Hawaiian island has a specific bloom designated as its island flower; Kauai's pick is the *mokihana*, which is actually a light green berry. These berries, which produce an aroma reminiscent of anise, only grow in the Garden Isle's rainforests. *Mokihana* is often woven into leis with fragrant *maile* leaves.

The *olulu*, also know as *alula*, is endemic to Kauai and Niihau. Found on the Na Pali Coast and Haupu Ridge, this endangered plant is one of only two true succulents native to Hawaii. A dense rosette of green leaves cradles white blooms with tubular stalks.

Although many people equate the tropics with the swaying palm tree, Kauai is home to a variety of exotic trees. The famed banyan tree, known for pillarlike aerial roots that grow vertically downward from the branches, spreads to form a natural canopy. When the roots touch the ground, they thicken, providing support for the tree's branches to continue expanding. The state tree is the *kukui* or candlenut tree, which provided early Hawaiians with oil, light and a natural remedy. Originally brought to Kauai from the South Pacific islands, the *kukui* tree is big, bushy and prized for its nuts, which can be used for oil or polished and strung together to make leis. With its cascades of bright yellow or pink flowers, the cassia tree earns its moniker—the shower tree. Covered with tiny pink blossoms, the canopied monkeypod tree has fernlike leaves that close up at night.

Found in a variety of shapes and sizes, the ubiquitous palm does indeed sway to the breezes on white-sand beaches, but it also comes in a short, stubby form, the Samoan coconut, featuring more frond than trunk. The fruit, or nuts, of these trees are prized for their oil, which can be utilized for making everything from margarine to soap. The wood (rattan, for example) is often used for making furniture.

FRUITS AND VEGETABLES   There's a lot more to Kauai's tropical wonderland than gorgeous flowers and overgrown rainforests. The island also teems with edible plants. Roots, fruits, vegetables, herbs and spices grow like weeds from the shoreline to the mountains. Following is a list of some of the more commonly found edibles.

Avocado: Covered with either a tough green or purple skin, this pear-shaped fruit sometimes weighs as much as three pounds. It grows on ten- to forty-foot-high trees, and ripens from June through November.

Bamboo: The bamboo plant is actually a grass with a sweet root that is edible and a long stem frequently used for making furniture. Often exceeding eight feet in height, the most common bamboo is green until picked, when it turns a golden brown.

Banana: Polynesians use banana trees not only for food but also for clothing, medicines, dyes and even alcohol; culturally, it represents man. The fruit, which grows upside down on broad-leaved trees, can be harvested as soon as the first banana in the bunch turns yellow.

Opihi, with their dome-shaped shells, are a delicacy in Hawaii. Not only are they good to eat, they are also considered *aumakua*, or family gods, protecting the family from sharks and heavy surf.

Breadfruit: This large round fruit grows on trees that reach up to 60 feet in height. Like the banana and plantain, the breadfruit may be roasted in an underground oven on preheated rocks or baked with a little water in a pan. Sometimes it is cored and stuffed with coconut before roasting. Breadfruit is also candied, or sometimes prepared as a sweet pickle.

Coconut: The coconut tree is probably the most important plant in the entire Pacific. Every part of the towering palm is used. Most people are concerned only with the hard brown nut, which yields delicious milk as well as a tasty meat. If the coconut is still green, the meat is a succulent jellylike substance. Otherwise, it's a hard but delicious white rind.

Guava: A roundish yellow fruit that grows on a small shrub or tree, guavas are extremely abundant in the wild. They ripen between June and October.

Lychee: Found hanging in bunches from the lychee tree, this popular summer fruit is encased in red, prickly skin that peels off to reveal the sweet-tasting, translucent flesh.

Mango: Known as the king of fruits, the mango grows on tall shade trees. The oblong fruit ripens in the spring and summer.

Mountain apple: This sweet fruit grows in damp, shaded valleys at an elevation of about 1800 feet. The flowers resemble fluffy crimson balls; the fruit, which ripens from July to December, is also a rich red color.

Papaya: This delicious fruit, which is picked as it begins to turn yellow, grows on unbranched trees. The sweet flesh can be bright orange or coral pink in color. Summer is the peak harvesting season.

Passion fruit: Known as *lilikoi* in the islands, this tasty yellow fruit is oval in shape and grows to a length of about two or three inches. It's produced on a vine and ripens in summer or fall.

Taro: The tuberous root of this Hawaiian staple is pounded into a grayish purple paste known as *poi*. One of the most nutritious foods, it has a rather bland taste. The plant, called *kalo* in Hawaiian, has wide, shiny, thick leaves with reddish stems; the root is white with purple veins. The Western palate may prefer taro in the form of chips. It can also be baked like a breadfruit.

FAUNA

On Kauai, it seems there is more wildlife in the water and air than on land. A scuba-diver's paradise, the ocean is also a promised land for many other creatures. Coral, colorful fish and migrating whales are only part of this underwater community. Sadly, many of Hawaii's coral reefs have been dying mysteriously in the last several years. No one is sure why, but many believe this is partially due to runoff from pesticides used in agriculture.

Green sea turtles are common on all of the Hawaiian islands, although this was not always the case. Due to the popularity of their shells and meat, they spent many years on the endangered species list, but are now making a comeback. Measuring three to four feet in diameter, these large reptiles frolic in saltwater only, and are often visible from the shore.

Not many wild four-footed creatures roam the island. Deer, feral goats and pigs were brought here early on and have found a home in the forests. Some good news for people fearful of snakes: There is nary a serpent (or a sea serpent) in Kauai, although lizards such as skinks and geckos abound.

One can only hope that with the renewed interest in Hawaiian culture, and growing environmental awareness, Hawaii's plants and animals will continue to exist as they have for centuries.

WHALES & DOLPHINS Every year, humpback whales converge in the warm waters off the islands to give birth to their calves. Beginning their migration in Alaska, they can be spotted in Hawaiian waters from November through May. The humpback, named for its practice of showing its dorsal fin when diving, is quite easy to spy. They feed in shallow waters, usually diving for periods of no longer than 15 minutes. They often sleep on the surface and breathe fairly frequently. Unlike other whales, humpbacks have the ability to sing.

Loud and powerful, their songs carry above and below the water for miles. The songs change every year, yet, incredibly, all the whales always seem to know the current one. Quite playful, they can be seen leaping, splashing and flapping their 15-foot tails over their backs. The best time for whale watching is from January to April.

Spinner dolphins are also favorites among visitors. Named for their "spinning" habit, they can revolve as many as six times during one leap. They resemble the spotted dolphin, another frequenter of Hawaiian waters, but are more likely to venture closer to the shore. Dolphins have clocked in with speeds ranging from 9 to 25 mph, a feat they often achieve by propelling themselves out of the water (or even riding the bow wave of a ship). Their thick, glandless skin also contributes to this agility. The skin is kept smooth by constant renewal and sloughing. Playful and intelligent, dolphins are a joy to watch. Many research centers are investigating the mammals' ability to imitate, learn and communicate; some believe that dolphin intelligence may be comparable to that of humans.

FISH It'll come as no surprise to anyone that Kauai's waters literally brim with an extraordinary assortment of fish—over 400 different species, in fact.

The goatfish, with more than 50 species in its family worldwide, boasts at least ten in Kauai waters. This bottom dweller is recognized by a pair of whiskers, used as feelers for searching out food, that are attached to its lower jaw. The *moano* sports two stripes

SUNTAN SPECIALISTS

A stroll on almost any beach in Kauai might bring you face to face with a Hawaiian monk seal, one of Hawaii's two endemic mammals. (Hawaii's only other endemic mammal is the Hoary bat.) Although monk seals have successfully adapted to life in the sea, their species, pinnipeds, are thought to have evolved from terrestrial mammals millions of years ago and continue to retain strong ties to land. Closely related to the elephant seal, the monk seal is not as agile or as fond of land as other seals. Often found on the sand sunning themselves on shore, federal law requires that you give these endangered species a 50-foot berth. Besides, as cute as they look, they can give nasty bites.

across its back and has shorter whiskers. The red-and-black banded goatfish has a multihued color scheme that also includes yellow and white markings; its light yellow whiskers are quite long. The head of the goatfish is considered poisonous and is not eaten.

Occasionally found on the sharper end of your line is the bone-fish, or *oio*. One of the best game fish in the area, its head extends past its mouth to form a somewhat transparent snout. The *awa*, or milkfish, is another common catch. This silvery, fork-tailed fish can grow longer than three feet and puts up a good fight.

A kaleidoscope of brilliantly colored specimens can be viewed around the reefs of Kauai; you'll feel like you're in a technicolor movie when snorkeling. Over 20 known species of butterfly fish are found in this area. Highlighted in yellow, orange, red, blue, black and white, they swim in groups of two and three. The long, tubular body of the needlefish, or *aha*, can reach up to 40 inches in length; this greenish, silvery species is nearly translucent. The masked angelfish flits around in deeper waters on the outer edge of reefs. The imperial angelfish is distinguishable by fantastic color patterns of dark blue hues. The Hawaiian fish with the longest name, the colorful *humuhumunukunukuapuaa*, is found in the shallow waters along the outer fringes of reefs.

Sharks, unlike fish, have skeletons made of cartilage; the hardest parts of their bodies are their teeth (once used as tools by the Hawaiians). If you spend a lot of time in the water, you may spot a shark. But not to worry; Hawaiian waters are just about the safest around. The harmless, commonly seen blacktipped and whitetipped reef sharks (named for the color of their fins) are as concerned about your activities as you are about theirs. The gray reef shark (gray back, white belly with a black tail) and tiger shark, however, are predatory and aggressive, but they are rarely encountered.

KAUAI IS FOR THE BIRDS

Kauai offers a unique opportunity for spotting a wide variety of Hawaiian birds, such as the *akekee*, the *anianiau* and the *amakihi*. **Terran Tours** provides one- to three-day tours. A professional guide will escort you.
~ P.O. Box 1018, Waimea, HI 96796; 808-335-3313, fax 808-335-5849; e-mail dkuhn@rare-dear.com.

Another cartilaginous creature you might see in shallow water near the shoreline is the manta ray, a "winged" plankton feeder with two appendages on either side of its head that work to direct food into its mouth. The eagle ray, a bottom dweller featuring "wings" and a tail longer than its body, feeds in shallow coastal waters. When it's not feeding, it lies on the ocean floor and covers itself with a light layer of sand. Since some eagle rays have stingers, take precautions by shuffling the sand as you walk. Not only will you not be impaled, you will also be less likely to squash smaller, unsuspecting sea creatures.

While on Kauai, you'll inevitably see fish out of water as well —on your plate. The purple-blue-green-hued mahimahi, or dolphin fish, can reach six feet and 70 pounds. The *opakapaka* is another common dish and resides in the deeper, offshore waters beyond the reef. This small-scaled snapper is a reddish-olive color and can grow up to four feet long. Elongated with a sharply pointed head, the *ono* (also known as the wahoo) is a carnivorous, savage striped fish with dark blue and silver coloring. Perhaps the most ubiquitous fish is the ahi, or tuna, often used for sashimi.

BIRDS The island is also home to many rare and endangered birds. Like the flora, the birds in the Hawaiian Islands are highly specialized. The state bird, the nene, or Hawaiian goose, is a cousin to the Canadian goose and mates for life. (You'll find more birds residing on Kauai than on the other islands. Why? Because it is the one main island that the mongoose, which thrives on bird eggs and birds, has not settled down in.)

Known in Hawaiian mythology for its protective powers, the *pueo*, or Hawaiian owl, a brown-and-white-feathered bird, resides on Kauai, the Big Island and in Haleakala crater.

Endemic to the island, the *puaiohi* (small Kauai thrush) is a dark-brown forest bird that nests in fern-choked cliffs. The tiny bright-yellow *anianiau* is the smallest of the native Hawaiian honeycreepers. More likely to be heard than seen, the plain gray *akikiki* (Kauai creeper) travels in family groups while foraging in the canopy. These endangered birds, found only on Kauai, all reside in the Alakai Swamp.

There *are* a few birds native to Hawaii that have thus far avoided the endangered species list. Two of the most common birds are the yellow-green *amakihi* and the red *iiwi*.

The *koae kea*, or "tropic bird," lives in Kauai's Waimea Canyon, in the Big Island's Kilauea Crater and on Maui's Haleakala but are more often seen soaring along the coastline. Resembling a seagull in size, it has a long, thin white tail and a striking striping pattern on the back of the wings.

One common seabird is the *iwa*, or frigate, a very large creature measuring three to four feet in length, with a wing span averaging seven feet. The males are solid black, while the females have a large white patch on their chest and tail. A predatory bird, they're easy to spot raiding the nesting colonies of other birds along the offshore rocks. If you see one, you may want to seek cover; legend says they portend a storm. Other native birds that make the islands their home are the endangered Hawaiian stilt and the Hawaiian coot—both water birds—along with the black noddy, American plover, wedge-tailed shearwater, and the endangered Newell's shearwater (most commonly found on Kauai and Molokai).

Outdoor Adventures

FISHING

Fishing in Kauai is superb year-round, and the offshore waters are crowded with many varieties of edible fish. For deep-sea fishing you'll have to charter a boat, and freshwater angling requires a license, which can be obtained at sportfishing stores. For information on seasons, licenses and official regulations, check with the **Division of Aquatic Resources**, which is part of of the State Department of Land and Natural Resources. ~ 3060 Eiwa Street, Room 306, Lihue, HI 96766; 808-274-3344, fax 808-274-3448.

TORCHFISHING

The old Hawaiians often fished at night by torchlight. They fashioned torches by inserting nuts from the kukui tree into the hollow end of a bamboo pole, then lighting the flammable nuts. When fish swam like moths to the flame, the Hawaiians speared, clubbed or netted them. Today, it's easier to use a flashlight or lantern and spear. (In fact, it's all *too* easy and tempting to take advantage of this willing prey: Take only edible fish and only what you will eat, and follow state rules on size and season limits for some species.) It's also handy to bring a facemask or a glass-bottomed box to aid in seeing underwater. The best time for torchfishing is a dark night when the sea is calm and the tide low.

The easiest, most economical way to fish is with a hand-held line. Just get a 50- to 100-foot line, and attach a hook and a ten-ounce sinker. Wind the line loosely around a smooth block of wood, then remove the wood from the center. If your coil is free from snags, you'll be able to throw-cast it easily. You can either hold the line in your hand, feeling for a strike, or tie it to the frail end of a bamboo pole.

Beaches and rocky points are generally good places to surf-cast; the best times are during the incoming and outgoing tides. Popular baits include octopus, eel, lobster, crab, frozen shrimp and sea worms.

Both saltwater and freshwater fishing opportunities make Kauai popular with anglers. Intriguing possibilities include over-night adventures off the Niihau coast, fishing for giant tuna and marlin. Keep a sharp eye out on your trip and you may spot spin-ner dolphins or breaching whales along the way.

Wild Bill Sport Fishing provides everything you need to fish for marlin, ahi, *ono* and *aku* on Kauai's south and east coasts. The four-hour charter accommodates up to six people; six- and eight-hour charters are also available. ~ Nawiliwili Harbor, Lihue; 808-822-5963.

Head inland to fish for bass on Kauai's reservoirs with **Cast and Catch Freshwater Bass Guides**. Half- and full-day trips are con-ducted at reservoirs all over the island. An 18-foot bass boat takes anglers out to try for largemouth, smallmouth and peacock bass. Bait, tackle and beverages are included. ~ Koloa; 808-332-9707.

SPEARFISHING During daylight hours, the best place to spear-fish is along coral reefs and in areas where the bottom is a mix-ture of sand and rock. Equipped with speargun, mask, fins and snorkel, you can explore underwater grottos and spectacular coral formations while seeking your evening meal. Spearguns can be purchased inexpensively throughout the island.

For the hungry adventurer, there are several crab species in Hawaii. The most sought-after are the Kona and Samoan varieties. Kona crabs are found in relatively deep water, and can usually be caught only from a boat. Samoan crabs inhabit sandy and muddy areas in bays and near river mouths. All you need to catch them are a boat and a net fastened to a round wire hoop secured by a string.

CRABBING

The net is lowered to the bottom; then, after a crab has gone for the bait, the entire contraption is raised to the surface.

SQUIDDING Between June and December, squidding is another popular sport. Actually, the term is a misnomer: squid inhabit deep water and are not usually hunted. What you'll really be after are octopuses. There are two varieties here, both of which are commonly found in water three or four feet deep: the *hee*, a greyish-brown animal that changes color like a chameleon, and the *puloa*, a red-colored mollusk with white stripes on its head.

Both are nocturnal and live in holes along coral reefs. At night by torchlight you can spot them sitting exposed on the bottom. During the day, they crawl inside the holes, covering the entrances with shells and loose coral.

The Hawaiians used to pick the octopus up, letting it cling to their chest and shoulders. When they were ready to bag their prize, they'd dispatch the creature by biting it between the eyes. You'll probably feel more comfortable spearing the beast.

SHELLFISH GATHERING Other excellent food sources are the shellfish that inhabit coastal waters. The ancient Hawaiians used pearl shells to attract the fish, and hooks, some made from human bones, to snare them. Your friends will probably be quite content to see you angling with store-bought artificial lures. Spiny lobsters are illegal to spear, but can be taken in season with short poles to which cable leaders and baited hooks are attached. You can also just grab them with a gloved hand but be careful—spiny lobsters live up to their name! Lobster hunting is not allowed between May and September. You can also gather limpets, though I don't recommend it. These tiny black shellfish, locally known as *opihi*, cling tenaciously to rocks in the tidal zone. In areas of very rough surf, the Hawaiians gather them by leaping into the water after one set of waves breaks, then jumping out before the next set arrives. Being a coward myself, I simply order them in Hawaiian restaurants.

SEAWEED GATHERING There are still some people who don't think of seaweed as food, but it's very popular among Japanese, and it once served as an integral part of the Hawaiian diet. It's extremely nutritious, easy to gather and very plentiful. Rocky shores are the best places to find the edible species of seaweed. Some of them float in to shore

Ocean Safety

For swimming, surfing and scuba diving, there's no place quite like Kauai. With endless miles of white-sand beach, the island attracts aquatic enthusiasts worldwide. They come to enjoy Kauai's colorful coral reefs and matchless surf conditions. Many water lovers, however, don't realize how dangerous the sea can be. Particularly on Kauai, where waves can reach 30-foot heights and currents flow unobstructed for thousands of miles, the ocean is sometimes as treacherous as it is spectacular. Dozens of people drown every year in Hawaii, many others are dragged from the crushing surf with broken backs, and countless numbers sustain minor cuts and bruises.

These accidents can be avoided if you approach the ocean with a respect for its power as well as an appreciation of its beauty. Just heed a few simple guidelines. First, never turn your back on the sea. Waves come in sets: one group may be small and quite harmless, but the next could be large enough to sweep you out to sea. Never swim alone.

Don't try to surf, or bodysurf, until you're familiar with the sports' techniques and precautionary measures. Be careful when the surf is high.

If you get caught in a rip current, don't swim *against* it: swim *across* it, parallel to the shore. These currents, running from the shore out to sea, can often be spotted by their ragged-looking surface water and foamy edges.

Around coral reefs, wear something to protect your feet against cuts. Recommended are inexpensive Japanese *tabis*, or reef slippers. If you do get a coral cut, clean it with hydrogen peroxide, then apply an antiseptic or antibiotic substance.

When stung by a Portuguese man-of-war or a jellyfish, rinse the affected area with sea water to remove any tentacles. Use gloves or towels—not your bare fingers—to remove remaining tentacles. Human urine, once considered an effective remedy, is no longer a recommended treatment. With jellyfish stings only, you might also try vinegar or isopropyl alcohol.

If you step on the sharp, painful spines of a sea urchin, be sure the entire spine is removed. Soaking the wound in vinegar helps to dissolve the spine; for pain, soak the affected area in very hot water for 30 to 90 minutes. If the pain persists for more than a day, or you notice swelling or other signs of infection, consult a doctor.

Oh, one last thing. The chances of encountering a shark are about as likely as sighting a UFO. But should you meet one of these ominous creatures, stay calm. Simply swim quietly to shore. By the time you make it back to terra firma, you'll have one hell of a story to tell.

and can be picked up; other species cling stubbornly to rocks and must be freed with a knife; still others grow in sand or mud. Low tide is the best time to collect seaweed: more plants are exposed, and some can be taken without even getting wet.

CAMPING   Camping on Kauai usually means pitching a tent or reserving a cabin. Throughout the islands there are secluded spots and hidden beaches, plus numerous county, state and federal parks. All of these campsites, together with hiking trails, are described in the following chapters; it's a good idea to consult those detailed listings when planning your trip. The camping equipment you'll require is listed in the "Packing" section of the preceding chapter.

Before you set out on your camping trip, there are a few very important matters that I want to explain more fully. First, bring a campstove: firewood is scarce in most areas and soaking wet in others.

Another problem that you're actually more likely to encounter are those nasty varmints that buzz your ear just as you're falling asleep—mosquitoes. Kauai contains neither snakes nor poison ivy, but it has plenty of these dive-bombing pests. Like me, you probably consider that it's always open season on the little bastards.

With most of the archipelago's other species, however, you'll have to be a careful conservationist. You'll be sharing the wilder-

SNORKELING SAFETY TIPS

Don't miss out on an opportunity to explore the depths of Kauai's busy ocean life (even if you only venture a few feet down). You're apt to find fish and coral in a dazzling array of colors, sizes and shapes. But take the following precautions before you dip into the water:

- always snorkel with someone else
- avoid big waves, surfers and windy conditions
- bring a flotation device like an inner tube, noodle or life jacket, especially if you are with kids or are a novice swimmer
- don't poke your hands into crevices in a reef (a favorite eel hangout)
- look up now and again to watch the weather conditions—if you're having trouble getting back to shore because the waves are too high, wait for the set to break
- wear lots of waterproof sunscreen (and perhaps a T-shirt) because your back will be lobster red if you don't!

ness with pigs, goats, tropical birds and deer, as well as a spectacular array of exotic and indigenous plants. All exist in one of the world's most delicate ecological balances. There are more endangered species in Hawaii than in all the rest of the United States. So keep in mind the maxim that the Hawaiians try to follow. *Ua mau ke ea o ka aina i ka pono:* The life of the land is perpetuated in righteousness.

To visit Kauai without enjoying at least one camping trip is to miss a splendid opportunity. This lovely isle is dotted with county and state parks that feature ideal locations and complete facilities. There are also many hidden beaches where unofficial camping is common.

Camping at **county parks** requires a permit. These are issued for seven days. You are allowed to camp seven consecutive days at one county park and a total of 60 days per year at all county parks. Permits cost $3 per person per night; children under 18 are free. Permits can be obtained weekdays at the Division of Parks and Recreation. You can also buy permits from a ranger at the campsite for $5 per person per night. ~ 4444 Rice Street, Suite 330, Lihue; 808-241-4460.

State park permit fees vary by location. They allow camping five consecutive days at each park, and should be requested at least one month in advance for winter, at least a year in advance for summer reservations. These permits are issued by the Department of Land and Natural Resources. ~ 3060 Eiwa Street, Lihue, HI 96766; 808-274-3445.

The State Division of Forestry also maintains camping areas in the **forest reserves**. Currently, these are free (but call the Division of Forestry to see about new fees); permits are available at the State Division of Forestry. ~ 3060 Eiwa Street, Room 306, Lihue, HI 96766; 808-274-3433. Camping is limited at each site, and there's a four-night maximum at the Kukui Trail campsites near Waimea Canyon and a three-night limit at the Sugi Grove and Kawaikoi sites in the rainforest area at the top of Waimea Canyon.

Camping elsewhere on the island is officially prohibited. While local people and visitors do sometimes camp on hidden beaches anyway, the authorities crack down on this regularly. By the way, an extra effort should be made to keep these areas clean. One of the best suggestions I've ever heard is to leave your campsite cleaner than when you arrived.

Rainfall is much heavier along the North Shore than along the south coast, but be prepared for showers anywhere. The Kokee area gets chilly, so pack accordingly. And remember, boil or chemically treat all water from Kauai's streams. Water from some of these streams can cause dysentery and leptospirosis, a serious illness with flu-like symptoms, and none of the waterways are certified safe by the Health Department.

DIVING   The Garden Isle offers snorkeling and scuba opportunities at such spots as Haena Beach, Tunnels Beach, Moloaa and Koloa Landing. In the Poipu area, Koloa Landing has a number of green sea turtles in its midst and is mainly for experienced snorkelers. The beach in front of Lawai Beach Resort is another popular spot for snorkelers. Brennecke's Beach is now completely restored from the damage wrought by Hurricane Iniki. Even if you have your own equipment, it's a good idea to stop by one of the local dive shops to pick up a map, as well as advice on local conditions.

POIPU AREA   To familiarize yourself with the area's treasures you may want to begin with a group tour. **Fathom Five Divers** rents diving and snorkeling equipment and takes groups to hot spots such as Sheraton Caverns and Brennecke's Ledge. Divers often spot fish unique to Kauai such as bandit angel fish, long-nosed hawkfish and boarfish. Half-day dives leave every morning and afternoon. ~ Poipu Road, Koloa; 808-742-6991; www.fathom five.com. **Seasport Divers** rents snorkeling and scuba equipment and offers lessons, tours, and day and night dives. ~ 2827 Poipu Road, Poipu; 808-742-9303; www.kauaiscubadiving.com.

WAILUA–KAPAA AREA   **Snorkel Bob's Kauai** rents snorkeling equipment returnable at branches on all the other islands. The shop puts together a tip sheet of the best current snorkel spots (factoring in the weather, tides and so forth). They can also arrange helicopter tours, boat rides and luaus. ~ 4-734 Kuhio Highway, Kapaa, 808-823-9433; and also at 3236 Poipu Road, Koloa, 808-742-2206; www.snorkelbob.com.

NORTH SHORE   **Hanalei Water Sports Inc.** offers certification classes. Beginners start right at Princeville Beach; more advanced divers may join small groups in exploring the lava tubes and caverns of Tunnels Beach. ~ Princeville Resort, Princeville; 808-826-7509. Another good possibility for snorkeling rentals is **Hanalei Surf Company**. Check out their supply of boogieboards, wet suits and surfboards. ~ 5-5161 Kuhio Highway, Hanalei; 808-826-9000; www.hanaleisurf.com. **Pedal 'N Paddle** has snorkels, masks and fins as well as single and double kayaks for rent. ~ Ching Young Village, Hanalei; 808-826-9069.

SNUBA

Somewhere between snorkeling and scuba diving is Snuba, a relatively new watersport that's catching on in resort areas around the world. You don't need certification, and it's quite safe.

Snuba was created for those who would like to take snorkeling a step further but may not be quite ready for scuba diving. It's a shallow-water dive system that allows underwater breathing. Basically this is how it works. Swimmers wear a breathing device (the same one used in scuba diving) that is connected to a built-in scuba tank that floats on a raft. They also wear a weight belt, mask and fins. The air comes through a 20-foot tube connected to the raft, which follows the swimmer. Groups are taken out with a guide. They can dive up to 20 feet. **Snuba Tours of Kauai** provides just that, leaving from Lawai Beach in Poipu and consisting of groups of one to eight divers. The personalized instruction extends to the underwater tour; all equipment (and fish food) is provided. Closed weekends. ~ 808-823-8912; www.snubakauai.com, e-mail snuba@snubakauai.com.

SURFING & WIND-SURFING

Kauai isn't exactly the surfing capital of the islands, but there are several places where both beginners and experts can give it a try. My best advice is to check with a surf shop to find out the best places for both surfing and windsurfing. Tell them how much experience you *really* have. Don't exaggerate, you could get hurt. Conditions at the Poipu beaches are usually gentler than on the other side of the island. But if you're qualified, you might want

HEY DUDES, SURF'S UP

Surf is usually up somewhere on Kauai. If you're interested in finding the best breaks check with the local surf shop. They can direct you to the following spots:

- *In winter*: Cannons, Tunnels, Hanalei Bay, Kalihiway Bay (experts only) and Hideaways
- *In summer*: Brennecke's, Poipu, Prince Kuhio and Pakala
- *Year-round*: Rock Quarry Beach, Kealia Beach, Kalapaki Bay, Shipwreck, Kekaha Beach and Barking Sands

to take on challenging North Shore beaches like Hanalei. Keep in mind that conditions can be extremely dangerous during the winter months. Don't try this area unless you're an expert.

POIPU AREA Surfers head for the Poipu coastline. **Progressive Expressions** not only sells and rents surfboards, they make their own. Bodyboards and swim fins are also available. ~ 5420 Koloa Road, Koloa; 808-742-6041. Surfing champion Margo Oberg's **Nukaumoi Beach and Surf Center** offers beginner's surfing lessons on Poipu Beach. Boogieboards, snorkel gear and accessories are for rent. ~ Next to Brennecke's Beach Broiler, Poipu; 808-742-8019.

If you're new to surfing, or just want a refresher course, sign up for a lesson with the **Kauai Surf School**. They give two-hour private and group lessons, mainly aimed at beginners although advanced classes are also available. Groups are limited to four so that everyone receives personalized instruction. ~ Poipu; 808-332-7411; www.kauaisurfschool.com.

WAILUA–KAPAA AREA The **Kauai Water Ski and Surf Company** rents surfboards and offers all levels of lessons, usually conducted on Wailua Beach. They also have a boat on Wailua River for knee boarding or wake boarding. Boards and accessories are also for sale. ~ 4-356 Kuhio Highway, Wailua; 808-822-3574.

NORTH SHORE Both fiberglass and soft surfboards, boogieboards and swim fins can be rented at **Hanalei Surf Company**. ~ 5-5161 Kuhio Highway, Hanalei; 808-826-9000; www.hanaleisurf.com. Rentals and beginner-to-expert windsurfing lessons are offered at **Windsurf Kauai**. The North Shore's Anini Beach, with its reef-protected lagoon, is often the setting for the lessons. ~

HELP PROTECT THE REEF

Exploring underwater in Kauai is one of the most wonderful experiences available in the islands, but we must protect that environment while we enjoy it. Did you know that coral reefs are living animals that live in large colonies? They are also home to hundreds of creatures, including colorful reef fish. It takes years and years for coral reefs to regenerate themselves when damaged, and if they are badly damaged they die. We can help protect the reefs by not touching them (they are protected by Hawaiian law—it is illegal to take live coral from their beds); not walking or standing on them; and not feeding the fish that inhabit them (this upsets the eco-balance).

Near Anini Park, Hanalei; 808-828-6838. Windsurfing lessons of all levels are conducted right on Anini Beach at **Anini Beach Windsurfing**. ~ 808-826-9463; www.windsurfingandkitesurfing onkauai.com.

The latest craze to hit the water is kitesurfing. Following principles similar to paragliding, windsurfing and even snowboarding, you're strapped to a light board and pulled across the water by, well, a big kite. Most folks in decent physical condition pick up the sport quickly, especially if they've had experience with a related activity. After some concentrated study, you'll graduate to bigger kites and speeds of up to 40 mph. Kitesurfers have been known to jump 30 feet off the water. For a kitesurfing spot on Kauai, look for an area clear of trees and powerlines, preferably an uncrowded beach; also talk to local kitesurfers before you start—the Kauai coastline is pretty unpredictable. If a 30-foot leap seems like a little too much excitement, you'll still enjoy watching the riders jump, jibe and "kite the surfzone." Because the sport is relatively new, and Kauai remains off the beaten path, it's a bit difficult to find an instructor here. But call **Anini Beach Windsurfing** on the North Shore and speak with Foster. He'll conduct private kitesurfing lessons with folks of all levels, and fix you up with the gear. His office address is "the beach," but you can make reservations and get information by phone. ~ 808-826-9463.

KITE-SURFING

The trade winds ensure excellent sailing in Kauai waters. From a catamaran trip along the southern shore to a thrilling trip along the rugged Na Pali Coast, these waters are ideal for cruising. Many of the cruises stop at isolated beaches and also offer excellent snorkeling opportunities.

BOAT TOURS

LIHUE AREA True Blue Charters offers sailboat rentals. With exclusive boating rights to Kalapaki Bay, they conduct one-hour rides of the area; personalized tours will take you to remote destinations of your choice. All levels of sailing lessons are offered, as well as kayak tours of Huleia River. Boogieboards and snorkel gear are also rented. ~ Kalapaki Beach, Lihue; 808-245-9662; www.truebluecharters.com.

WAIMEA AREA For south coast sailing tours on the 55-foot-long *Spirit of Kauai* catamaran, weigh anchor with **Captain Andy's**

Sailing Adventures. Along the way, you may spot humpback whales or giant green sea turtles. Sunset sails are among the intriguing possibilities. ~ Port Allen; 808-335-6833. **Holoholo Charters** runs five-and-a-half-hour snorkel sails to the Na Pali Coast, and seven-hour trips to Niihau. ~ Port Allen Boat Harbor; 808-335-0815, 800-848-6130; www.sail-kauai.com. **Na Pali Riders** has a rafting trip that explores the entire Na Pali Coast including the sea caves, and offers snorkeling at the Nualolo Kai reef. Lunch and equipment included. ~ P.O. Box 1082, Kalaheo, HI 96741; 808-742-6331; www.napaliriders.com. **Captain Andy's** also serves the Na Pali Coast with motor-powered catamarans. Snorkeling equipment is provided on these narrated tours of historic Kauai, while from December through March the focus is on whale watching. ~ Port Allen; 808-335-6833.

Captain Zodiac offers rafting expeditions along the Na Pali Coast. Six-hour trips include visits to sea caves, beautiful reefs and an ancient fishing village. All trips include some snorkeling, and equipment is provided. Sunrise and sunset cruises are offered in the summertime, while whale watching along the north shore in the winter months is also featured. ~ Port Allen; 808-826-9371; www.captainzodiackauai.com, e-mail capt_zodiac@hotmail.com.

Zodiac and catamaran tours of the Na Pali Coast are also offered by **Kauai Sea Tours.** Half-day snorkeling tours take you to a landing on a secluded beach for first-rate snorkeling during the summer, while winter and spring whale-watching tours are led by naturalists. ~ Port Allen; 808-826-7254, 800-733-7997; www. seatours.net, e-mail seatour@aloha.net.

AUTHOR FAVORITE

Expect more than a cruise along the extraordinary Kauai coastline when you board the **Na Pali Explorer.** In addition to providing descriptions of flora, fauna and Hawaiian culture that make the experience educational, the crew is always on the lookout for dolphins and sea turtles. They are attentive to your needs, ecologically oriented, and will lead you along one of the most beautiful coastlines in the world, past craggy cliffs and into remote sea caves. Then they'll take you snorkeling amid the region's colorful coral reefs. You can't miss with one of their trips. These five-hour expeditions run from May through September; snorkeling gear and light snacks are provided. ~ 9935 Kaumualii Highway, Waimea; 808-338-9999; www.napali-explorer.com.

WAILUA–KAPAA AREA Paradise Outdoor Adventures leads tours and rents kayaks, ideal for exploring rivers and wildlife refuges. Snorkel gear and boogie boards are also for rent. ~ 4-1596 Kuhio Highway, Kapaa; 808-822-1112, 800-662-6287.

Kayaking is one of Kauai's fastest growing water sports. And why not? Choose from verdant river valleys or, if you like, go down to the sea again.

KAYAKING

LIHUE AREA Aloha Canoes & Kayaks conducts tours up the Huleia River through the midst of the Huleia National Wildlife Refuge. Among the sights you'll pass are ancient taro fields and the Menehune Fishpond. The tour continues with a hike through the *Jurassic Park* rainforest and a gourmet lunch beside a waterfall. The way back is the easy part: gliding on a motorized canoe, you'll be entertained with stories of the history and legends of Kauai. Closed Sunday. ~ Lihue; 808-246-6804, 877-473-5446; www.hawaiikayaks.com, e-mail info@hawaiikayaks.com.

A similar tour is conducted by **True Blue Kauai**, which departs from the Nawiliwili Small Boat Harbor. The tour follows the Huleia River, "blown upstream," you're assured. After a short hike through the wildlife refuge, you'll be driven back to the harbor by van. (See "From the Menehune to Indiana Jones," page 96.) ~ 808-245-9662; www.kauaifun.com, e-mail info@kauaifun.com.

POIPU AREA Outfitters Kauai offers paddling around Poipu during the winter months, and North Shore trips in the summer. Bring your snorkel gear along, as there will be time to explore. ~ 2827-A Poipu Road, Poipu Beach; 808-742-9667, 888-742-9887; www.outfitterskauai.com, e-mail info@outfitterskauai.com.

WAILUA–KAPAA AREA Kayak Kauai rents kayaks and runs snorkel trips. They also sponsor river tours of waterfalls on the Wailua River, as well as all-day tours of the Na Pali Coast from May to September. This trip includes a lunch break at the ruins of an ancient Hawaiian fishing village. ~ Kapaa, 808-822-9179; Hanalei, 808-826-9844, 800-437-3507; www.kayakkauai.com, e-mail info@kayakkauai.com.

If you want to go out on your own, you can rent a kayak from **Kauai Waterski and Surf Company**. Kayakers are provided with a map leading them to such Wailua River highlights as Secret Falls, a waterfall and a remote Hawaiian village. Guided trips are also available. ~ 4-356 Kuhio Highway, Wailua; 808-822-3574; www.kauai-waterski-kayak-surf.com, e-mail surfski@aloha.net.

Kayak Wailua has a similar self-guided adventure: they'll provide equipment and a laminated map to guide you two and a half miles up Wailua River. At a Hawaiian village along the way, you can secure your boats and continue on foot. Here you'll discover canyons, waterfalls, a swimming hole where ancient Hawaiian kings and high chiefs once bathed, as well as other natural treasures. They also have guided tours. ~ 808-822-3388; www.kayakwailua.com, e-mail info@kayakwailua.com.

Bzzzz. You can thank the ship Wellington for bringing the first mosquitoes to the islands in 1826.

NORTH SHORE **Kayak Hanalei** will take you on a relaxing tour of the river, stopping to snorkel, eat and laze. Or, if you prefer, they'll introduce you to the rich history of Kauai on a narrated tour. All equipment is provided. ~ In the Ching Yong Shopping Center, Kuhio Highway, Hanalei; 808-826-1881; www.kayakhanalei.com, email a1kayak@aloha.net.

WATER-SKIING
If you've ever wondered what it feels like to waterski through paradise, why not head for the town of Wailua. The serene Wailua River is the perfect place to glide through verdant canyons graced by waterfalls. You can practice your slalom technique, try out a pair of trick skis or enjoy yourself on the hydroslide.

Kauai Waterski and Surf Company offers trips for intermediate to advanced waterskiers. Hot doggers will want to try out the competition slalom course; 15-minute, half-hour or hour-long runs can be arranged. ~ 4-356 Kuhio Highway, Wailua; 808-822-3574; www.kauai-waterski-kayak-surf.com, e-mail surfski@aloha.net.

RIDING STABLES
From scenic coastal trail rides to journeys up North Shore valleys, Kauai is an equestrian's delight.

In the Poipu area, try **CJM Country Stables**. Possibilities include two-hour rides along the south shore to Mahaulepu and Haupu beaches. They also offer a three-hour "breakfast ride" departing at 8:30 a.m. and covering some of the best beaches in the Poipu area. You may be tempted to return later on foot to explore these hidden spots. (No rides on Sunday.) ~ At the end of Poipu Road; 808-742-6096.

In the Hanalei area, contact **Princeville Ranch Stables** for three- or four-hour picnic rides to waterfalls (includes a moder-

The New
Travel

Travel has become a personal art form. A destination no longer serves as just a place to relax: It's also a point of encounter. To many, this new wave in travel customs is labeled "adventure travel" and involves trekking glaciers or dusting the cliffs in a hang glider; to others, it connotes nothing more daring than a restful spell in a secluded resort. Actually, it's a state of mind, a willingness not only to accept but seek out the uncommon and unique.

Few places in the world are more conducive to this imaginative travel than Hawaii. Several organizations in the islands cater specifically to people who want to add local customs and unusual adventures to their vacation itineraries.

Hawaiian Adventure Tours features a ten-day tour of Kauai, Maui and the Big Island, including hiking and snorkeling. ~ P.O. Box 1269, Kapaau, HI 96755; 808-889-0227, 800-659-3544; www.hawaiianadventure tours.com.

The **Sierra Club** sponsors regular hikes on Kauai, as well as trail building and other projects aimed at helping to preserve the island's natural heritage. ~ P.O. Box 3412, Lihue, HI 96766; www.hi.sierraclub.org.

When you're ready to take up the challenge of this style of freewheeling travel, check with these outfits. Or plan your own trip. To traditional tourists, Hawaii means souvenir shops and fast-food restaurants. But for those with spirit and imagination, it's a land of untracked beaches and ancient volcanos waiting to be explored.

ately strenuous hike), as well as 90-minute country rides to the bluff overlooking Anini Reef. ~ Kuhio Highway, Princeville; 808-826-6777.

GOLF Some of the best golfing in Hawaii is found on the Garden Isle. In addition to outstanding resort courses at Princeville, the Kauai Marriott and the Hyatt Regency Kauai, you can enjoy several excellent public courses. Beautifully situated with dramatic ocean and mountain backdrops, all of these links will make your game a pleasure.

LIHUE AREA **Kiele Course** and the **Mokihana Course**, both created by Jack Nicklaus, are two of the island's best-known golfing spots. Both courses have 18 holes, full equipment rental, spectacular ocean views and guava and mango forests. ~ Both are adjacent to the Kauai Marriott, Nawiliwili; 808-241-6000, 800-634-6400.

POIPU AREA Next door to the Hyatt Regency Kauai is the Robert Trent Jones, Jr.–designed 18-hole **Poipu Bay Resort Golf Course**. Full equipment rental is available at this course that was specifically designed to provide an ocean view from each hole. ~ 2250 Ainako Street, Koloa; 808-742-8711.

WAIMEA AREA On the south side of the island, the semiprivate **Kukuiolono Golf Course** in Kalaheo is also popular. This nine-hole course offers views of ocean and Kalaheo mountains. ~ 854 Puu Road, Kalaheo; 808-332-9151.

WAILUA–KAPAA AREA The golfing public is well served at the 18-hole, oceanfront **Wailua Golf Course**, and the low green fees make this course a best buy. ~ Wailua; 808-241-6666.

NORTH SHORE The 27-hole **Princeville Makai Golf Course** was designed by Robert Trent Jones. Full equipment rental is available and the scenery is beautiful. ~ Princeville; 808-826-3580. It is complemented by the demanding 18-hole **Prince Country Club** course next door. There's also a driving range to help sharpen your skills. ~ 428 Kuhio Highway, Princeville; 808-826-5000.

BIKING There are no bikeways on Kauai and most roads have very narrow shoulders, but the Garden Isle is still the most popular island for bicycling. Roads are good and, except for the steep 20-mile climb along Waimea Canyon, the terrain is either flat or gently rolling. The spectacular scenery and network of public parks make this a cyclist's dream.

One local spot for biking is along **Route 56**. This is a narrow road with one-lane bridges that keep tour buses and large trucks out of the area, though car traffic can be quite heavy.

For hearty mountain bikers, the **Powerline Trail** (15 miles) is an arduous but rewarding challenge. It follows a powerline that connects the North Shore with the east side of Kauai. The trail takes you into the interior of the island, offering views of Mt. Waialeale, one of the wettest spots on earth. Be sure to bring a U.S. Survey map (available at local camping stores), water and food with you. This journey is for experienced mountain bikers who are in the best of shape. ~ To get to the trailhead, turn in-land at the corner of Princeville stables and continue beyond the row of houses.

Bike Rentals   **Outfitters Kauai** rents hybrid, full-suspension and road bikes as well as children's mountain bikes and baby seats. ~ 2827-A Poipu Road, Poipu; 808-742-9667; www.outfitters kauai.com. In Hanalei, **Pedal 'N Paddle** rents mountain bikes and beach cruisers. Popular destinations from here include Princeville and the lagoon at Kee Beach. Car racks are also available. ~ Ching Young Village; 808-826-9069.

Bike Repairs   **Bicycle John's** in Lihue offers a full-service sales and repair shop. Closed Sunday and Monday. ~ 3215 Kuhio Highway, Lihue; 808-245-7579.

Bike Tours   **Outfitters Kauai** has an afternoon tour that is especially fun, and includes sunset gazing over Niihau. The tour stops along the way for photo ops and interesting lectures on the history and folklore of the area. The best part is: they'll bring you

FLY LIKE AN EAGLE (OR A GOONIE BIRD)

What better way to see Kauai than to soar on high with the birds? Okay, so you don't have wings. How about trying a motorized hang glider, accompanied by a fully certified flight instructor from **Birds in Paradise**? Be assured, you'll get a briefing on the basics of flying in a "weight-shift aircraft," and you will always be in communication with the pilot through an intercom on your helmet. ~ 808-822-5309; www.birdsinparadise. com, e-mail birds@birdsinparadise.com.

up the hill in a van. ~ Poipu Plaza, 2827A Poipu Road, Poipu; 808-742-9667, 888-742-9887; www.outfitterskauai.com, e-mail info@outfitterskauai.com.

HIKING

Hiking is among the finest, and certainly least expensive, ways of touring the Garden Isle. Kauai's trails are concentrated in the Na Pali Coast and Waimea Canyon–Kokee regions, with a few others near the Wailua River. Most are well maintained and carefully charted. For further information, contact the State Department of Land and Natural Resources. ~ 808-984-8100; www.hawaiitrails.org.

> On a clear day, watch the horizon as the sun sets. You may be able to see the "green flash," a refraction of the sun's rays.

Most trails you'll be hiking are composed of volcanic rock. Since this is a very crumbly substance, be extremely cautious when climbing any rock faces. In fact, you should avoid steep climbs if possible. Stay on the trails: Kauai's dense undergrowth makes it very easy to get lost. If you get lost at night, stay where you are. Because of the low latitude, night descends rapidly here; there's practically no twilight. Once darkness falls, it can be very dangerous to move around.

It's advisable to wear long pants when hiking in order to protect your legs from rock outcroppings, spiny plants and insects. You should also be careful to purify all of your drinking water. And be extremely cautious near streambeds as flash-flooding sometimes occurs, particularly on the windward coasts. This is particularly true during the winter months, when heavy storms from the northeast lash the islands.

All distances listed for hiking trails are one way unless otherwise noted.

WAILUA RIVER While none of these hikes actually follow the Wailua, all begin near Route 580, which parallels the river.

Nounou Mountain Trail—East Side (1.75 miles) begins off Haleilio Road at the parking lot in the Wailua Houselots and climbs 1250 feet to the Sleeping Giant's head at Mount Nounou summit. This trail is strenuous.

Nounou Mountain Trail—West Side (1.5 miles) begins off Route 581 and ascends with moderate difficulty 1000 feet to join the East Side trail.

Keahua Arboretum Trail (0.5 mile) begins two miles past the University of Hawaii Wailua Experiment Station on Route 580. This easy nature trail is lined with foreign plants.

Kuilau Ridge Trail (1.2 miles) begins on Route 580 near the Keahua Arboretum. This moderate, scenic hike goes past several vista points and picnic areas.

WAIMEA CANYON–KOKEE   Kokee State Park has about 45 miles of hiking trails through rugged, beautiful country. Along the mountain paths listed here, you'll discover some of the finest hiking in all Hawaii.

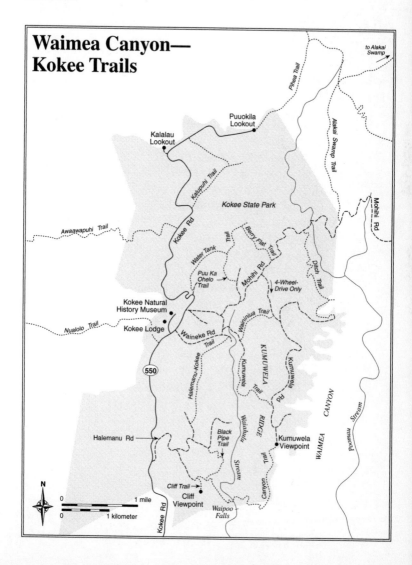

Waimea Canyon—
Kokee Trails

Alakai Swamp Trail (3.5 miles) passes through bogs and scrub rainforests to the Kilohana Lookout. This moderate once-muddy trail is now partially covered with boardwalks. It begins off Mohihi (Camp 10) Road, but is also accessible by the Pihea Trail.

Awaawapuhi Trail (3.25 miles) starts on Route 550 midway between Kokee Museum and Kalalau Lookout. This physically challenging trail leads through a forest to a vista at 2500-feet elevation that overlooks sheer cliffs and the ocean. The trail then connects with Nualolo Trail for a 13-mile loop.

Berry Flat Trail (0.6 mile) and **Puu Ka Ohelo Trail** (0.5 mile) combine off Mohihi (Camp 10) Road to form an easy loop that passes an interesting assortment of trees, including California redwood, *ohia*, *sugi* pine and *koa*.

Black Pipe Trail (0.5 mile) links Canyon Trail with Halemanu Road. It follows a cliff past stands of the rare *iliau* plant, a relative of Maui's famous silversword.

Canyon Trail (1.8 miles) forks off Cliff Trail and follows a relatively easy path around Waimea Canyon's northern rim to a vista sweeping down the canyon to the sea.

Cliff Trail (0.1 mile) begins at the end of the right fork of Halemanu Road and offers a pleasant walk to a viewpoint above Waimea Canyon. Feral goats are often spotted.

Ditch Trail (1.7 miles) runs from Mohihi Road at one end to Waininiua Road at the other. It's a moderate trail with spectacular views of forest areas and the Poomau River.

Halemanu-Kokee Trail (1.2 miles) sets out from the old ranger station. Birdwatchers should especially enjoy this easy jaunt.

Iliau Nature Loop (0.3 mile roundtrip) starts along Route 550 on a short course past 20 local plant species, including the *iliau*, endemic only to the Garden Isle. This easy trail offers good views of both Waimea Canyon and Waialae Falls.

Kalupuhi Trail (1.6 miles) begins at Route 550 en route to a plum grove. The plums are in season every other year. In a good year, you can enjoy both plums and a pleasant hike.

Kawaikoi Stream Trail (1.7 miles roundtrip), an easy loop trail, starts on Mohihi (Camp 10) Road across from Sugi Grove and follows near the stream through a manmade forest.

Koaie Canyon Trail (3 miles) branches off the Waimea Canyon trail near Poo Kaeha. It's a moderate hike that crosses the Waimea River and passes ancient terraces and rock walls en route to

Hiking
Kalalau

Kauai's premier hike, one of the finest treks in all the islands, follows an 11-mile trail along the rugged Na Pali Coast. This ancient Hawaiian trail to Kalalau Valley descends into dense rainforests and climbs along windswept cliffs. Streams and mountain pools along the path provide refreshing swimming holes. Wild orchids, guavas, *kukui* nuts, mangos and mountain apples grow in abundance.

The trail begins near Kee Beach at the end of Kuhio Highway. After a strenuous two-mile course the trail drops into Hanakapiai Valley. From here, it climbs through the valley and up to Hanakapiai Falls. Fringed by cliffs and possessing a marvelous sand beach, Hanakapiai makes an excellent rest point or final destination.

If you bypass the side trails and continue along the Kalalau Trail, you'll find that as it climbs out of Hanakapiai Valley, it becomes slightly rougher. Sharp grass presses close to the path as it leads through thick foliage, then along precipitous cliff faces. Four miles from Hanakapiai Valley, the trail arrives at Hanakoa Valley. There is an open-air shelter for public use here, as well as a steep one-third-mile trail that goes up to Hanakoa Falls.

The final trek to Kalalau, the most difficult section of the trail, passes scenery so spectacular it seems unreal. Knife-point peaks, illuminated by shafts of sunlight, rise thousands of feet. Frigate birds hang poised against the trade winds. Wisps of cloud fringe the cliffs. The silence is ominous, almost tangible. A foot from the trail, the ledge falls away into another sheer wall, which plummets a thousand feet and more to the surf below.

The narrow, serpentine trail then winds down to Kalalau Valley. A well-fed stream rumbles through this two-mile-wide vale. If you must use the water here, be sure to boil or otherwise purify it. Farther along, a white-sand beach sweeps past a series of caves to the far end of the valley. You may want to stop awhile and explore the caves, but if you swim here or at Hanakapiai, exercise extreme caution. The undertow and riptides are wicked.

Kalalau has many fine campsites near the beach, but firewood is scarce and cutting trees is *kapu*, so you'd best bring a campstove. Camping at Hanakapiai, Hanakoa or Kalalau will necessitate a state permit. Anyone hiking beyond Hanakapiai also needs a permit. These are available from the State Parks office. ~ 3060 Eiwa Street, Lihue; 808-274-3445.

Lonomea camp, a wilderness campsite. Here you'll find a shelter and a stream chock-full of swimming holes.

Kumuwela Trail (1 mile) begins off Mohihi (Camp 10) Road and passes through a fern-choked gulch. Good for birdwatchers.

Nature Trail (0.1 mile) begins behind the Kokee Museum and passes through a *koa* forest.

Nualolo Trail (3.75 miles) starts near Park Headquarters. Along the strenuous path you'll be able to see Nualolo Valley on the Na Pali Coast.

Pihea Trail (3.7 miles) offers excellent views of Kalalau Valley and the Alakai Swamp. This moderate trail also features a variety of birds and plant life. It begins at Puuokila Lookout.

Poomau Canyon Lookout Trail (0.3 mile) heads through a stand of Japanese *sugi* trees and a native rainforest. It begins from Mohihi (Camp 10) Road and ends at a vista overlooking Poomau and Waimea Canyons.

Waimea Canyon Trail (8 miles) can be reached from the Kukui Trail. Its very challenging path follows the Waimea River through the center of the canyon.

Waininiua Trail (0.6 mile) leads from the unpaved Kumuwela Road through a forest where ginger grows.

NORTH SHORE The **Powerline Trial** (15 miles) is a strenuous hike through Kauai's interior. Beginning in Princeville, it follows the Hanalei River, offering views of countless waterfalls and Mt. Waialeale, ending on the east side of the island near Kapaa. If you're feeling less adventurous, hike in a few miles and enjoy the waterfalls and lush vegetation before turning back the way you came.

SERVICE IN THE SUN

If you're looking for a fun and fulfilling way to spend ten days, contact **Sierra Club Outings**. Their guided service trips lead you into the islands' most desolate wilderness areas, through lush tropical forests and to coastal waters, restoring natural settings by removing manmade structures and fencing and conducting research on marine wildlife. Adventurers are able to snorkel, hike and enjoy beautiful views while helping to preserve Hawaii's paradise. ~ 85 2nd Street, 2nd Floor, San Francisco, CA 94105; 415-977-5522; www.sierraclub.org/outings/national, e-mail national. outings@sierraclub.org.

~ To get to the trailhead, turn inland at the corner of Princeville stables and continue beyond the row of houses.

Hiking Tours   Combine an education about the history, flora and fauna of Kauai's interior with a hiking/kayaking adventure. **Princeville Ranch Adventures** offers a number of options. Hikes include the "Hidden Hanalei" (a trek into the hills towards Mt. Namolokama to a perfect picture-taking spot) and the "Jungle Waterfall Kayak Adventure" (a combination kayaking/hiking/inner-tubing experience). There is also a range of private excursions available, with length and destinations tailored to your interests. Children over five are welcome. ~ Princeville; 808-826-7669, 888-955-7669; www.adventureskauai.com.

Kauai Nature Tours is a company that encourages "effective co-existence of earth's environment and its human inhabitants." To this end, all tours are led by local scientists and provide a detailed look into the natural wonders of Hawaii. The "Waimea Canyon Explorer" tour explores Kauai's geologic past. The "Mahaulepu Coast" hike shows you Kauai's limestone ledges and discusses the history of the coastline. This is a perfect way to learn to "take only pictures, leave only footprints." ~ Koloa; 808-742-8305, 888-233-8365; www.teok.com, e-mail teok@aloha.net.

THREE

History and Culture

POLYNESIAN ARRIVAL The island of Kauai was the first land mass created in the ongoing dramatic geologic upheaval that formed the Hawaiian islands. And, according to some historians, it was possibly the first island to be inhabited by humans. Perhaps as early as the third century, Polynesians sailing from the Marquesas Islands, and then later from Tahiti, landed in Hawaii. In Europe, mariners were rarely venturing outside the Mediterranean Sea, and it would be centuries before Columbus happened upon the New World. Yet in the Pacific, entire families were crossing 2500 miles of untracked ocean in hand-carved canoes with sails woven from coconut fibers. The boats were formidable structures, catamaran-like vessels with a cabin built on the platform between the wooden hulls and sails woven from *hala* (pandanus) leaves. Some of the vessels were 100 feet long and could do 20 knots, making the trip to Hawaii in a month. Entire families crossed the 2500 miles of untracked ocean with all the provisions they needed for their new home.

The Polynesians had originally come from the coast of Asia about 3000 years before. They had migrated through Indonesia, then pressed inexorably eastward, leapfrogging across archipelagoes until they finally reached the last chain, the most remote—Hawaii.

These Pacific migrants were undoubtedly the greatest sailors of their day, and stand among the finest in history. When close to land they could smell it, taste it in the seawater, see it in a lagoon's turquoise reflection on the clouds above an island. They knew 150 stars. From the color of the water they determined ocean depths and current directions. They had no charts, no compasses, no sextants; sailing directions were simply recorded in legends and chants. Yet Polynesians discovered the Pacific, from Indonesia to Easter Island, from New Zealand to Hawaii. They made the Vikings and Phoenicians look like landlubbers.

CAPTAIN COOK They were high islands, rising in the northeast as the sun broke across the Pacific. First one, then a second and, finally, as the tall-masted ships drifted west, a third island loomed before them. Landfall! The British crew was ecstatic. It meant fresh water, tropical fruits, solid ground on which to set their boots and a chance to carouse with the native women. For their captain, James Cook, it was another in an amazing career of discoveries. The man whom many call history's greatest explorer was about to land in one of the last spots on earth to be discovered by the West.

He would name the place for his patron, the British earl who became famous by pressing a meal between two crusts of bread. The Sandwich Islands. Later they would be called Owhyhee, and eventually, as the Western tongue glided around the uncharted edges of a foreign language, Hawaii.

It was January 1778, a time when the British Empire was still basking in a sun that never set. The Pacific had been opened to Western powers over two centuries before, when a Portuguese sailor named Magellan crossed it. Since that time, the British, French, Dutch and Spanish had tracked through in search of future colonies.

They happened upon Samoa, Fiji, Tahiti and the other islands that spread across this third of the globe, but somehow they had never sighted Hawaii. Even when Cook finally spied it, he little realized how important a find he had made. Hawaii, quite literally, was a jewel in the ocean, rich in fragrant sandalwood, ripe for agricultural exploitation and crowded with sea life. But it was the archipelago's isolation that would prove to be its greatest resource. Strategically situated between Asia and North America, it was the only place for thousands of miles to which whalers, merchants and bluejackets could repair for provisions and rest.

Cook was 49 years old when he shattered Hawaii's quiescence. The Englishman hadn't expected to find islands north of Tahiti. Quite frankly, he wasn't even trying. It was his third Pacific voyage and Cook was hunting bigger game, the fabled Northwest Passage that would link this ocean with the Atlantic.

But these mountainous islands were still an interesting find. He could see by the canoes venturing out to meet his ships that the lands were inhabited; when he finally put ashore in Waimea on Kauai, Cook discovered a Polynesian society. He saw irrigated fields, domestic animals and high-towered temples. The women were bare-breasted, the men wore loincloths. As his crew bartered for pigs, fowls and bananas, he learned that the natives knew about metal and coveted iron like gold.

If iron was gold to these "Indians," then Cook was a god. He soon realized that his arrival had somehow been miraculously timed, coinciding with the Makahiki festival, a months-long celebration highlighted by sporting competitions, feasting, hula and exaltation of the ruling chiefs. Even war ceased during this gala affair. Makahiki honored the roving deity Lono, whose return to Hawaii on "trees that would move over seas" was foretold in ancient legend. Cook was a strange white man sailing tall-masted ships—obviously he was Lono. The Hawaiians gave him gifts, fell in his path and rose only at his insistence.

But even among religious crowds, fame is often fickle. After leaving Kauai, Cook sailed north to the Arctic Sea, where he failed to discover the Northwest Passage. He returned the next year to Kealakekua Bay on the Big Island, arriving at the tail end of another exhausting Makahiki festival. By then the Hawaiians had tired of his constant demands for provisions and were suffering from a new disease that was obviously carried by Lono's archangelic crew—syphilis. This Lono was proving something of a freeloader.

Tensions ran high. The Hawaiians stole a boat. Cook retaliated with gunfire. A scuffle broke out on the beach and in a sudden violent outburst, which surprised the islanders as much as the interlopers, the Hawaiians discovered that their god could bleed. The world's finest mariner lay face down in foot-deep water, stabbed and bludgeoned to death.

Cook's end marked the beginning of an era. He had put the Pacific on the map, his map, probing its expanses and defining its fringes. In Hawaii he ended a thousand years of solitude. The archipelago's geographic isolation, which has always played a crucial role in Hawaii's development, had finally failed to protect it, and a second theme had come into play—the islands' vulnerability. Together with the region's "backwardness," these conditions would now mold Hawaii's history. All in turn would be shaped by another factor, one which James Cook had added to Hawaii's historic equation: the West.

The Landing

January 20, 1778:

"Between three and four in the afternoon, the captain went ashore with three armed boats and twelve of the marines, with a view of examining the water, and trying the disposition of the natives, who had assembled in considerable numbers on a sand beach before the village; behind it was a valley, in which was the piece of water. The moment he leaped on shore, all the islanders fell prostrate upon their faces, and continued in that posture, till, by signs, he prevailed on them to rise. They then presented to him many small pigs, with plantain trees, making use of nearly the same ceremonies which we had seen practiced, on similar occasions, at the Society, and other isles, and a long oration or prayer being pronounced by an individual, in which others of the assembly joined occasionally. The captain signified his acceptance of their proffered friendship, by bestowing on them, in return, such presents as he had brought ashore."

—An excerpt from *Captain Cook's Third and Last Voyage*
by George William Anderson

KAMEHAMEHA AND KAAHUMANU   The next man whose star would rise above Hawaii was present at Cook's death. Some say he struck the Englishman, others that he took a lock of the great leader's hair and used its residual power, its *mana*, to become king of all Hawaii.

Kamehameha was a tall, muscular man with a furrowed face, a lesser chief on the powerful island of Hawaii. When he began his career of conquest a few years after Cook's death, he was a mere upstart, an ambitious, arrogant young chief. But he fought with a general's skill and a warrior's cunning, often plunging into the midst of a melee. He had an astute sense of technology, an intuition that these new Western metals and firearms could make him a king.

In Kamehameha's early years, the Hawaiian islands were composed of many fiefdoms. Several kings or great chiefs, continually warring among themselves, ruled individual islands. At times, a few kings would carve up one island or a lone king might seize several. Never had one monarch controlled all the islands.

But fresh players had entered the field: Westerners with ample firepower and awesome ships. During the decade following Cook, only a handful had arrived, mostly Englishmen and Americans, and they had not yet won the influence they soon would wield. However, even a few foreigners were enough to upset the balance of power. They sold weapons and hardware to the great chiefs, making several of them more powerful than any of the others had ever been. War was imminent.

King Kamehameha I was a true diplomat. When Kauai finally (peacefully) fell under his control, he granted the former king of Kauai, Kaumualii, governorship of the island.

Kamehameha stood in the center of the hurricane. Like any leader suddenly caught up in the terrible momentum of history, he never quite realized where he was going or how fast he was moving. And he cared little that he was being carried in part by Westerners who would eventually want something for the ride. Kamehameha was no fool. If political expedience meant Western intrusion, then so be it. He had enemies among chiefs on the other islands; he needed the guns.

When two white men came into his camp in 1790, he had the military advisers to complement a fast-expanding arsenal. Within months he cannonaded Maui. In 1792, Kamehameha seized the Big Island by inviting his main rival to a peaceful parley, then slaying the hapless chief. By 1795, he had consolidated his control of Maui, grasped Molokai and Lanai, and begun reaching greedily toward Oahu. He struck rapidly, landing near Waikiki and sweeping inland, forcing his enemies to their deaths over the precipitous cliffs of the Nuuanu Pali.

The warrior had become a conqueror, controlling all the islands except Kauai, which he finally gained in 1810 by peaceful negotiation with King Kaumualii. Kamehameha proved to be as able a bureaucrat as he had been a general. He became a benevolent despot who, with the aid of an ever-increasing number of Western advisers, expanded Hawaii's commerce, brought peace to the islands and moved his people inexorably toward the modern age.

He came to be called Kamehameha the Great, and history first cast him as the George Washington of Hawaii, a wise and resolute leader who gathered a wartorn archipelago into a kingdom. Kamehameha I. But with the revisionist history of the

1960s and 1970s, as Third World people questioned both the Western version of events and the virtues of progress, Kamehameha began to resemble Benedict Arnold. He was seen as an opportunist, a megalomaniac who permitted the Western powers their initial foothold in Hawaii. He used their technology and then, in the manner of great men who depend on stronger allies, was eventually used by them.

As long a shadow as Kamehameha cast across the islands, the event that most dramatically transformed Hawaiian society occurred after his death in 1819. The kingdom had passed to Kamehameha's son Liholiho, but Kamehameha's favorite wife, Kaahumanu, usurped the power. Liholiho was a prodigal son, dissolute, lacking self-certainty, a drunk. Kaahumanu was a woman for all seasons, a canny politician who combined brilliance with boldness, the feminist of her day. She had infuriated Kamehameha by eating forbidden foods and sleeping with other chiefs, even when he placed a taboo on her body and executed her lovers. She drank liquor, ran away, proved completely uncontrollable and won Kamehameha's love.

It was only natural that when he died, she would take his *mana*, or so she reckoned. Kaahumanu gravitated toward power with the drive of someone whom fate has unwisely denied. She carved her own destiny, announcing that Kamehameha's wish had been to give her a governmental voice. There would be a new post and she would fill it, becoming in a sense Hawaii's first prime minister.

And if the power, then the motion. Kaahumanu immediately marched against Hawaii's belief system, trying to topple the old idols. For years she had bristled under a polytheistic religion regulated by taboos, or *kapu*, which severely restricted women's rights. Now Kaahumanu urged the new king, Liholiho, to break a very strict *kapu* by sharing a meal with women.

Since the act might help consolidate Liholiho's position, it had a certain appeal to the king. Anyway, the *kapu* were weakening: these white men, coming now in ever greater numbers, defied them with impunity. Liholiho vacillated, went on a two-day drunk before gaining courage, then finally sat down to eat. It was a last supper, shattering an ancient creed and opening the way for a radically new divinity. As Kaahumanu had willed, the old order collapsed, taking away a vital part of island life and leaving the Hawaiians more exposed than ever to foreign influence.

Already Western practices were gaining hold. Commerce from Honolulu, Lahaina and other ports was booming. There was a fortune to be made dealing sandalwood to China-bound merchants, and the chiefs were forcing the common people to strip Hawaii's forests. The grueling labor might make the chiefs rich, but it gained the commoners little more than a barren landscape. Western diseases struck virulently. The Polynesians in Hawaii, who numbered 300,000 in Cook's time, were extremely susceptible. By 1866, their population had dwindled to less than 60,000. It was a difficult time for the Hawaiian people.

MISSIONARIES AND MERCHANTS   Hawaii was not long without religion. The same year that Kaahumanu shattered tradition, a group of New England missionaries boarded the brig *Thaddeus* for a voyage around Cape Horn. It was a young company—many were in their twenties or thirties—and included a doctor, a printer and several teachers. They were all strict Calvinists, fearful that the second coming was at hand and possessed of a mission. They were bound for a strange land called Hawaii, 18,000 miles away.

Hawaii, of course, was a lost paradise, a hellhole of sin and savagery where men slept with several wives and women neglected to wear dresses. To the missionaries, it mattered little that the Hawaiians had lived this way for centuries. The churchmen would save these heathens from hell's everlasting fire whether they liked it or not.

The delegation arrived in Kailua on the Big Island in 1820 and then spread out, establishing important missions in Honolulu and Lahaina. Soon they were building schools and churches, conducting services in Hawaiian and converting the natives to Christianity.

The missionaries rapidly became an integral part of Hawaii, despite the fact that they were a walking contradiction to everything Hawaiian. They were a contentious, self-righteous, fanatical people whose arrogance toward the Hawaiians blinded them to the beauty and wisdom of island lifestyles. Where the natives lived in thatch homes open to the soothing trade winds, the missionaries built airless clapboard houses with New England–style fireplaces. While the Polynesians swam and surfed frequently, the new arrivals, living near the world's finest beaches, stank from not bathing. In a region where the thermometer rarely drops much below 70°, they wore long-sleeved woolens, ankle-length dresses and claw-hammer coats. At dinner they preferred salt pork to fresh beef, dried meat to fresh fish. They considered coconuts an abomination and were loath to eat bananas.

And yet the missionaries were a brave people, selfless and God-fearing. Their dangerous voyage from the Atlantic had brought them into a very alien land. Many would die from disease and overwork; most would never see their homeland again. Bigoted though they were, the Calvinists committed their lives to the Hawaiian people. They developed the Hawaiian alphabet, rendered Hawaiian into a written language and, of course, translated the Bible. Theirs was the first printing press west of the Rockies. They introduced Western medicine throughout the islands and created such an effective school system that, by the mid-19th century, 80 percent of the Hawaiian population was literate. Unlike almost all the other white people who came to Hawaii, they not only took from the islanders, they also gave.

But to these missionaries, *giving* meant ripping away everything repugnant to God and substituting it with Christianity. They would have to destroy Hawaiian culture in order to save it. Though instructed by their church elders not to meddle in island politics, the missionaries soon realized that heavenly wars had to be fought on earthly battlefields. Politics it would be. After all, wasn't government just another expression of God's bounty?

They allied with Kaahumanu and found it increasingly difficult to separate church from state. Kaahumanu converted to Christianity, while the missionaries became government advisers and helped

A SLICE OF THE PIE

In ancient Hawaii, the chiefs used an *ahupuaa* system to divide and manage the islands. The pie-shaped wedges of land varied in size, depending on a chief's status, but each ran from the mountains to the sea, providing the residents with all the resources they needed to exist. Those who lived in the uplands traded food they raised with their *ohana* (family) that resided by the sea. People rarely ventured beyond their own *ahupuaa*, and while they might trade with neighboring *ahupuaa*, they would never hunt or harvest outside their own boundaries. Even today, folks in Hawaii tend to stick close to home in deference to the old system.

pass laws protecting the sanctity of the Sabbath. Disgusting practices such as hula dancing were prohibited.

Politics can be a dangerous world for a man of the cloth. The missionaries were soon pitted against other foreigners who were quite willing to let the clerics sing hymns, but were damned opposed to permitting them a voice in government. Hawaii in the 1820s had become a favorite way station for the whaling fleet. As the sandalwood forests were decimated, the island merchants began looking for other industries. By the 1840s, when over 500 ships a year anchored in Hawaiian ports, whaling had become the islands' economic lifeblood.

After King Kamehameha died, his successor forced Kaumualii to leave Kauai and marry Queen Kaahumanu. The former king of Kauai never returned to his island.

Like the missionaries, the whalers were Yankees, shipping out from bustling New England ports. But they were a hell of a different cut of Yankee. These were rough, crude, boisterous men who loved rum and music, and thought a lot more of fornicating with island women than saving them. After the churchmen forced the passage of laws prohibiting prostitution, the sailors rioted along the waterfront and fired cannons at the mission homes. When the smoke cleared, the whalers still had their women.

Religion simply could not compete with commerce, and other Westerners were continuously stimulating more business in the islands. By the 1840s, as Hawaii adopted a parliamentary form of government, American and British fortune hunters were replacing missionaries as government advisers. It was a time when anyone, regardless of ability or morality, could travel to the islands and become a political powerhouse literally overnight. A consumptive American, fleeing the mainland for reasons of health, became chief justice of the Hawaiian Supreme Court while still in his twenties. Another lawyer, shadowed from the East Coast by a checkered past, became attorney general two weeks after arriving.

The situation was no different internationally. Hawaii was subject to the whims and terrors of gunboat diplomacy. The archipelago was solitary and exposed, and Western powers were beginning to eye it covetously. In 1843, a maverick British naval officer actually annexed Hawaii to the Crown, but the London government later countermanded his actions. Then, in the early 1850s, the threat of American annexation arose. Restless Californians, fresh from the gold fields and hungry for revolution, plotted unsuccessfully in Honolulu. Even the French periodically sent gunboats in to protect their small Catholic minority.

Finally, the three powers officially stated that they wanted to maintain Hawaii's national integrity. But independence seemed increasingly unlikely. European countries had already begun claiming other Pacific islands, and with the influx of Yankee missionaries and whalers, Hawaii was being steadily drawn into the American orbit.

THE SUGAR PLANTERS   There is an old Hawaiian saying that describes the 19th century: The missionaries came to do good, and they did very well. Actually the early evangelists, few of whom profited from their work, lived out only half the maxim. Their sons would give the saying its full meaning.

This second generation, quite willing to sacrifice glory for gain, fit neatly into the commercial society that had rendered their fathers irrelevant. They were shrewd, farsighted young Christians who had grown up in Hawaii and knew both the islands' pitfalls and potentials. They realized that the missionaries had never quite found Hawaii's pulse, and they watched uneasily as whaling became the lifeblood of the islands. Certainly it brought wealth, but whaling was too tenuous—there was always a threat that it might dry up entirely. A one-industry economy would never do; the mission boys wanted more. Agriculture was the obvious answer, and eventually they determined to bind their providence to a plant that grew wild in the islands—sugar cane.

The first sugar plantation, the Koloa Sugar Company, was started on Kauai in 1835, but not until the 1870s did the new industry blossom. By then, the Civil War had wreaked havoc with the whaling fleet, and a devastating winter in the Arctic whaling grounds practically destroyed it. The mission boys, who had prophesied the storm, weathered it quite comfortably. They had already begun fomenting an agricultural revolution.

THE GREAT MAHELE   Agriculture, of course, means land, and until the 19th century all Hawaii's acreage was held by chiefs. So in 1848, the mission sons, together with other white entrepreneurs, pushed through the Great Mahele, one of the slickest real estate laws in history. Rationalizing that it would grant chiefs the liberty to sell land to Hawaiian commoners and white men, the mission sons established a Western system of private property.

The Hawaiians, who had shared their chiefs' lands communally for centuries, had absolutely no concept of deeds and leases. What resulted was the old $24-worth-of-beads story. The benevolent Westerners wound up with the land, while the lucky Hawaiians got practically nothing. Large tracts were purchased for cases of whiskey; others went for the cost of a hollow promise. The entire island of Niihau, which is still owned by the same family, sold for $10,000. It was a bloodless coup, staged more than 40 years before the revolution that would topple Hawaii's monarchy. In a sense it made the 1893 uprising anticlimactic. By then Hawaii's future would already be determined: white interlopers would own four times as much land as Hawaiian commoners.

> Before the Great Mahele Hawaiians flourished because they had the rights of access and were able to use the resources of both land and the sea. Their traditions were based on sharing and common use.

Following the Great Mahele, the mission boys, along with other businessmen, were ready to become sugar planters. The *mana* once again was passing into new hands. Obviously, there was money to be made in cane, a lot of it, and now that they had land, all they needed was labor. The Hawaiians would never do. Cook might have recognized them as industrious, hardworking people, but the sugar planters considered them shiftless. Disease was killing them off anyway, and the Hawaiians who survived seemed to lose the will to live. Many made appointments with death, stating that in a week they would die; seven days later they were dead.

Foreign labor was the only answer. In 1850, the Masters and Servants Act was passed, establishing an immigration board to import plantation workers. Cheap Asian labor would be brought over. It was a crucial decision, one that would ramify forever through Hawaiian history and change the very substance of island society. Eventually these Asian workers transformed Hawaii from a chain of Polynesian islands into one of the world's most varied and dynamic locales, a meeting place of East and West.

The Chinese were the first to come, arriving in 1852 and soon outnumbering the white population. Initially, with their long pigtails and uncommon habits, the Chinese were a joke around the islands. They were poor people from southern China whose lives were directed by clan loyalty. They built schools and worked hard so that one day they could return to their native villages in glory. They were ambitious, industrious and—ultimately—successful.

Too successful, according to the sugar planters, who found it almost impossible to keep the coolies down on the farm. The Chinese came to Hawaii under labor contracts, which forced them to work for five years. After their indentureship, rather than reenlisting as the sugar bosses had planned, the Chinese moved to the city and became merchants. Worse yet, they married Hawaiian women and were assimilated into the society.

These coolies, the planters decided, were too uppity, too ready to fill social roles that were really the business of white men. So in the 1880s, they began importing Portuguese, more than 20,000 of them. But the Portuguese thought they already *were* white men, while any self-respecting American or Englishman of the time knew they weren't.

The Portuguese spelled trouble, and in 1886 the sugar planters turned to Japan, with its restricted land mass and burgeoning population. The new immigrants were peasants from Japan's southern islands, raised in an authoritarian, hierarchical culture in which the father was a family dictator and the family was strictly defined by its social status. Like the Chinese, they built schools to protect their heritage and dreamed of returning home someday; but unlike their Asian neighbors, they only married other Japanese. They sent home for "picture brides," worshipped their ancestors and Emperor and paid ultimate loyalty to Japan, not Hawaii.

The Japanese, it soon became evident, were too proud to work long hours for low pay. Plantation conditions were atrocious; workers were housed in hovels and frequently beaten. The Japanese simply did not adapt. Worst of all, they not only bitched, they organized, striking in 1909.

So in 1910, the sugar planters turned to the Philippines for labor. For two decades the Filipinos arrived, seeking their fortunes and leaving their wives behind. They worked not only with sugar cane but also with pineapples, which were becoming a big business in the 20th century. They were a boisterous, fun-loving people, hated by the immigrants who preceded them and used by the whites who hired them. The Filipinos were given the most menial jobs, the worst working conditions and the shoddiest housing. In time, another side of their character began to show—a despondency, a hopeless sense of their own plight, their inability to raise passage money back home. They became the untouchables of Hawaii. (Between 1850 and 1930, 180,000 Japanese, 125,000 Filipinos, 50,000 Chinese and 20,000 Portuguese immigrated to Hawaii.)

REVOLUTIONARIES AND ROYALISTS   Sugar, by the late 19th century, was king. It had become the center of island economy, the principal fact of life for most islanders. Like the earlier whaling industry, it was drawing Hawaii ever closer to the American sphere. The sugar planters were selling the bulk of their crops in California; having already signed several tariff treaties to protect their American market, they were eager to further strengthen mainland ties. Besides, many sugar planters were second-, third- and fourth-generation descendants of the New England missionaries; they had a natural affinity for the United States.

There was, however, one group that shared neither their love for sugar nor their ties to America. To the Hawaiian people, David Kalakaua was king, and America was the nemesis that had long threatened their independence. The whites might own the land, but the Hawaiians, through their monarch, still held substantial political power. During Kalakaua's rule in the 1870s and 1880s, anticolonialism was rampant.

The sugar planters were growing impatient. Kalakaua was proving very antagonistic; his nationalist drumbeating was becoming louder in their ears. How could the sugar merchants convince the United States to annex Hawaii when all these silly Hawaiian royalists were running around pretending to be the Pacific's answer to the British Isles? They had tolerated this long enough. The Hawaiians were obviously unfit to rule, and the planters soon joined with other businessmen to form a secret revolutionary organization. Backed by a force of well-armed followers, they pushed through the "Bayonet Constitution" of 1887, a self-serving document that weakened the king and strengthened the white landowners. If Hawaii was to remain a monarchy, it would have a Magna Carta.

But Hawaii would not be a monarchy long. Once revolution is in the air, it's often difficult to clear the smoke. By 1893, Kalakaua was dead and his sister, Liliuokalani, had succeeded to the throne. She was an audacious leader, proud of her heritage, quick to defend it and prone to let immediate passions carry her onto dangerous ground. At a time when she should have hung fire, she charged, proclaiming publicly that she would abrogate the new constitution and reestablish a strong monarchy. The revolutionaries had the excuse they needed. They struck in January, seized government buildings and, with four boatloads of American marines and the support of the American minister, secured Honolulu. Liliu-okalani surrendered.

It was a highly illegal coup; legitimate government had been stolen from the Hawaiian people. But given an island chain as isolated and vulnerable as Hawaii, the revolutionaries reasoned, how much did it really matter? It would be weeks before word reached Washington of what a few Americans had done without official sanction, then several more months before a new American president, Grover Cleveland, denounced the renegade action. By then the revolutionaries would already be forming a republic.

> George Kaumualii, the son of former King Kaumualii, educated in New England at the Foreign Mission School at South Farms, Massachusetts, brought missionaries back with him to Kauai. One was Sam Whitney, who planted the first sugar on the island.

Not even revolution could rock Hawaii into the modern age. For years, an unstable monarchy had reigned; now an oligarchy composed of the revolution's leaders would rule. Officially, Hawaii was a democracy; in truth, the Chinese and Japanese were hindered from voting, and the Hawaiians were encouraged not to bother. Hawaii, reckoned its new leaders, was simply not ready for democracy. Even when the islands were finally annexed by the United States in 1898 and granted territorial status, they remained a colony.

More than ever before, the sugar planters, alias revolutionaries, held sway. By the early 20th century, they had linked their plantations into a cartel, the Big Five. It was a tidy monopoly composed of five companies that owned not only the sugar and pineapple industries, but the docks, shipping companies and many of the stores, as well. Most of these holdings, happily, were the property of a few interlocking, intermarrying mission families—the Doles, Thurstons, Alexanders, Baldwins, Castles, Cookes and others—who had found heaven right here on earth. They golfed together and dined together, sent their daughters to Wellesley and their sons to Yale. All were proud of their roots, and as blindly paternalistic as their forefathers. It was their destiny to control Hawaii, and they made very certain, by refusing to sell land or provide services, that mainland firms did not gain a foothold in their domain.

What was good for the Big Five was good for Hawaii. Competition was obviously not good for Hawaii. Although the Chinese and Japanese were establishing successful businesses in Honolulu and some Chinese were even growing rich, they posed no immediate threat to the Big Five. And the Hawaiians had never been good at capitalism. By the early 20th century, they had become one of the world's most urbanized groups. But rather than competing with white businessmen in Honolulu, unemployed Hawaiians were forced to live in hovels and packing crates, cooking their poi on stoves fashioned from empty oil cans.

Political competition was also unhealthy. Hawaii was ruled by the Big Five, so naturally it should be run by the Republican Party. After all, the mission families were Republicans. Back on the mainland, the Democrats had always been cool to the sugar planters, and it was a Republican president, William McKinley, who eventually annexed Hawaii. The Republicans, quite simply, were good for business.

The Big Five set out very deliberately to overwhelm any political opposition. When the Hawaiians created a home-rule party around the turn of the 20th century, the Big Five shrewdly co-opted it by running a beloved descendant of Hawaii's royal family as the Republican candidate. On the plantations they pitted one ethnic group against another to prevent the Asian workers from organizing. Then, when labor unions finally formed, the Big Five attacked them savagely. In 1924, police killed 16 strikers on Kauai. Fourteen years later, in an incident known as the "Hilo massacre," the police wounded 50 picketers.

The Big Five crushed the Democratic Party by intimidation. Polling booths were rigged. It was dangerous to vote Democratic—workers could lose their jobs, and if they were plantation workers, that meant losing their houses as well. Conducting Democratic meetings on the plantations was about as easy as holding a hula dance in an old missionary church. The Democrats went underground.

Those were halcyon days for both the Big Five and the Republican Party. In 1900, only five percent of Hawaii's population was white. The rest was composed of races that rarely benefitted from Republican policies. But for the next several decades, even during the Depression, the Big Five kept the Republicans in power.

While the New Deal swept the mainland, Hawaii clung to its colonial heritage. The islands were still a generation behind the rest of the United States—the Big Five enjoyed it that way. There was nothing like the status quo when you were already in power.

Other factors that had long shaped Hawaii's history also played into the hands of the Big Five. The islands' vulnerability, which had always favored the rule of a small elite, permitted the Big Five to establish an awesome cartel. Hawaii's isolation, its distance from the mainland, helped protect their monopoly.

THE JAPANESE AND THE MODERN WORLD   All that ended on December 7, 1941. On what would afterwards be known as the "Day of Infamy," a flotilla of six aircraft carriers carrying over 400 planes unleashed a devastating assault on Pearl Harbor. Attacking the Pacific Fleet on a Sunday morning, when most of the American ships were unwisely anchored side by side, the Japanese sank or badly damaged six battleships, three destroyers and several other vessels. Over 2400 Americans were killed.

The Japanese bombers that attacked Pearl Harbor sent shock waves through Hawaii that are still rumbling today. World War II changed all the rules of the game, upsetting the conditions that had determined island history for centuries.

Ironically, no group in Hawaii would feel the shift more thoroughly than the Japanese. On the mainland, Japanese Americans were rounded up and herded into relocation camps. But in Hawaii that was impossible; there were simply too many (160,000—fully one-third of the island's population), and they comprised too large a part of the labor force.

Many were second-generation Japanese, *nisei*, who had been educated in American schools and assimilated into Western society. Unlike their immigrant parents, the *issei*, they felt few ties to Japan. Their loyalties lay with America, and when war broke out they determined to prove it. They joined the U.S. armed forces and formed a regiment, the 442nd, which became the most frequently decorated outfit of the war. The Japanese were heroes, and when

NIIHAU NINJA

Niihau had its World War II claim to fame when one of the Japanese airplanes involved in the bombing of Pearl Harbor had to make a forced landing on the island. The pilot was captured and his documents were seized. It is said that those papers would later assist in the breaking of the Japanese communication code. The pilot tried to escape the island but was overpowered by a Niihau resident and killed.

the war ended many heroes came home to the United States and ran for political office. Men like Daniel Inouye and Spark Matsunaga began winning elections and would eventually become United States senators.

By the time the 442nd returned to the home front, Hawaii was changing dramatically. The Democrats were coming to power. Leftist labor unions won crucial strikes in 1941 and 1946. Jack Burns, an ex-cop who dressed in tattered clothes and drove around Honolulu in a beat-up car, was creating a new Democratic coalition.

Jack London's story, "Koolau, The Leper," was about a Kauaian leper who refused to be moved to Kalaupapa on Molokai, taking his family to the mountains of Na Pali instead to survive.

Burns, who would eventually become governor, recognized the potential power of Hawaii's ethnic groups. Money was flowing into the islands—first military expenditures and then tourist dollars, and non-whites were rapidly becoming a new middle class. The Filipinos still constituted a large part of the plantation force, and the Hawaiians remained disenchanted, but the Japanese and Chinese were moving up fast. Together they formed a majority of Hawaii's voters.

Burns organized them, creating a multiracial movement and thrusting the Japanese forward as candidates. By 1954, the Democrats controlled the legislature, with the Japanese filling one out of every two seats in the capital. Then, when Hawaii attained statehood five years later, the voters elected the first Japanese ever to serve in Congress. Today one of the state's U.S. senators and a congressman are Japanese. On every level of government, from municipal to federal, the Japanese predominate. They have arrived. The *mana*, that legendary power coveted by the Hawaiian chiefs and then lost to the sugar barons, has passed once again—to a people who came as immigrant farm-workers and stayed to become the leaders of the 50th state.

The Japanese and the Democrats were on the move, but in the period from World War II until the present day, everything was in motion. Hawaii was in upheaval. Jet travel and a population boom shattered the islands' solitude. While in 1939 about 500 people flew to Hawaii, now about seven million visitors land every year. The military population escalated as Oahu became a key base not only during World War II but throughout the Cold War and the Vietnam War, as well. Hawaii's overall population exploded from about a half-million just after World War II to over one million at the present time.

No longer did the islands lag behind the mainland; they rapidly acquired the dubious quality of modernity. Hawaii became America's 50th state in 1959, Honolulu grew into a bustling high-rise city, and hotels and condominiums mushroomed along the beaches of Maui, a neighboring island. Outside investors swallowed up two of the Big Five corporations, and several partners in the old monopoly began conducting most of their business outside Hawaii. Everything became too big and moved too fast for Hawaii to be entirely vulnerable to a small interest group. Now, like the rest of the world, it would be prey to multinational corporations.

By the 1980s, it would also be of significant interest to investors from Japan. In a few short years they succeeded in buying up a majority of the state's luxury resorts, including every major beachfront hotel in Waikiki, sending real-estate prices into an upward spiral that did not level off until the early 1990s. During the rest of the decade, the economy was stagnant, with real-estate prices dropping, agriculture declining and tourism leveling off at seven million visitors annually.

One element that has not plateaued during the last ten years is the Native Hawaiian movement. Nativist sentiments were spurred in January 1993 by the 100th anniversary of the American overthrow of the Hawaiian monarchy. Over 15,000 people turned out to mark the illegal coup. Later that year, President Clinton signed a statement issued by Congress formally apologizing to the Hawaiian people. In 1994, the United States Navy returned the island of Kahoolawe to the state of Hawaii. Long a rallying symbol for the Native Hawaiian movement, the unoccupied island had been used for decades as a naval bombing target. By 1996, efforts to clean away bomb debris and make the island habitable were well under way, although completion of the clean-up is still years off. Then in 1998, the issue of Hawaii's monarchy arose again when demonstrators marched around the entire island of Oahu and staged rallies to protest the 100th anniversary of the United States' annexation of Hawaii.

Today, numerous perspectives remain to be reconciled, with grassroots movements working to secure a degree of autonomy for Hawaii's native people. The most common goal seems to be a status similar to that accorded the American Indians by the federal government, although there are still those who seek a return to an independent Hawaii, either as a restored monarchy or along democratic lines. Also pending resolution is the distribution of land to Native Hawaiians with documented claims, as well as a financial settlement with the state government. It's a complex situation involving the setting right of injustices of a century past.

Hawaiian Culture

Hawaii, according to Polynesian legend, was discovered by Hawaii-loa, an adventurous sailor who often disappeared on long fishing trips. On one voyage, urged along by his navigator, Hawaii-loa sailed toward the planet Jupiter. He crossed the "many-colored ocean," passed over the "deep-colored sea," and eventually came upon "flaming Hawaii," a mountainous island chain that spewed smoke and lava.

History is less romantic. The Polynesians who found Hawaii were probably driven from their home islands by war or some similar calamity. They traveled in groups, not as lone rangers, and shared their canoes with dogs, pigs and chickens, with which they planned to stock new lands. Agricultural plants such as coconuts, yams, taro, sugar cane, bananas and breadfruit were also stowed on board.

Most important, they transported their culture, an intricate system of beliefs and practices developed in the South Seas. After undergoing the stresses and demands of pioneer life, this traditional lifestyle was transformed into a new and uniquely Hawaiian culture.

It was based on a caste system that placed the *alii*, or chiefs, at the top and the slaves, *kauwa*, on the bottom. Between these two groups were the priests, *kahuna*, and the common people, or *makaainana*. The chiefs, much like feudal lords, controlled all the land and collected taxes from the commoners who farmed it.

Life centered around the *kapu*, a complex group of regulations that dictated what was sacred or profane. For example, women were not permitted to eat pork or bananas; commoners had to prostrate themselves in the presence of a chief. These strictures were vital to Hawaiian religion; *kapu* breakers were directly violating the will of the gods and could be executed for their actions. And there were a lot of gods to watch out for, many quite vindictive. The four central gods were *Kane*, the creator; *Lono*, the god of agriculture; *Ku*, the war god; and *Kanaloa*, lord of the underworld.

They had been born from the sky father and earth mother, and had in turn created many lesser gods and demigods who controlled various aspects of nature.

It was, in the uncompromising terminology of the West, a stone-age civilization. Though the Hawaiians lacked metal tools, the wheel and a writing system, they managed to include within their inventory of cultural goods everything necessary to sustain a large population on a chain of small islands. They fashioned fish nets from native *olona* fiber, made hooks out of bone, shell and ivory, and raised fish in rock-bound ponds. The men used irrigation in their farming. The men and women made clothing by pounding mulberry bark into a soft cloth called *tapa*, dyeing elaborate patterns into the fabric. They built peak-roofed thatch huts from native *pili* grass and *hala* leaves. The men fought wars with spears, slings, clubs and daggers. The women used mortars and pestles to pound the roots of the taro plant into poi, the islanders' staple food. Bread, fruit, yams and coconut were other menu standards.

The West labeled these early Hawaiians "noble savages." Actually, they often lacked nobility. The Hawaiians practiced human sacrifice during religious ceremonies and often used human bone to fashion fish hooks. They constantly warred among themselves and would mercilessly pursue a retreating army, murdering as many of the vanquished soldiers as possible.

HAWAIIAN SOVEREIGNTY

Over the past few decades since the advent of Hawaiian Renaissance, there has been a loud call for Hawaiian sovereignty. A bitter feeling of mistrust is held by many Hawaiians against the U.S. government because the monarchy was overthrown by a band of U.S. merchant renegades. Hawaiians have been outspoken in their demand for righting the wrong that was done to them; however, there is confusion among various Hawaiian groups as to what should be done. Some activists see the sovereignty movement as a struggle to elevate the native Hawaiian people to a higher place *within* the structure of the United States of America. Others believe that Hawaii should be moved *out* of the United States—with the monarchy reinstated, giving Hawaii an independent status. Many think something in between should be done. Some activists demand that reparations should be inclusive of all the people of Hawaii, others think it should include only the native Hawaiian people. It is a movement marked with passion and ambiguity.

But they weren't savages either. The Hawaiians developed a rich oral tradition of genealogical chants and created beautiful lilting songs to accompany their hula dancing. Their musicians mastered several instruments including the *ukeke* (a single-stringed device resembling a bow), an *ohe hano ihu* or nose flute, rattles and drums made from gourds, coconut shells or logs. Their craftsmen produced the world's finest featherwork, tying thousands of tiny feathers onto netting to produce golden cloaks and ceremonial helmets. The Hawaiians helped develop the sport of surfing. They also swam, boxed, bowled and devised an intriguing game called *konane*, a cross between checkers and the Japanese game of go. They built networks of trails across lava flows, and created an elemental art form in the images—petroglyphs—that they carved into lava rock along the trails.

They also achieved something far more outstanding than their varied arts and crafts, something that the West, with its awesome knowledge and advanced technology, has never duplicated. The Hawaiians created a balance with nature. They practiced conservation, establishing closed seasons on certain fish species and carefully guarding their plant and animal resources. They led a simple life, without the complexities the outside world would eventually thrust upon them. It was a good life: food was plentiful, people were healthy and the population increased. For a thousand years, the Hawaiians lived in delicate harmony with the elements. It wasn't until the West entered the realm, transforming everything, that the fragile balance was destroyed. But that is another story entirely.

PEOPLE   The most isolated population center on earth, Hawaii is 2390 miles from the mainland United States and 4900 miles from China. Because of its unique history and isolated geography, Hawaii is truly a cultural melting pot. It's one of the few states in the union in which caucasians are a minority group. Whites, or *haole* as they're called in the islands, comprise only about 21 percent of Hawaii's 1.2 million population. Japanese constitute 18 percent, Filipinos 12 percent, Hawaiians and part-Hawaiians account for 22 percent, Chinese about 4 percent and other racial groups 23 percent. It's a very vital society, with one fifth of the people born of racially mixed parents.

One trait characterizing many of these people is Hawaii's famous spirit of *aloha*, a genuine friendliness, an openness to strangers, a willingness to give freely. Undoubtedly, it is one of the finest qualities any people has ever demonstrated. *Aloha* originated with the Polynesians and played an important role in ancient Hawaiian civilization.

The aloha spirit is alive and well in the islands, although bad attitudes toward *haole*, the term used for whites, are not unknown. All parties, however, seem to understand the crucial role tourism has come to play in Hawaii's economy, which means you're not likely to experience unpleasantness from the locals you'll meet—unless you behave unpleasantly. A smile goes a long way.

CUISINE

Nowhere is the influence of Hawaii's melting pot population stronger than in the kitchen. While in the islands, you'll probably eat not only with a fork, but with chopsticks and fingers as well. You'll sample a wonderfully varied cuisine. In addition to standard American fare, hundreds of restaurants serve Hawaiian, Japanese, Chinese, Korean, Portuguese and Filipino dishes. There are also fresh fruits aplenty—pineapples, papayas, mangos, bananas and tangerines—plus local fish such as mahimahi, marlin and snapper.

The mainstay of the traditional Hawaiian diet is poi, a purplish paste pounded from baked or steamed taro tubers. It's pretty bland fare, but it does make a good side dish with *imu*-cooked pork or tripe stew. Poi was considered such a sacred a part of daily Hawaiian life that whenever a bowl of poi was uncovered at a family gathering, it was believed that the spirit of Haloa, the ancestor of the Hawaiian people, was present. That meant that all conflict among family members had to stop.

LUAUS IN KAUAI

Hawaii folks love to eat, especially at luaus, where the food is always plentiful and *ono* (good) and entertainment is guaranteed. A luau is traditionally held to celebrate a baby's first birthday, high school graduation and marriage, and friends and family all pitch in to help. The tourist luau is a different beast, but still worth checking out. You can expect hula dancing, singing, plentiful mai tais, *imu*-roasted pork and poi, along with a vast spread of other Hawaiian and local-style dishes. On Kauai, the major resorts and Kilohana do a very good job of it, or check out such classic venues as Smith's Tropical Gardens in Wailua and Tahiti Nui's in Hanalei.

You should also try *laulau*, a combination of fish, pork and taro leaves wrapped in a *ti* leaf and steamed. And don't neglect to taste baked *ulu* (breadfruit) and *opihi* (limpets). Among the other Hawaiian culinary traditions are *kalua* pig, a shredded pork dish baked in an *imu* (underground oven); *lomilomi* salmon, which is salted and mixed with onions and tomatoes; and chicken *luau*, prepared in taro leaves and coconut milk.

A good way to try all these dishes at one sitting is to attend a luau. I've always found the tourist luaus too commercial, but you might watch the newspapers for one of the special luaus sponsored by civic organizations.

Japanese dishes include sushi, sukiyaki, teriyaki and tempura, plus an island favorite—sashimi, or raw fish. On most any menu, including McDonald's, you'll find *saimin*, a noodle soup filled with meat, vegetables and *kamaboko* (fishcake).

You can count on the Koreans for *kim chi*, a spicy salad of pickled cabbage, and *kalbi*, barbecued beef short ribs prepared with soy and sesame oil. The Portuguese serve up some delicious sweets including *malasadas* (donuts minus the holes) and *pao doce*, or sweet bread. For Filipino fare, I recommend *adobo*, a pork or chicken dish spiced with garlic and vinegar, and *pochero*, a meat entrée cooked with bananas and several vegetables. In addition to a host of dinner dishes, the Chinese have contributed treats such as *manapua* (a steamed bun filled with barbecued pork) and oxtail soup. They also introduced crack seed to the islands. Made from dried and preserved fruit, it provides a treat as sweet as candy.

As the Hawaiians say, *"Hele mai ai."* Come and eat!

SOUNDS FISHY

What are all those strange-sounding fish dishes on the menu? A quick translation will help you when choosing a seafood platter from Hawaiian waters. Firm-textured with a light taste, the most popular fish is *mahimahi*, or dolphin fish (no, it's not one of those amazing creatures that do fancy tricks on the waves); its English equivalent is dorado. *Ahi* is yellowfin tuna and is especially delicious as sashimi (raw) or blackened. *Opakapaka* is pink snapper and is a staple of Pacific Rim cuisine. Other snappers include *uku* (gray snapper), *onaga* (ruby snapper) and *ehu* (red snapper). *Ono* (which means delicious in Hawaiian) is king mackerel, or wahoo, a white fish that lives up to its name.

The language common to all Hawaii is English, but because of **LANGUAGE** its diverse cultural heritage, the archipelago also supports several other tongues. Foremost among these are Hawaiian and pidgin. Hawaiian, closely related to other Polynesian languages, is one of the most fluid and melodious languages in the world. It's composed of only twelve letters: five vowels—*a, e, i, o, u* and seven consonants—*h, k, l, m, n, p, w*. The glottal stop ('), when used, counts as a thirteenth letter.

At first glance, the language appears formidable: How the hell do you pronounce *humuhumunukunukuapuaa*? But actually it's quite simple. After you've mastered a few rules of pronunciation, you can take on any word in the language.

The first thing to remember is that every syllable ends with a vowel, and the next to last syllable usually receives the accent.

The next rule to keep in mind is that all the letters in Hawaiian are pronounced. Consonants are pronounced the same as in English (except for the *w*, which is pronounced as a *v* when it introduces the last syllable of a word—as in *ewa* or *awa*. Vowels are pronounced the same as in Spanish: *a* as in *among*, *e* as in *they*, *i* as in *machine*, *o* as in *no* and *u* as in *too*. Hawaiian has four vowel combinations or diphthongs: *au*, pronounced *ow*; *ae* and *ai*, which sound like *eye*; and *ei*, pronounced *ay*. As noted above, the glottal stop (') occasionally provides a thirteenth letter.

By now, you're probably wondering what I could possibly have meant when I said Hawaiian was simple. I think the glossary that follows will simplify everything while helping you pronounce common words and place names. Just go through the list, starting with words like aloha and luau that you already know. After you've practiced pronouncing familiar words, the rules will become second nature; you'll no longer be a *malihini*.

Just when you start to speak with a swagger, cocky about having learned a new language, some young Hawaiian will start talking at you in a tongue that breaks all the rules you've so carefully mastered. That's pidgin. It started in the 19th century as a lingua franca among Hawaii's many races. Pidgin speakers mix English and Hawaiian with several other tongues to produce a spicy creole. It's a fascinating language with its own vocabulary, a unique syntax and a rising inflection that's hard to mimic.

Pidgin is definitely the hip way to talk in Hawaii. A lot of young Hawaiians use it among themselves as a private language. At times they may start talking pidgin to you, acting as though they don't speak English; then if they decide you're okay, they'll break into English. When that happens, you be one *da kine brah*.

So *brah*, I take *da kine* pidgin words, put 'em together with Hawaiian, make one big list. Savvy?

aa (ah-**ah**)—a type of rough lava
ae (eye)—yes
aikane (eye-**kah**-nay)—friend, close companion
akamai (ah-kah-**my**)—wise
alii (ah-**lee**-ee)—chief
aloha (ah-**lo**-ha)—hello; greetings; love
aole (ah-**oh**-lay)—no
auwe (ow-**way**)—ouch!; oh no!
brah (bra)—friend; brother; bro'
bumby (**bum**-bye)—after a while; by and by
da kine (da kyne)—whatdyacallit; thingamajig; the best
dah makule guys (da mah-**kuh**-lay guys)—senior citizens
duh uddah time (duh **uh**-duh time)—once before
e komo mai (eh kohmoh mai)—welcome, come in
hale (**hah**-lay)—house
haole (**how**-lee)—Caucasian; white person
hapa (**hah**-pa)—half
hapa-haole (**hah**-pa **how**-lee)—half-Caucasian
heiau (hey-**yow**)—temple
hele on (**hey**-lay on)—go, move, outta here
hoaloha (ho-ah-**lo**-ha)—friend
holo holo (**ho**-low **ho**-low)—to visit
howzit? (hows-it)—how you doing? what's happening?
huhu (hoo-hoo)—angry
hukilau (**who**-key-lau)—community fishing party
hula (**who**-la)—Hawaiian dance
imu (ee-moo)—underground oven
ipo (ee-po)—sweetheart
kahuna (kah-**who**-nah)—priest; specialist or expert
  in any field
kai (kye)—ocean
kaka-roach (**kah**-kah roach)—ripoff; theft
kamaaina (kah-mah-**eye**-nah)—one born and raised
  in Hawaii; a longtime island resident
kane (**kah**-nay)—man
kapu (**kah**-poo)—taboo; forbidden
kaukau (cow-cow)—food; eat
keiki (**kay**-key)—child
kiawe (key-**ah**-vay)—mesquite tree
kokua (ko-**coo**-ah)—help

kona winds (**ko**-nah winds)—winds that blow against the trades

kuli kuli (koo-lee koo-lee)—be quiet; be still

lanai (lah-**nye**)—porch; also island name

lauhala (lau-**hah**-lah) or *hala* (**hah**-lah)—a pandanus tree whose leaves are used in weaving

lei (lay)—flower garland

lolo (low-low)—stupid

lomilomi (**low**-me-**low**-me)—massage; salted raw salmon

luau (**loo**-ow)—Hawaiian meal

mahalo (mah-**hah**-low)—thank you

mahalo nui loa (mah-**ha**-low **new**-ee **low**-ah)—thank you very much

mahu (**mah**-who)—gay; homosexual

makai (mah-**kye**)—toward the sea

malihini (mah-lee-**hee**-nee)—newcomer; stranger

mauka (**mau**-kah)—toward the mountains

nani (**nah**-nee)—beautiful

ohana (oh-**hah**-nah)—family

okole (oh-**ko**-lay)—rear; ass

okolemaluna (oh-ko-lay-mah-**loo**-nah)—a toast: bottoms up!

ono (**oh**-no)—tastes good

pahoehoe (pah-**hoy**-hoy)—smooth or ropy lava

pakalolo (pah-kah-**low**-low)—marijuana

pali (**pah**-lee)—cliff

paniolo (pah-nee-**oh**-low)—cowboy

pau (pow)—finished; done

pilikia (pee-lee-**key**-ah)—trouble

popakiki (poh-pah-**key**-key)—stubborn; hard head

puka (**poo**-kah)—hole

pupus (**poo**-poos)—hors d'oeuvres

shaka (**shah**-kah)—hand greeting

swell head—"big head"; egotistical

tapa (**tah**-pah)—also *kapa*; fabric made from the beaten bark of mulberry trees

wahine (wah-**hee**-nay)—woman

wikiwiki (**wee**-key-**wee**-key)—quickly; in a hurry

you get stink ear—you don't listen well

MUSIC

Music has long been an integral part of Hawaiian life. Most families keep musical instruments in their homes, gathering to play at impromptu living room or backyard jam sessions. Hawaiian folk tunes are passed down from generation to generation. In the earliest days, it was the sound of rhythm instruments and chants that filled the air. Drums were fashioned from hollowed-out gourds, coconut shells or hollowed sections of coconut palm trunks, then covered with sharkskin. Gourds and coconuts, adorned with tapa cloth and feathers, were also filled with shells or pebbles to produce a rattling sound. Other instruments included the nose flute, a piece of bamboo similar to a mouth flute, but played by exhaling through the nostril; the bamboo organ; and *puili*, sections of bamboo split into strips, which were struck rhythmically against the body.

Western musical scales and instruments were introduced by explorers and missionaries. As ancient Hawaiian music involved a radically different musical system, Hawaiians had to completely re-adapt. Actually, western music caught on quickly, and the hymns brought by missionaries fostered a popular musical style—the *himeni,* or Hawaiian church music.

Hawaii has been the birthplace of several different musical instruments and styles. The ukulele, modeled on a Portuguese guitar, quickly became the most popular Hawaiian instrument. Its small size made it easy to carry, and with just four strings, it was simple to play. The ukulele is enjoying a surge of popularity on the mainland, and several craftsmen throughout the islands have begun making beautiful instruments from native woods for collectors and those who want to play in style. During the early 1900s, the steel guitar was exported to the mainland. Common in country-and-western music today, it was invented by a young man who experimented by sliding a steel bar across guitar strings.

The slack-key style of guitar playing also comes from Hawaii, where it's called *ki ho'alu.* When the guitar was first brought to Hawaii in the 1830s by Mexican and Spanish cowboys, the Hawaiians adapted the instrument to their own special breed of music. In tuning, the six (or twelve) strings are loosened so that they sound a chord when strummed and match the vocal range of the singer. Slack-key is played in a variety of ways, from plucking or slapping the strings to sliding along them. A number of different tunings exist, and many have been passed down orally through families for generations.

During the late 19th century, "*hapa*-haole" songs became the rage. The ukulele was instrumental in contributing to this Hawaiian fad. Written primarily in English with pseudo-Hawaiian themes, songs like "Tiny Bubbles" and "Lovely Hula Hands" were later introduced to the world via Hollywood.

The Hawaiian craze continued on the mainland with radio and television shows such as "Hawaii Calls" and "The Harry Owens Show." In the 1950s, little mainland girls donned plastic hula skirts and danced along with Hilo Hattie and Ray Kinney.

It was not until the 1970s that both the hula and music of old Hawaii made a comeback. Groups such as the Sons of Hawaii and the Makaha Sons of Niihau, along with Auntie Genoa Keawe and the late Gabby Pahinui, became popular. Before long, a new form of Hawaiian music was being heard, a combination of ancient chants and contemporary sounds, performed by such islanders as Henry Kapono, Kalapana, Olomana, the Beamer Brothers, the Peter Moon Band and the Brothers Cazimero.

Today many of these groups, along with other notables such as the Kaau Crater Boys, Brother Noland, Willie K., Butch Helemano and Obrien Eselu, bring both innovation to the Hawaiian music scene and contribute to the preservation of an ancient tradition. The trend continues with hybrid infusions of reggae and rock, while performers like Kealii Reichel and groups like Kapena maintain the soft-edged sounds so well-suited to the islands.

An entire new category of music has become established in Hawaii: dubbed "Jawaiian," the sound incorporates Jamaican reggae and contemporary Hawaiian music, and is especially popular amongst the state's younger population. In addition, now-deceased masters of Hawaiian song like Gabby Pahinui and Israel Kamakawiwoole have gained renewed popularity and respect for the links they created between old and contemporary Hawaiian music. Pro-sovereignty groups like Sudden Rush have taken this trend one step further, laying down their message-imbued rap lyrics on reggae tunes and Hawaiian classics to create a truly unique genre.

For both classic and contemporary Hawaiian music, tune your radio dial to KONG (93.5 FM), KSRF (95.9 FM), KUAI (720 AM) and KTOH (99.9 FM).

NO OOMPAH-PAH! MO' BETTAH BRAH!
Strangely enough, a Prussian bandmaster named Henry Berger had a major influence on contemporary Hawaiian music. Brought over in the 19th century by King Kalakaua to lead the Royal Hawaiian Band, Berger helped Hawaiians make the transition to Western instruments.

HULA

Along with palm trees, the hula—swaying hips, grass skirts, colorful leis—is linked forever in people's minds with the Hawaiian Islands. This Western idea of hula is very different from what the dance has traditionally meant to native Hawaiians.

Hula is an old dance form, its origin shrouded in mystery. The ancient hula, *hula kahiko*, was more concerned with religion and spirituality than entertainment. Originally performed only by men, it was used in rituals to communicate with a deity—a connection to nature and the gods. Accompanied by drums and chants, *hula kahiko* expressed the islands' culture, mythology and history in hand and body movements. It later evolved from a strictly religious rite to a method of communicating stories and legends. Over the years, women were allowed to study the rituals and eventually became the primary dancers.

> "Hula is the language of the heart, and therefore the heart beat of the Hawaiian people."
> —KING KALAKAUA

When Westerners arrived, the *hula kahiko* began another transformation. Explorers and sailors were more interested in its erotic element, ignoring the cultural significance. Missionaries simply found it scandalous and set out to destroy the tradition. They dressed Hawaiians in Western garb and outlawed the *hula kahiko*.

The hula tradition was resurrected by King David Kalakaua. Known by the moniker "Merrie Monarch," Kalakaua loved music and dance. For his coronation in 1883, he called together the kingdom's best dancers to perform the chants and hulas once again. He was also instrumental in the development of the contemporary hula, the *hula auwana*, which added new steps and movements and was accompanied by ukuleles and guitars rather than drums.

By the 1920s, modern hula had been popularized by Hollywood, westernized and introduced as kitschy tropicana. Real grass skirts gave way to cellophane versions, plastic leis replaced fragrant island garlands, and exaggerated gyrations supplanted the hypnotic movements of the traditional dance.

Fortunately, with the resurgence of Hawaiian pride in recent decades, Polynesian culture has been reclaimed and *hula kahiko* and traditional chants have made a welcome comeback.

FOUR

Lihue Area

Although Lihue is a rather dreary little town of 5700, visitors will likely pass through this tiny city several times because it's so centrally located. This is where the island's two highways converge—Kuhio heading north and Kaumualii going south. Here you'll find Kauai's airport and helicopter facilities, Nawiliwili Harbor and its commodity barges and cruise ships, government offices that issue camping and hiking permits, fast-food joints, industrial parks and big box retailers, and the island's largest shopping mall, Kukui Grove Center. In short, it's the civic and commercial center of the island.

But that doesn't mean the area is devoid of charm. The beautiful Haupu Ridge dominates the landscape to the south while the rambling peaks of Kalepa Ridge loom in the interior, and the Huleia River, which feeds the legendary Menehune (Alekoko) Fishpond, is one of the island's prettiest. And for those seeking convenience, or lacking transportation, Lihue is an excellent choice for home base.

Among the attractions you will find in Lihue is the **Kauai Museum**, a two-building complex rich in Hawaiiana. This is a prime spot to learn about the history, culture and natural history of the island. The main building focuses on Hawaiian heritage with its displays of feather leis, Hawaiian quilts, *koa* furniture and ancient calabashes. In the adjacent exhibition, 19th-century plantation life is revealed in a collection of old photographs, shot by W. J. Senda, a Japanese immigrant. Closed Sunday. Admission. ~ 4428 Rice Street, Lihue; 808-245-6931, fax 808-245-6864; e-mail kauaimuseum@museum.org.

Providing an even wider window on Kauai's sugar-cane heritage, **Grove Farm** is a beautifully preserved 80-acre homestead. Acquired in 1864 by the son of missionaries, the plantation is like a living museum with the main house, farm office, workers' homes and a private cottage still intact. Surrounding these tinroof buildings are banana patches, gardens and pastures. Two-hour guided tours of this fascinating facility are available (Monday, Wednesday and Thursday at 10 a.m. and 1 p.m.) by reservation. ~ 808-245-3202, fax 808-245-7988.

Another interesting side trip from Lihue is down Rice Street to busy **Nawiliwili Harbor**. This deep-water port, with its cruise ships and cargo vessels, is the island's major seaport. On December 31, 1941, it was shelled by the Japanese during World War II but sustained little damage. Nearby **Kalapaki Beach** is one of Kauai's most popular strands, both because of its proximity to Lihue and its pretty white sands.

Fronting Kalapaki Beach is the **Kauai Marriott Resort & Beach Club**. Some believe that Mother Nature, in the form of Hurricane Iniki, wreaked havoc on its previous incarnation, the Westin Kauai, because it was so un-Hawaiian in nature—it looked like a Las Vegas version of Rome. Today its lush gardens, massive swimming pool (complete with waterfalls)—the largest in the state—and an extensive art collection spread throughout the public spaces warrant a look and see. If nothing else, a stroll along the granite pathway along the white-sand beach is worth the detour. ~ 3610 Rice Street, Lihue; 808-245-5050, 800-220-2925, fax 808-245-5049; www.marriott.com/lihhi.

With more cruise ships stopping on Kauai, the area around the waterfront has developed considerably and begun catering to passengers. They can easily walk from their ship to the cluster of shops and restaurants that have sprung up on both sides of Rice Street between the harbor and the Kauai Marriott.

From Nawiliwili Harbor, you can continue on to the **Menehune** (or **Alekoko**) **Fishpond**. This 900-foot-long pond, spread across a valley floor and backdropped by the Hoary Head Mountain Range, dates back well before the Polynesians. Or so the mythmakers would like you to believe. Legend has it that a line of leprechaun-like *Menehune* 25 miles long passed rocks from hand to hand and built the pond in a single night. Their only request of the prince and princess for whom they built the structure was that these two mortals not watch them while they worked. When the *Menehune* discovered that curiosity had overcome the two, who were watching the midget workers by the light of the moon, the *Menehune* turned them into the pillars of stone you see on the mountainside above the fishpond. ~ Take

Rice Street to Nawiliwili, then right on Route 58, a quick left on Niumalu Road and finally right on Hulemalu Road.

Lihue has three old churches worth a look. Almost directly north of the fishpond off of Route 50 you'll find the **Lihue Lutheran Church**. Built in 1881 by German immigrants supervising plantation work, it was severely damaged in the hurricane of 1982. The rebuilt structure, however, is quite loyal to the original, and the congregation certainly is, too: it's been active since its incep-

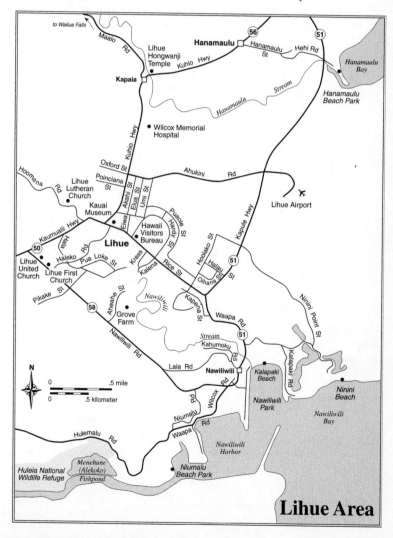

Lihue Area

tion, making this the oldest Lutheran church on the islands. ~ 4602 Hoomana Road; 808-245-2145, fax 808-246-8626; www.lihuelutheran.com. Near the Kukui Grove Center, behind the Kings Auto Center, is the stone **Lihue First Church**, founded in 1840. ~ 4320 Nawiliwili Road; 808-245-2274. The simple tombstones and construction of the **Lihue United Church** testify to the cane workers who worshipped here, beginning in 1901. The beautiful stained-glass windows were recently refurbished. The church also holds a Tongan service on Sunday. ~ 4340 Nawiliwili Road; 808-245-6253.

A short distance from Lihue, Kuhio Highway (Route 56), the main road to Kauai's north shore, descends into the rustic village of **Kapaia**. Classic plantation-style structures and a gulch choked with banana plants mark this valley. On the right, **Lihue Hongwanji Temple**, one of the island's oldest, smiles from beneath a modern-day facelift.

Off Kuhio Highway, Maalo Road threads through three miles of fields to **Wailua Falls**. These twin cascades tumble 80 feet into a heavenly pool fringed with *hala* trees. An easily accessible pool lies just a couple hundred yards past the falls.

Follow Kuhio Highway and you'll arrive in **Hanamaulu**, an old plantation town where falsefront stores and tinroof houses line the roadway. If you follow Hanamaulu Road to Hehi Road you'll come to **Hanamaulu Beach Park**. Shaded by coconut palms and ironwood trees, it's a lovely place to picnic. (See "Beaches & Parks" below.)

Or you can head a mile and a half southwest from Lihue on Kaumualii Highway (Route 50) to **Kilohana** for a view of the

AUTHOR FAVORITE

Visible from the vista overlooking the Menehune Fishpond, and accessible only to kayakers, is the **Huleia National Wildlife Refuge** (808-828-1413), a 238-acre preserve that rises from the river basin up the wooded slopes of Huleia Valley. This estuary is home to 31 bird species including four different endangered species of waterbirds—the Hawaiian stilt, Hawaiian duck, Hawaiian gallinule and Hawaiian coot. If a trip upriver begins to look familiar, it's because it was the setting for scenes in *Raiders of the Lost Ark*. Hawaiian medicinal plants and wild fruit line the banks of the river.

luxurious side of island life. This 16,000-square-foot Tudor mansion was home to the plantation that once covered these grounds. Today, the 1935 house serves as a center for arts-and-crafts shops and museum displays, and the 35 surrounding acres are devoted to a re-creation of traditional plantation life. Wander down the "coral path" and you'll pass a tropical garden and a succession of corrugated-roof houses. Papaya, banana and avocado trees line the route and roosters crow in the distance. Carriages pulled by Clydesdales tour the grounds and wagon tours lead out into the fields behind the house. There are weekly luaus. ~ Kaumualii Highway; 808-245-5608, fax 808-245-7818; e-mail kilohana@hawaiian.net.

If you are in search of budget-priced lodging facilities, there are few places in all Hawaii as inviting as Lihue. And being located near the airport or a block or two from downtown Lihue is convenient for those folks without wheels.

LODGING

At the **Tip Top Motel** you'll find trim rooms with tile floors, stall showers and air conditioning. The sheer size of this two-story, two-building complex makes it impersonal by Kauai standards, but I found the management to be very warm. You'll have to eat meals in the adjoining restaurant or elsewhere, since none of the rooms have kitchenettes. ~ 3173 Akahi Street, Lihue; 808-245-2333, fax 808-246-8988. BUDGET.

The **Motel Lani**, located three blocks from the Rice Shopping Center, has eight small rooms facing a small patio where guests can lounge about in lawn chairs. The units are clean and comfortable, though sparsely furnished. About half are air-conditioned; all have fans and refrigerators. This place has a noisy lobby (with a television) just off busy Rice Street. ~ 4240 Rice Street, Lihue; 808-245-2965. BUDGET.

Over 100 years old (and the first hotel on the island), **Kauai Inn** was extensively renovated at the end of the millennium, resulting in a comfortable hotel with remnants of old Hawaii. Convenient to the airport, it sits on three acres near the Hapu Mountains and Huleia River, with 48 units, a pool and laundry facilities. All guest rooms have a refrigerator and microwave. ~ 2430 Hulemalu Road, Lihue; 808-245-9000, 800-808-2330, fax 808-245-3004; www.kauai-inn.com, e-mail info@kauai-inn.com. MODERATE.

Situated across the street from Nawiliwili Park is the **Garden Island Inn**. You'll find it near the corner of Waapa Road and Wilcox Road, a short walk from Kalapaki Beach. Each room is light and airy with comfortable furnishings, fresh flowers, attractive appointments and overhead fans. You'll hear occasional noise from passing trucks and planes. Children are welcome, and several of the large rooms are sufficiently spacious for families. All of the fully equipped units have refrigerators, wet bars and microwave ovens. Second- and third-story rooms have air conditioning. Beach gear, including boogieboards, is loaned free to guests. The grounds are trimly landscaped and highlighted by a koi pond in which several dozen carp flash their colors. ~ 3445 Wilcox Road, Lihue; 808-245-7227, 800-648-0154, fax 808-245-7603; www.gardenislandinn.com, e-mail info@gardenislandinn.com. MODERATE TO DELUXE.

> Check in with the Kauai Historical Society to find out what's on tap—they offer free lectures and field trips. ~ 808-245-3373.

Sitting all alone on windswept Nukolii Beach, just north of Lihue, is the luxurious **Radisson Kauai Beach Resort**. It's a pretty property, with four swimming pools, one of which has a sand bottom. The beach here isn't great for swimming, but you can walk for miles; its reef is frequented by local fishermen. It's also near the airport, making it popular for conventions and meetings (airport noise can be distracting). Guests can play tennis or use the adjacent municipal golf course for a fee. All rooms have internet access; there's also an onsite internet café with a high-speed connection. While not spectacular, it's nice enough and one of only two brand-name hotels in Lihue. ~ 4331 Kauai Beach Drive, Lihue; 808-245-1955, 800-333-3333, fax 808-246-9085; www.radissonkauai.com. DELUXE TO ULTRA-DELUXE.

Fronting a quarter-mile of white sandy beach, one of the island's loveliest, the **Kauai Marriott Resort & Beach Club** is the Lihue area's premier resting spot. The 356-room timeshare property is a stone's throw from the airport and Lihue. Most rooms, appointed in island-style decor featuring Hawaiian tropical floral designs, offer views of the ocean and come with a lanai. A beach promenade of granite tile leads from one end of the beach to the other. For those not interested in swimming in the ocean, the resort sports the largest swimming pool in the islands, replete with waterfalls. A myriad of water sports is available to guests. Restaurants and a fitness center round out the amenities. ~ 3610

Rice Street, Lihue; 808-245-5050, 800-872-6626, fax 808-245-5049; www.marriott.com/lihhi, e-mail kauai@marriott.com.
ULTRA-DELUXE.

Banyan Harbor Resort, a collection of woodframe buildings across a busy street from Nawiliwili Harbor, has condos with ocean and garden views; one-bedroom units are $120 per night while two-bedroom units are $150 per night. Each unit has a full kitchen and laundry facilities. Most of the 148 units here are leased by the month, but a handful rent by the night. ~ 3411 Wilcox Road, Lihue; 808-245-7333, 800-422-6926, fax 808-246-3687; www.vacation-kauai.com, e-mail reservations@banyanharbor.net.

CONDOS

For good food at modest prices, Lihue is a prime spot. This is the center of most island business so it contains numerous restaurants that cater largely to local folks.

DINING

You're liable to see lots of local faces lining **Hamura Saimin**'s curving counter. When I ate there the place was packed. I had the "*saimin* special," a combination of noodles, wontons, eggs, meat, onion, vegetables and fish cake in a delicious broth. ~ 2956 Kress Street, Lihue; 808-245-3271. BUDGET.

◄ *HIDDEN*

Oki Diner is open 19 hours a day. A small and spare eatery, this is a favorite place for locals to dine on ramen, wonton soup and various other Asian dishes. ~ 3125 Kuhio Highway, Lihue; 808-245-5899. BUDGET.

◄ *HIDDEN*

Want to go Japanese? Try **Restaurant Kiibo**, a contemporary-style restaurant with a tatami room. You'll find the menu filled with yakitori, tempura and tofu dishes, as well as sushi and sashimi. Closed Sunday. ~ 2991 Umi Street, Lihue; 808-245-2650. MODERATE.

A local institution since 1939, the **Lihue Barbecue Inn** offers Asian dishes in addition to all-American meals. Breakfasts at this comfortable establishment are pretty standard: the lunch menu includes salads, soups, sandwiches, hamburgers and a daily special that often features teriyaki and Pacific Rim–influenced dishes; at dinner, there's steak, shrimp tempura and scampi. Closed Sunday. ~ 2982 Kress Street, Lihue; 808-245-2921. MODERATE TO DELUXE.

◄ *HIDDEN*

A favorite among tourists is the **Tip Top Café and Bakery**. Visitors can take their pick from any in a succession of booths in this large and impersonal eatery. Breakfasts are inexpensive—the macadamia-nut pancakes are delicious. Lunch entrées, however, are not very imaginative and have received negative reviews from readers. The well-known bakery serves macadamia-nut cookies, the house specialty. No dinner. Closed Monday. ~ 3173 Akahi Street, Lihue; 808-245-2333, fax 808-246-8988. BUDGET.

HIDDEN ► For the money, the best breakfast spot on the island is **Ma's Family Restaurant**. This nondescript café makes up in clientele what it lacks in physical beauty. Early in the morning the place is crowded with locals on their way to work. In the world of breakfasts, this is the bargain basement. Or if you want to go Hawaiian, order a *laulau*, poi and *lomi* salmon dish. No dinner. ~ 4277 Halenani Street, Lihue; 808-245-3142. BUDGET.

The **Café Portofino** at the Kauai Marriott serves up several pasta dishes as well as house specialties like calamari, scampi, eggplant parmigiana and sautéed rabbit. Dinner only. ~ 3610 Rice Street, Lihue; 808-245-2121. DELUXE TO ULTRA-DELUXE.

HIDDEN ► Visit **Kalena Fish Market** for the best plate lunch in Lihue. Fish and meat specials, like breaded mahi, Korean-style barbecue spare ribs and local foods like *laulau* and *kalua* pig with cabbage, change daily. You can choose from a wide array of side dishes: macaroni salad, marinated bean sprouts and *kim chee*. It's clean and modern with a few tables. ~ 2985 Kalena Street (off Rice Street), Lihue; 808-246-6629, fax 808-246-2174. BUDGET.

Whatever the time of day or night, **Garden Island BBQ** is generally packed with customers, nearly all of them locals. The reason? Great food, ample portions, three pages of menu choices

FROM THE MENEHUNE TO INDIANA JONES

Board your kayak and head down the Huleia River, home to the legendary Menehune Fishpond. **Island Adventures**, an eco-friendly kayaking company, escorts you to the heart of the Huleia National Wildlife Refuge. Spottings of Koloa ducks, egrets, Hawaiian stilts and jumping fish are all part of the adventure. You can even play Indiana Jones at the rope swing used in *Raiders of the Lost Ark*. To complete the trip, you'll take a short hike through the wildlife refuge, where your local guide will point out Hawaiian medicinal plants and fruits as you squish along a muddy trail. A very enjoyable, laidback Hawaiian adventure. ~ Nawiliwili Small Boat Harbor, Lihue; 808-245-9662, fax 808-246-9661; www.kauaifun.com, e-mail funkauai@hawaiian.net.

that are the same for lunch and dinner, super casual setting and low prices. The menu is predominantly Chinese and the barbecue is more local or Korean-style than Texas, but you can also get burgers, sandwiches and plate lunches. Closed Sunday. ~ 4252 Rice Street, Lihue; 808-245-8868. BUDGET.

Just a coconut's throw from a sandy beach, **Duke's Canoe Club** is on Kalapaki Bay at the Kauai Marriott Resort & Beach Club. Besides the fresh fish, grill items and celebrated salad bar, this open-air restaurant has surfboards, photos and memorabilia commemorating the granddaddy of surfing, Duke Kahanamoku. Roaming musicians entertain nightly. ~ Kalapaki Beach, Lihue; 808-246-9599, fax 808-246-1047. MODERATE TO ULTRA-DELUXE.

Harbor Mall has several tasty options. One of the better choices is **Surf's Island Seafood Grill & Longboard Bar**, a comfortable, casual, ocean-view restaurant and watering hole that does a good job with surf and turf. The house-made linguine served with scampi is the specialty, and the Portuguese smoked ham shank braised in red wine with beans, potatoes, tomatoes and onions is a hearty meal. Closed Sunday. ~ 3501 Rice Street, Nawiliwili; 808-246-4725. DELUXE.

Aromas, which prides itself on using quality local ingredients, is also worth checking out. An eclectic, health-conscious, international menu, featuring island-raised beef, fresh fish and vegetarian entrées, is served up in an open-air dining area. Closed Monday. ~ 3501 Rice Street, Nawiliwili; 808-245-9192. MODERATE.

JJ's Broiler is a family-style eatery with standard steak dishes, seafood platters and a salad bar. The waterfront location overlooks Kalapaki Beach and has a sunny Southern California ambience. ~ 3416 Rice Street, Nawiliwili; 808-246-4422, fax 808-245-7019; www.jjsbroiler.com, e-mail jjsbroiler@hotmail.com. DELUXE TO ULTRA-DELUXE.

Also located in Nawiliwili is **The Beach Hut**. They offer a full breakfast menu; for lunch and dinner, there are hamburgers, sandwiches and salads. Order at the window and dine upstairs on a deck overlooking the water. ~ 3474 Rice Street, Nawiliwili; 808-246-6330. BUDGET.

At **Ara's Sakana-ya Fish House** you can kill two birds with one stone. Their deli has good plate lunches, sushi and fresh fish, but the best part is you can take your food to the laundromat next door and eat while you wash. Lunch and take-out only. ~

Hanamaulu Plaza at Kuhio Highway and Hanamaulu Road, Hanamaulu; 808-245-1707. BUDGET.

If it's atmosphere and a taste of the Orient you're after, reserve a tea room at the **Hanamaulu Café**. My favorite is the garden room overlooking a rock-bound pond filled with carp. Lunch and dinner are the same here, with an excellent selection of Japanese and Chinese dishes. There's also a sushi bar at night. Children's portions are available. Closed Monday. ~ Kuhio Highway, Hanamaulu; 808-245-2511, fax 808-245-2497. MODERATE.

Take a plantation manor, add a flowering garden, and you have the setting for **Gaylord's**. Elevating patio dining to a high art, this alfresco restaurant looks out on the spacious lawns and spreading trees of Kilohana plantation. The menu features fresh island fish, pasta, farm-raised venison, baby back ribs, slow-roasted prime rib and chicken Kauai in addition to exotic specials on Monday and a well-rounded wine list. Or consider attending their luau on Tuesday or Thursday. A rare combination of Old World elegance and tropical ambience; lunch, dinner and Sunday brunch served. Reservations required. ~ At Kilohana on Kaumualii Highway, one and one half miles southwest of Lihue; 808-245-9593, fax 808-246-1087; www.gaylordskauai.com, e-mail gaylords@hawaiian.net. DELUXE TO ULTRA-DELUXE.

GROCERIES Lihue has by far the greatest number of grocery, health food and fresh fish stores on the island. This commercial center is an ideal place to stock up for a camping trip, a hike or a lengthy sojourn in an efficiency apartment.

The **Big Save Market** is one of Lihue's main grocery stores. Its doors are open daily from 7 a.m. to 11 p.m. ~ Lihue Shopping Center, 4444 Rice Street, Lihue; 808-245-6571.

Star Market, located in the Kukui Grove Center, is another local grocery staple. They're open from 6 a.m. to 11 p.m. every day. ~ 3-2600 Kaumualii Highway, Lihue; 808-245-7777.

Vim 'N Vigor has an excellent line of vitamins, juices and bath supplies, plus natural foods and sandwiches. Closed Sunday. ~ Rice Shopping Center, 3122 Kuhio Highway, A-9, Lihue; 808-245-9053; www.vimnvigor.com.

HIDDEN ► Don't miss the **Sunshine Market** every Friday afternoon in the parking lot of the town stadium. Local folks turn out to sell homegrown produce, "talk story," and generally have a good time. It's a great place to buy island fruits and vegetables at bargain prices, and an even better spot to meet Kauai's farmers. Early morning is the best time to arrive—before the best produce has disappeared. ~ Kapule Highway.

If you hanker for fresh fish, be sure to check out **The Fish Express**. ~ 3343 Kuhio Highway, Lihue; 808-245-9918.

Love's Bakery sells day-old products including delicious breads at a discount. ~ 4100 Rice Street, Nawiliwili; 808-245-6113.

Kukui Grove Center is the island's largest shopping mall, an ultramodern complex. Here are department stores, bookshops, specialty stores and other establishments. Though lacking the intimacy of Kauai's independent handicraft outlets, the center provides such a concentration of goods that it's hard to bypass. ~ 3-2600 Kaumualii Highway, Lihue; 808-245-7784.

SHOPPING

Why not stop in at the **Kauai Museum Shop** if you're interested in taking home some Niihau shell leis, local crafts or books? They have a nice selection. Closed Sunday. ~ 4428 Rice Street, Lihue; 808-246-2470.

For everyday needs and common items, try the local shopping centers. **Anchor Cove** (808-246-0634), a beachside mall, stands along Rice Street near Kalapaki Beach in Nawiliwili. **Harbor Mall** (808-245-6255) rests nearby at 3501 Rice Street.

The **Kauai Fruit & Flower Company** can put together custom-made baskets of coffee, macadamia nuts, papaya salsa, coconut syrup, fresh bread, dried fruit, etc. They make a great gift for anyone you left at home. The store also sells traditional Hawaiian musical instruments. Closed Sunday. ~ 3-4684 Kuhio Highway, Lihue; 808-245-1814, 800-943-3108; www.kauaifruit.com.

Kilohana (808-245-5608) is one of Hawaii's most beautiful complexes to shop. Set in a grand sugar plantation house, it rests

At the **Kapaia Stitchery** half the items are designed and stitched by local women. There's an array of T-shirts, aloha shirts, Hawaiian quilting pillow kits and patterns, plus stunning patchwork quilts. This is an excellent place to buy Hawaiian fabrics and hand-dyed batiks from Bali. Closed Sunday. ~ Kuhio Highway, just north of the hamlet of Kapaia; 808-245-2281, fax 808-245-1772.

amid acres of manicured grounds. Many rooms in this museum-cum-mall are furnished in period style to recapture 1930s-era plantation life. The galleries, boutiques and crafts shops are equally enchanting. Here you'll find pillows, hand-blown glassware, Niihau shell leis, pottery and much, much more. ~ Kaumualii Highway, one and one half miles southwest of Lihue.

Two Frogs Hugging got its campy name from a statue the owners saw that began their foray into imports. Their merchandise consists mainly of intricate, imported wood furniture and stone carvings. Closed Sunday. ~ 3215 Kuhio Highway, Lihue; 808-246-8777; www.twofrogshugging.com, e-mail kauaimp@aloha.net.

The **Kauai Marriott Resort** has a selection of shops and galleries along its colonnaded walkways. Everything from designer clothing to Hawaiian artworks created by local artisans can be found. ~ Kalapaki Beach, Lihue; 808-245-5050.

NIGHTLIFE   You'll find a lot of local color at the **Lihue Café**. The drinks are cheap, the tourists are few. ~ 2978 Umi Street, Lihue; 808-245-6471.

Rob's Good Times Grill is definitely the most happening place in Lihue, with a full food menu, sports bar, pool tables, country line dancing, karaoke and nightly dancing to music mixed by deejays. ~ Rice Shopping Center, Lihue; 808-246-0311.

Every small town needs its quirky band of players, and Lihue is no exception. The island's only theater troupe is located here, in the **Kauai Community Players**. The non-profit has been around since 1971, producing old standbys like *Joseph and the Amazing Technicolor Dreamcoat*, *The Miracle Worker* and *Sweeney Todd*, as well as lesser-known productions. ~ Lihue; 808-245-7700; www.kauaicommunityplayers.org, e-mail kcp@hawaiian.net.

Or you can always head to the **Lihue Bowling Center** and knock down a few pins. ~ 4303 Rice Street, Lihue; 808-245-5263.

Grab a beer at **Whaler's Brewpub**; the suds are especially enjoyable when coupled with the pub's gorgeous view of Kalapaki Bay. ~ 3132 Ninini Point Street, Lihue; 808-245-2000.

BEACHES & PARKS   **KALAPAKI BEACH** 🏄 🏊 🛶 This wide strand stretches for a quarter-mile in front of the Kauai Marriott hotel. Popular with surfers since ancient Hawaiian times, Kalapaki is situated right on Nawiliwili Bay, an appealing but busy harbor. It is also one of the best swimming beaches on the island since the harbor protects it from heavy shorebreak. Out past the harbor, the Hoary Head mountains rise in the background. Beginner's surfing is best in the center of Nawiliwili Bay, where there is a right slide. More experienced surfers will find good breaks next to the rock wall near the lighthouse, where there's a left slide. There's also good surfing on the right side of the bay. Nicknamed "Hang Ten," these left slide breaks are a good place for nose-riding. Snorkeling is so-so at Kalapaki, but anglers should have better luck.

Good news for those who want to get away from city life—only 3 percent of Kauai is "urbanized."

Both off the pier and near the lighthouse are good spots for mullet, big-eyed scad, *papio*, bonefish and threadfin; sometimes *ulua*, *oama* and red bigeye can be caught here, too. Nawiliwili Park, next to the beach, has a picnic area and restrooms. ~ Take Rice Street from Lihue to Nawiliwili Park. Enter from the park.

NIUMALU BEACH PARK This tree-lined park is tucked into a corner of Nawiliwili Harbor near a small-boat harbor. With neighbors like this and no swimming facilities, the park's key feature is its proximity to Lihue. It is popular nonetheless with picnickers, and the adjacent Huleia River attracts kayakers, fishermen and crabbers. Facilities include a picnic area, restrooms and showers. ~ Take Rice Street to Nawiliwili, turn right on Route 58, then left on Niumalu Road.

▲ Camping allowed with county permit.

NININI BEACH Hidden along a rocky coastline between Nawiliwili Bay and the lighthouse on Ninini Point are two small sand beaches. Lying at the base of a sea cliff, these pocket beaches are separated by a lava rock formation. The smaller beach is about a quarter-mile from Ninini Point and the larger is known as **Running Waters Beach**, named for the numerous springs that bubble out of the lava and percolate up into the sand. Both are excellent for sunbathing but generally not safe for other water activities due to strong currents and undertow; bodysurfers, however, frequent Running Waters Beach. Since both beaches are pretty close to civilization, I don't recommend camping at either beach. There are no facilities here. ~ Take the road leading through the Kauai Marriott property in Nawiliwili. Follow this road to the golf course clubhouse. Park and walk across the golf course in a direction several degrees to the right of the lighthouse. The smaller beach can be reached by walking from Running Water Beach toward the lighthouse for about three-tenths of a mile.

◀ HIDDEN

HANAMAULU BEACH PARK 🏊 Here's an idyllic park nestled in Hanamaulu Bay and crowded with ironwood and coconut trees. The beach is a narrow corridor of sand at the head of Hanamaulu Bay. The bay is well-protected, but the water is usually murky and of questionable quality so swim at your own risk. I found this a great place for picnicking and shell collecting. Anglers can expect to hook bonefish, mullet and bigeyed scad. A picnic area, restrooms, showers and a playground are some of the facilities here. ~ Take Kuhio Highway to Hanamaulu, then turn down the road leading to the bay.

△ Needles from the ironwood trees make a natural bed at this lovely site. Tent and trailer camping (closed Wednesday); county permit required.

NAWILIWILI PARK Not the most beautiful setting on the island, this park nevertheless offers a swath of grass and picnic tables as well as access to good surf and fishing grounds. There's also playground equipment for the little ones. Picnic tables, a pavilion and restrooms round out the facilities. ~ Located north of Nawiliwili Harbor. Take Waapa Road north until it connects with Rice Street (Route 51). The park is east of the junction.

FIVE

Poipu Area

The Poipu area, crown jewel of the southside of Kauai, specializes in beaches—along with a steady stream of sunshine. What you'll find in this warm, dry, white-sand corner of the island is a prime example of everyone's favorite combination—the old and the new. The traditional comes in the form of Koloa Town, site of Hawaii's first successful sugar mill, a 19th-century plantation town that has been splashed with tropical colors. For the modern, you need look only a couple miles down the road to Poipu, a series of scalloped beaches that has become action central for real-estate developers.

Anchoring these enclaves to the east is Puuhi Mount, scene of the last volcanic eruption on Kauai. To the north rises Haupu Ridge, a wall of wooded mountains that divides the district from the Huleia Valley and Lihue. Everywhere else you'll find abandoned sugar fields or acres planted with corn.

The tiny, old communities of Lawai and Omao comprise the rest of what is known locally as the southside. Poipu has a low-key, tropical beauty that is achieved in part through dense landscaping around the resorts and building-height restrictions. The sunsets can be truly remarkable here, and during the summer months, the surf is frequently up. Certainly it can be gray and blustery during the winter months and, yes, it even rains at times in Poipu. Let's not forget the shrieking winds and storm surge of Hurricane Iniki, which devastated much of Poipu's coastal development in 1992. But that's in the past now and its traces are almost impossible to tell today. For the most part, Poipu and the southside are generally sunny and more than inviting.

Without doubt, you'll want to drive out from Lihue along Kaumualii Highway (Route 50) to explore the south coast. Along the way, if you possess a Rorschach test imagination, you'll see **Queen Victoria's Profile** etched in the Hoary

Head Range. (Need a helping eye? Watch for the Hawaii Visitors Bureau sign on the side of the highway.)

When you turn south toward Poipu on Maluhia Road (Route 520), you won't need a road sign to find what locals refer to as **Tree Tunnel**, an arcade of towering eucalyptus trees that forms a shadowy tunnel en route to the timeworn town of **Koloa**. The remains of the original sugar plantation stand in an unassuming pile on the right side of the road as you enter town; a plaque and sculpture near this old chimney commemorates the birth of Hawaii's sugar industry, a business that dominated life in the islands throughout most of the 19th and 20th centuries. A sugar mill continued to operate until 1996 just outside town and Koloa still consists primarily of company-town houses and humble churches surrounded by former sugar cane fields. But the main street was gentrified during the 1980s as tropical-colored paints were added to the old woodframe and falsefront town center.

The tiny **Koloa History Center**, located in the Old Koloa Town mall, provides a brief introduction to the history of the area in the form of artifacts from the old plantation days. ~ Koloa Road, Koloa.

A dirt road at the end of Weliweli Road near the sugar mill leads to the largest manmade reservoir in Kauai and on the islands. Covering over 350 acres **Waita Reservoir** (closed to the public) is built on former marshlands on the eastside of Koloa.

Aside from the ruins of the sugar mill and the small museum in town, two churches round out the "sights" of Koloa. The **Koloa Church** has been used by sailors, and now tourists, as a landmark for docking near Poipu; its New England–style steeple is easy to spot from the water. The church was established and built in the mid-1850s. ~ Poipu Road, Koloa; 808-742-9956.

Christians of a different stripe established a Catholic mission, the first in the islands, near present-day **St. Raphael's Catholic Church**. The church, located on the outskirts of Koloa, was originally built in the mid-1800s but damaged by Hurricane Iniki. It has since been repaired and supports a sizeable congregation. ~ Hapa Road, Koloa; 808-742-1955.

From Koloa, Poipu Road takes you through fields two miles to the coast and the vacation community of **Poipu**. If a one-word association test were applied to Poipu, the word would be "beach." There really is no town here, just a skein of hotels, condominiums and stores built along a series of white-sand beaches. Nevertheless, this is Kauai's premier playground, a sun-soaked realm that promises good weather and good times.

Near the center of Poipu, tucked into the grounds of Kiahuna Plantation, are the **Moir Gardens.** What was once a labor of love for the Koloa Sugar Plantation manager's wife has grown over the years from a small cactus garden into its present-day incarnation, filled with a variety of tropical plants as well as a broad collection of succulents. If you're staying in Poipu, it's worth strolling through. ~ Kiahuna Plantation, 2253 Poipu Road, Poipu; 808-742-6411, fax 808-742-1698.

While civilization has encroached to the very side of the sea, nature continues to display some of its gentle wonders along the colorful reefs and pearly sands. Most remarkable of all is **Spouting Horn,** an underwater lava tube with an opening along the shore. Surf crashing through the tube dramatically transforms this blowhole into a miniature Old Faithful. The mournful sounds issuing from Spouting Horn are said to be the plaintive cries of a legendary lizard or *mo'o*. It seems that he was returning from another island where he had been told of the death of his two sisters. Blinded by tears he missed his landing and was swept into

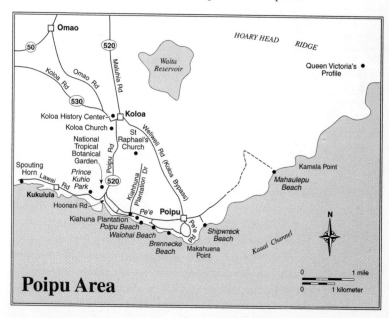

Poipu Area

the blowhole. Try to time your visit with the high tide when the spumes from Spouting Horn reach their greatest heights. You should look around at this intriguing coastline, which is covered by coral outcroppings and tidepools. ~ End of Lawai Road.

During the 1800s, **Koloa Landing** was a major port for whalers in the islands and was, until the 20th century, the main port of Kauai. Now it's a major spot for scuba divers.

On Lawai Road, a small park commemorates the life of Prince Kuhio, who died in 1922 and was the last designated heir to the Hawaiian throne. A statue of the prince graces **Prince Kuhio Park**, as well as the well-preserved **Hoai Heiau**, the foundation of the prince's home and the remains of an ancient fishpond. This is a pretty palm-framed greensward steeped in history. ~ Lawai Road, Poipu.

Beyond the park is **Kukuiula Bay**, a popular spot for fishing and scuba diving. There's an offshore reef and boaters and kayakers often launch their vessels here.

The **National Tropical Botanical Garden** encompasses 300 acres in the Lawai Valley, and within its lush grounds are offered two distinct tours: the Allerton Garden Tour and the McBryde Garden Tour. The Allerton tour is guided and includes the summer cottage of the late Queen Emma and the former home of Chicago millionaire Robert Allerton. The McBryde tour is self-guided and explores the scientific garden as well as some historic buildings that were part of the old McBryde sugar plantation tours. Both tours offer a wealth of information about the 10,000 species of plants cultivated in the valley, as well as NTBG's mission to save rare tropical plants from around the world. Each tour costs $30 per person. The NTBG Visitor Center is located across from Spouting Horn. ~ Lawai Road, Poipu; 808-742-2623 (reservations); www.ntbg.org.

For a real "Hidden Hawaii" adventure, follow Poipu Road east past the Hyatt Regency Kauai. The pavement will end and you'll find yourself on an old cane road. Follow it for about two miles. Minor cane roads will intersect the main one—ignore them. When you come to a major cane road (you'll know it by the telephone poles), turn right and follow this road. After about a mile you'll see roads leading to the beach. There's a guard shack at the turnoff (you're venturing into private property) and **HIDDEN ▶** you may have to sign a waiver to continue on to **Mahaulepu Beach**—the south shore's hidden strands. In addition to being incredibly beautiful and ripe with potential for outdoor sports, Mahaulepu Beach is important scientifically. Look around for petroglyphs or play in the 100-foot-high sand dunes. (See "Beaches & Parks" below for more information.)

LODGING

One place for people wanting to rough it or to establish a base camp is **Kahili Mountain Park,** run by the Seventh Day Adventist Church. Facing Haupu Ridge and backdropped by Kahili Mountain, this 197-acre domain offers an easy compromise between hoteling and camping. The two-bedroom cabin comes equipped with lanai and private bathroom, plus a funky kitchenette; the other cabins are one-bedroom units. The facilities also include cabinettes with shared baths. Both types of facilities should be reserved several months in advance. Though cooking utensils and bed linens are provided, furnishings are a bit spartan: The floors are uncarpeted and the sole decoration is the surrounding mountains. Thank God for nature. At this rustic resort you can enjoy the swimming pond or hike the nearby trails. ~ Write to Kahili Mountain Park, P.O. Box 298, Koloa, HI 96756. The park is five miles from Koloa town and about one mile off Kaumualii Highway; 808-742-9921, fax 808-742-6628; www. kahilipark.org, e-mail reservations@kahilipark.org. BUDGET TO MODERATE.

◄ HIDDEN

Located on a small bluff overlooking the ocean is **Garden Isle Cottages Oceanfront**. These pretty one-bedroom hideaways are decorated with artistic flair: Oil paintings and woven pieces adorn the walls, the furnishings are rattan and the kitchens are modern. The rooms, which are decorated with Asian, Polynesian and Indo-

AUTHOR FAVORITE

For a place located right on the water, there's **Gloria's Spouting Horn Bed & Breakfast**. This custom-designed beachhouse features three oceanfront guest rooms outfitted with canopy beds, handmade Hawaiian quilts and *koa* furniture. Open and airy, Gloria's is a place where you can relax on the lanai that sits just above the waves, lie in a hammock, swim in the pool, or go surfing outside your front door. Full breakfast served. ~ 4464 Lawai Beach Road, Poipu; phone/fax 808-742-6995; www.glorias bedandbreakfast.com, e-mail glorbb@gte.net. ULTRA-DELUXE.

nesian themes, overlook Koloa Landing, site of the best snorkeling on the island. There is usually a two-night minimum stay. Closed Saturday and Sunday. ~ 2660 Puuholo Road, Koloa; 808-742-6717, 800-742-6711, fax 808-742-1933; www.oceancottages.com, e-mail vacation@oceancottages.com. DELUXE.

In a renovated plantation house near Poipu Beach you'll find the **Old Koloa House**. The rooms are pleasant, and decorated à la old Hawaii, complete with flowered drapes and ceiling fans; they all have private entrances. One room has a private bath (with clawfoot tub and shower); the other two share a bathroom. A continental breakfast is served in your room on the first morning. After that, you have to fend for yourself, but you'll be armed with a refrigerator and a microwave. ~ 3327 Waikomo Road, Koloa; 808-742-2099; www.oldkoloahouse.com, e-mail information@oldkoloahouse.com. MODERATE.

Koloa Landing Cottages in Poipu offers five cottages, a studio, a one-bedroom unit, and three two-bedroom units, one of which sleeps up to six; all are walking distance to the ocean. These are attractive facilities with kitchens. With a garden setting and family atmosphere, they evoke a comfortable sense of old Hawaii. Four-night minimum. ~ 2704-B Hoonani Road, Poipu; 808-742-1470, 800-779-8773; www.koloalanding.com, e-mail infokoloalanding@aol.com. MODERATE.

Poipu Bed & Breakfast Inn is a lovely woodframe house with four guest rooms. The decor is dominated by white wicker furniture and merry-go-round horses (there's one in the living room and in three of the bedrooms). You can also expect wall-to-wall carpeting and overhead fans. There are large covered lanais in front

A FRUIT FOR ALL SEASONS

Coconuts are one of those blessings from heaven, providing food, fuel, water, shade and building materials. The fronds were used with *pili* grass to thatch roofs, the hollowed trunks are made into *pahu*, or drums, and the fiber can be dried for fuel. It was also fashioned into ropey sandals that allowed Hawaiians to walk across razor-sharp lava. Nutritionally, the water inside is sterile and full of healthful enzymes, and the meat can be eaten or pressed into cream and oil. Most importantly, coconuts grow well close to the ocean, offering welcome shade from the harsh tropical sun.

and back plus a yard complete with garden and fruit trees. ~ 2720 Hoonani Road, Poipu; 808-743-0100, 800-808-2330, fax 808-245-3004; www.kauai-inn.com, e-mail info@kauai-inn.com. DELUXE.

It would be an elastic stretch of the imagination to call the **Grand Hyatt Regency Kauai Resort & Spa** a hidden destination. This *is*, after all, a Hyatt Regency—with over 600 guest rooms, several pools, six restaurants, six lounges and several acres of manmade lagoons. But before this luxury resort was built, the beach on which it sits was one of the great hidden locales on Kauai. Shipwreck Beach is still a magnificent crescent of white sand, and the Hyatt Regency Kauai Resort & Spa, backdropped by cane fields and deep-green mountains, enjoys some of the seclusion for which Keoneloa Bay was renowned. With its wood-paneled lobby, atrium garden and plush guest rooms, it is one of Kauai's prettier hotels. ~ 1571 Poipu Road, Poipu; 808-742-1234, 800-554-9288, fax 808-742-1557; www.kauai-hyatt.com. ULTRA-DELUXE.

With one of the southside's few truly oceanfront locations, as well as a pool that takes full advantage of the enviable view, the **Sheraton Kauai Resort** is a pleasant, subdued hotel. The 413 rooms, like the resort itself, are totally comfortable and standard Sheraton, but with an understated elegance. The grounds are lushly landscaped, giving the resort a private feel. ~ 2440 Hoonani Road, Poipu; 808-742-1661, 800-782-9488, fax 808-742-9777; www.sheratonkauai.com. ULTRA-DELUXE.

The posh **Embassy Vacation Resort** sits on 22 acres of garden, perched on a rocky cliff. One- and two-bedroom villas are available, all with a washer/dryer and a kitchenette. The property includes a fitness center, a manmade lagoon with jacuzzis, and a pool specifically designed for kids (not that you'll need it with the beach right next door). There's also a barbecue and picnic area; a golf course is nearby. ~ 1613 Pe'e Road, Koloa; 808-742-1888, 800-362-2779, fax 808-742-1924; www.embassy vacationresorts.com. ULTRA-DELUXE.

Marjorie's Kauai Inn overlooks grazing horses in the Lawai Valley, and you can enjoy the view from your private deck. All three spacious guest rooms have a refrigerator, a microwave, a coffee maker and a toaster; you'll receive bread, fruit, juice and coffee on your arrival. Guests have access to a swimming pool, and you can ask your hostess for use of a barbecue grill, a blender and beach chairs. Marjorie's a good resource for information about local attractions. Adults only. ~ Lawai; 808-332-8838, 800-717-8838; www.marjorieskauaiinn.com, e-mail marjorie@marjorieskauai inn.com. MODERATE.

CONDOS   The best way to shop for value and location among Poipu condos is to contact one of the local rental agencies. They include **Poipu Beach Resort Association** at 2440 Hoonani Road in Koloa (808-742-7444, 888-744-0888, fax 808-742-7887; www.poipu beach.org, e-mail info@poipubeach.org), **Grantham Resorts** at 3176 Poipu Road in Poipu (808-742-2000, 800-325-5701, fax 808-742-9093; www.grantham-resorts.com, e-mail info@grant ham-resorts.com) and **R & R Realty & Rentals** at 1763 Pee Road in Poipu (808-742-7555, 800-367-8022, fax 808-742-7434; www.r7r.com, e-mail randr@r7r.com). Talk to these agencies at length. Ask them about the best deals they have to offer in the season you're going.

A particularly well-known destination, **Kiahuna Plantation** is a 35-acre beachfront spread and an ideal family resting spot. This complex of resort condominiums is landscaped with lily ponds, lagoon and a spectacular cactus garden. The beach here provides lots of fun for bodysurfers. The units are housed in attractive plantation-style structures, which dot the resort's rolling lawns. In peak season, one-bedroom condos are $249 to $369; two-bedroom units are $319 to $449. Ask for a condo away from the street and parking lot. ~ 2253 Poipu Road, Poipu; 808-742-6411, 800-688-7444, fax 808-742-1698; www.outrigger.com.

When calling rental agencies about condo deals, also ask about packages that include rental cars.

Neatly situated near the oceanfront just a short jaunt to the beach, **Poipu Kapili** offers you a great place to unpack your bags. It's a 60-unit complex with a pool and tennis courts amid lush vegetation. Each condo, uniquely decorated by its owner, offers views (and sounds) of the blue Pacific. One-bedroom condos start at $220. ~ 2221 Kapili Road, Koloa; 808-742-6449, 800-443-7714, fax 808-742-9162; www.poipukapili.com, e-mail aloha@ poipukapili.com.

Whaler's Cove is a secluded condominium resort that serves up an idyllic shoreline setting. Its roomy, two-bedroom units (which sleep up to six and range from $507 to $656) feature oceanfront lanais that face onto the bright blue Pacific; one-bedroom units run from $349 to $469. Koloa Landing, an excellent snorkeling and shoreline dive spot, is right next door. Each condo has cheery, modern decor. The resort has a pool, a hot tub and the ubiquitous barbecue. ~ 2640 Puuholo Road, Koloa; 808-742-7571, 800-225-2683, fax 808-742-1185; www.whalers-cove.com, e-mail stay@whalers-cove.com.

One of the most unique condos around is **Poipu Crater Resort**.   ◄ HIDDEN
Located just 600 yards from the beach, it's also one of the best deals. This entire 30-unit facility rests in the crater of an extinct volcano. The accommodations are contained in attractive wood-frame houses; all are two-bedroom condos and rent for $137 to $187 in peak season, depending on length of stay. There's a pool, tennis courts, a sauna and a barbecue area. ~ Hoohu Road, Poipu; 808-742-7400, 800-367-8020, fax 808-742-9121; www.suite-paradise.com, e-mail mail@suite-paradise.com.

Poipu Kai Resort consists of a succession of separate buildings spread around a spacious lawn. There are seven pools and nine tennis courts plus a restaurant, jacuzzi and barbecues. The entire complex fronts Shipwreck and Brennecke's beaches. Economy Cottages start at $98 and one-bedroom condos start at $135, depending on the length of your stay. ~ 1941 Poipu Road, Poipu; 808-742-7400, 800-367-8020, fax 808-742-9121; www. suite-paradise.com, e-mail mail@suite-paradise.com.

Poipu Shores is a small (39-unit) complex right on the ocean with a swimming pool so close to the water the waves seem poised to break across it. One-bedroom units start at $268 ($222 off-season). ~ 1775 Pee Road, Poipu; 808-742-7400, 800-367-8020; www.suite-paradise.com.

At **Sunset Kahili Condominiums**, one-bedroom apartments start at $125 and sleep up to four, and two bedrooms house up to six and begin at $225. All units have ocean views. Four-night minimum stay gets a discount; two-week stay required during holiday season. ~ 1763 Pee Road, Poipu; 808-742-7434, phone/fax 800-827-6478; www.r7r.com, e-mail info@r7r.com.

At **Kuhio Shores**, one-bedroom apartments are $220 for one to four people; two bedrooms, two baths, cost $325 for one to six people. On the shore, but lacking a beach. Lower rates for stays longer than four days. ~ 5050 Lawai Road, Poipu; 808-742-7555,

800-367-8022, fax 808-742-1559; www.r7r.com, e-mail randr@ r7r.com

DINING

In Koloa town, drop by **Da'li Deli & Café** for coffee and house-made breakfast pastries, tasty gourmet sandwiches and simple Mediterranean-style dinner entrées served in a cozy dining room. ~ 5492 Koloa Road, Koloa; 808-742-8824. MODERATE.

South-of-the-border cuisine comes in the form of tamales, chile verde, enchiladas and tacos at **Mi Casita Mexican Restaurant**. With oilcloth on the tables and a desert-and-cactus mural covering an entire wall, this home-style eatery is a good bet for a filling meal. No lunch on Sunday. ~ 5470 Koloa Road, Koloa; 808-742-2323. BUDGET TO MODERATE.

For patio dining stroll down the street to **TomKats Grille**. Situated in a small interior courtyard, this easy-going restaurant has prime rib, lobster and fresh seafood, as well as sandwiches and chicken fingers for the kids. ~ 5400 Koloa Road, Koloa; 808-742-8887. MODERATE.

This area is not known for an abundance of restaurants, so you're lucky to find **Pizzetta**. Tastefully decorated with Italian scenes and tiles, the full bar will mix you up a drink while you wait for your order. The menu is basic Italian: calzones, mozzarella sticks, etc. But the pizza is particularly good, with its homemade crust and sauce, and reasonably priced. You can eat in, dine on the deck, or take it to go. Delivery is also an option. ~ 5408 Koloa Road, Koloa; 808-742-8881, fax 808-742-2715. MODERATE TO DELUXE.

HIDDEN ▶

For super fresh sashimi, a variety of fish *poke* and hearty plate lunches, stop in at the **Koloa Fish Market**. These plate lunches are several steps above the competitors in quality, and the raw fish items are fresh. Lunch only. ~ 5482 Koloa Road, Koloa; 808-742-6199, fax 808-742-1018. BUDGET.

The stars, the ocean and the **Beach House Restaurant** provide a perfect framework for some of Kauai's best Pacific Rim cuisine. Signature items include the "Ahi Taster," Kauai asparagus salad, lemongrass-and kaffir lime–crusted scallops, wasabi-crusted snapper and a kahlua taro cheesecake. Not only is the food worth the splurge, the oceanfront location, on the road to Spouting Horn, is an ideal place to catch the sunset. Dinner only. ~ 5022 Lawai Road, Koloa; 808-742-1424, fax 808-742-1369; www.the-beach-house.com. DELUXE TO ULTRA-DELUXE.

At **Pattaya Asian Cafe**, you can settle back at a teak dining table. This small patio eatery serves broccoli noodles, lemon chicken, fresh sweet basil beef, and numerous other Southeast Asian dishes. The food has never disappointed me the several times I've dined here. Worth a stop. ~ Poipu Shopping Village, 2360 Kiahuna Plantation Drive, Poipu; 808-742-8818. MODERATE.

It seems like everywhere you go in Hawaii these days, Roy Yamaguchi has a restaurant. On Kauai it is **Roy's Poipu Bar & Grill**, an informal dining room with the kitchen behind a glass partition. The menu is a sample of what the staff calls Hawaiian fusion cuisine. You can order steamed fresh fish, hibachi-style salmon or *kiawe*-grilled ribeye steak. Or at least that's what was on the ever-changing menu last time I was in. In any case, it's hard to go wrong. Reservations are strongly recommended. Dinner only. ~ Poipu Shopping Village, 2360 Kiahuna Plantation Drive, Poipu; 808-742-5000, fax 808-742-5050. MODERATE TO ULTRA-DELUXE.

Families will love **Poipu Tropical Burgers**, with its *keiki* meals, casual, open-air setting, low prices and wide range of items. Gourmet burgers, sandwiches, meal-sized salads, fresh fish, steak and pasta make up the menu. Portions are hearty, and it's open for three meals a day. ~ Poipu Shopping Village, 2360 Kiahuna Plantation Drive, Poipu; 808-742-1808. MODERATE.

Overlooking Poipu Beach is **Brennecke's Beach Broiler**. Downstairs at this two-level dining spot you'll find a budget-priced deli serving sandwiches and shave ice. The upper deck is occupied by an open-air restaurant that serves appetizers, lunch and dinner daily, then stokes the *kiawe* broiler for dinner selections that include fresh fish dishes, steak, chicken and seafood kebab. There is also pasta. ~ 2100 Hoone Road, Poipu; 808-742-7588, 888-

AUTHOR FAVORITE

Keoki's Paradise, a beautiful patio-style restaurant centered around a tropical garden and pond, is located in Poipu Shopping Village. They feature a steak-and-seafood menu. Some say the seafood is the best you'll get for the price. The setting alone makes it worth a visit. ~ Poipu Shopping Village, 2360 Kiahuna Plantation Drive, Poipu; 808-742-7534, fax 808-742-7847. MODERATE TO ULTRA-DELUXE.

384-8810, fax 808-742-1321; www.brenneckes.com, e-mail bob@ brenneckes.com. MODERATE TO ULTRA-DELUXE.

Huge (and tasty) portions that will last you two meals, or can be shared, are served up at **Taqueria Nortenos** in the Poipu Plaza. The decor isn't much to write home about, but you can take your Mexican food to go, and with prices like this it's hard to complain. You might want to try the *chalupas* or burritos. For dessert order the *bunuelos*. Closed Wednesday. ~ 2827 Poipu Road, Poipu; 808-742-7222. BUDGET.

The setting at **The Plantation Gardens Restaurant** is a restored Polynesian-style home tucked away in the densely landscaped grounds of Kiahuna Plantation Resort. Meals, served inside and on the open-air veranda, have a Pacific Rim influence. The menu emphasizes organic, locally grown herbs and vegetables as well as a grill using *kiawe*—the native Hawaiian mesquite. Filet mignon, double-cut lamb chops and a variety of fresh options will make your mouth water. Vegetarians will be pleased with a choice of creative entrées. Dinner only. ~ 2253 Poipu Road, Koloa; 808-742-2216, fax 808-742-1570. DELUXE TO ULTRA-DELUXE.

Casablanca at Kiahuna is the newest addition to the Poipu restaurant scene, and it's a welcome one. Its veranda dining makes good use of the southside's sunny weather, while warm lighting gives the high-ceilinged dining room a nighttime ambience that feels both spacious and snug. Best of all is the food, a tempting selection of Mediterranean and Italian fare. Try the tangine, a spicy Moroccan stew served with lamb or as a vegetarian option. ~ Kiahuna Swim and Tennis Club, 2290 Poipu Road, Koloa; 808-742-2929. DELUXE.

The Hyatt Regency Kauai Resort & Spa's most imaginative restaurant is without doubt **Tidepools**. The theme is grass-shack Polynesia, with each of the several dining rooms resembling a classic *hale pili*. Set in a quiet lagoon and graced with classic Hawaiian sunsets and ocean breezes, it's a great place to dine. The offerings include charred ahi sashimi and a mixed seafood grill with lobster, scallops, shrimp and fish. Dinner only. ~ 1571 Poipu Road, Poipu; 808-742-1234, fax 808-742-1557; www.kauai-hyatt.com. ULTRA-DELUXE.

GROCERIES The **Big Save Market** includes a dry goods section and is definitely the place to shop on the way to Poipu Beach. ~ Koloa Road, Koloa; 808-742-1614.

Also popular with local shoppers is **Sueoka Store**, a classic old grocery store with a takeout stand located right in the center of town. ~ Koloa Road, Koloa; 808-742-1611.

If you're stuck, you might want to check out the **Whaler's General Store**, which is open 7:30 a.m. to 10 p.m. The prices are higher and the grocery selection is limited, but the hours are handy. ~ Poipu Shopping Village, 2360 Kiahuna Plantation Drive, Poipu; 808-742-9431.

If you're already soaking up the sun at Poipu, you have a few grocery options. **Brennecke's Mini-Deli** is conveniently situated across the street from Poipu Beach Park. This mom-and-pop business has liquor, cold drinks and a limited selection of groceries. ~ 2100 Hoone Road, Poipu; 808-742-7583.

To increase your choices and decrease your food bill, head up Poipu Road to **Kukuiula Store**. This market has prices that are nearly competitive with the Big Save Market on Koloa Road. ~ 2827 Poipu Road, Poipu; 808-742-1601.

On the way to Poipu, the former plantation town of Koloa supports a cluster of shops as well as a miniature mall. Several clothing stores line Koloa Road. The minimall, called **Old Koloa Town** (even though it was totally overhauled in the 1980s), houses a string of small jewelry stores, a T-shirt shop and a photo studio. ~ Koloa Road, Koloa.

SHOPPING

Atlantis Gallery & Frames has contemporary Hawaiian paintings and prints. ~ 5400 Koloa Road, Koloa; 808-742-2555.

Walk into **Island Soap & Candle Works** and get an education in how to make both. This amazing little shop has soaps made

AUTHOR FAVORITE

My favorite shopping spot around Poipu has always been at the **Spouting Horn**. Here, next to the parking lot that serves visitors to the blowhole, local merchants set up tables to sell their wares. You're liable to find coral and *puka* shell necklaces, trident shell trumpets, rare Niihau shell necklaces and some marvelous mother-of-pearl pieces. You are free to barter, of course, though the prices are pretty good to begin with. If you're interested in jewelry and want to meet local artisans, this is an intriguing spot. ~ End of Lawai Road, Poipu.

from coconut, guava, plumeria and every other island product imaginable. There are bath gels, botanical hand lotions and, oh yes, candles—dozens of different kinds. ~ 5428 Koloa Road, Koloa; 808-742-1945.

Poipu Shopping Village is a resort-style shopping complex with several businesses, including restaurants, a store that sells only designer jewelry, two art galleries, a surf shop and a sundries shop. It's a good spot to stop at before a day at the beach. ~ 2360 Kiahuna Plantation Drive, Koloa; 808-742-2831.

Hale Mana offers a wonderful selection of designer island clothing, art prints, Chinese antiques, and "gifts for the spirited." Its sister store **Hale Mana Fine Arts** specializes in fine art and museum pieces. ~ 2360 Kiahuna Plantation Drive, Poipu; 808-742-1027.

You can also venture down to the **Hyatt Regency Kauai**. It's a spectacular resort property, well worth touring and also offering a variety of sleek shops. ~ 1571 Poipu Road, Poipu; 808-742-1234.

NIGHTLIFE   To catch a local crowd, head down to **Brennecke's Beach Broiler**. There's no music, but the crowds are young and the views otherworldly. ~ 2100 Hoone Road, Poipu; 808-742-7588.

Keoki's Paradise (808-742-7534) in Poipu Shopping Village features contemporary Hawaiian music every Tuesday, Thursday, Friday and Saturday nights and Sunday during the day. You can sit outdoors in a garden setting and enjoy the sounds. Also in the mall, check out the Polynesian dance show Tuesday and Thursday evenings on the mall's center stage. ~ 2360 Kiahuna Plantation Drive, Poipu.

Joe's On The Green has live Hawaiian music during their Wednesday and Thursday evening dinner. Locals love the place, so make reservations ahead of time or prepare to squeeze in at the bar. ~ 2545 Kiahuna Plantation Drive, Poipu; 808-742-9696.

There's live Hawaiian and light contemporary music at **The Point** Tuesday through Thursday from 8 to 11 p.m., and dancing on Friday and Saturday. The 225-degree view and wavefront location are an even stronger draw. Great at sunset. ~ Sheraton Kauai Beach Resort, 2440 Hoonani Road, Poipu; 808-742-1661 ext. 52.

The Hyatt Regency Kauai, with its spectacular location on Shipwreck Beach, hosts the area's upscale nightspots. **Stevenson's**

Library is a stately wood-paneled lounge that evokes a sense of colonial-era Polynesia. For a drink with a view of the beach, try the **Tidepools Restaurant**. Hawaiian sunsets and music go hand in hand at **Seaview Terrace**, located in the hotel's lobby. ~ Hyatt Regency Kauai Resort & Spa, 1571 Poipu Road, Poipu; 808-742-1234, 800-633-7313.

POIPU BEACH AND WAIOHAI BEACH 🏊 🏖 🚻 ⚓ Extending along the main hotel area in Poipu are two adjacent white-sand beaches crowded with visitors. Popular with sunbathers, swimmers and water-sport aficionados, both are protected by a series of off-shore reefs. At Poipu Beach there is good surfing for beginners near the beach, for intermediate surfers about 100 yards offshore and for expert surfers about a half-mile out at "First Break." This beach is also popular with windsurfers. Waiohai Beach has an offshore break near the reef known as "Waiohai." There's fishing from the nearby rocks (the beach area is usually crowded). There are lifeguards. ~ Located along Poipu Road near the closed Waiohai hotel.

BEACHES & PARKS

In addition to being incredibly beautiful and ripe with potential for outdoor sports, Mahaulepu Beach is important scientifically. Remains of extinct birds have been found here, and petroglyphs have been discovered along the shoreline.

POIPU BEACH PARK 🏊 🎣 ⚓ This has got to be one of the loveliest little parks around. There's a well-kept lawn for picnickers and finicky sunbathers, a crescent-shaped beach with a protecting reef and the sunny skies of Poipu. Since the water here is relatively flat, most days it's not good for surfing. However, swimming is excellent, and the entire area has some of the best diving on the island. An offshore sandbar makes for good bodysurfing. Bonefish, rockfish and *papio* are common catches; there's also good spearfishing on the nearby reefs. You'll find a picnic area, restrooms, showers and lifeguards. ~ Located on Hoone Road in Poipu.

SHIPWRECK BEACH 🏊 🎣 ⚓ Back in the 1980s, this was one of the greatest of Kauai's hidden beaches. Then condominiums began crawling along the coast and eventually the Hyatt Regency Kauai was built right on the strand. Today, it's a sandy but rock-studded beach, quite beautiful but bordered by the resort. Swimming is good when the surf is low. This is also an outstanding bodysurfing and windsurfing area (the best spot is at the east end of the beach). Fishing is good from nearby Makawehi Point. ~

From the Poipu Beach area, follow Poipu Road east and simply look for the Hyatt Regency Kauai, which borders the beach.

HIDDEN ▶   **MAHAULEPU BEACH** 🏊 🐟 🎣 ⛵ If you've come to Kauai seeking that South Seas dream, head out to these lovely strands. Mahaulepu is a tropical corridor of white sand winding for two miles along a reef-protected shoreline and including several strands and pocket beaches. Flocks of seabirds inhabit the area, and if that's not enough, the area boasts 100-foot-high sand dunes. There are well-protected sections of beach where you can swim, as well as rocky areas where you can fish. Snorkeling and surfing are also good here. The beach has no facilities. ~ From the Poipu Beach area, follow Poipu Road east past the Hyatt Regency Kauai at Shipwreck Beach. Beyond Shipwreck, the pavement ends and the thoroughfare becomes a cane road. Continue on the main cane road (which is like a dirt road continuation of Poipu Road). Follow this road for about two miles (even when it curves toward the mountains and away from the ocean). Numerous minor cane roads will intersect from the right and left: ignore them. Finally, you will come to a crossroads with a major cane road (along which a line of telephone poles runs). Turn right and follow this road for about a mile (you'll pass a quarry off in the distance to the right), then watch on the right for roads leading to the beach. You will encounter a guard shack at the turnoff where you are required to sign a waiver to continue onto the property. The beach entrance is closed from 7 p.m. to 7:30 a.m.

SIX

Waimea Area

The Western world's relationship with Hawaii, a tumultuous affair dating back more than two centuries, began in southwest Kauai when Captain James Cook set anchor at Waimea Bay. Cook landed on the leeward side of the island, a hot, dry expanse rimmed by white-sand beaches and dominated to the interior by Waimea Canyon, the "Grand Canyon of the Pacific."

The climate at the southwestern end of the island is conducive to sugar cane, which is partly why Gay & Robinson is the only plantation to still survive on Kauai. Its fields line the roads, along with Kauai Coffee groves.

The towns here have retained an old-Hawaii feel, even though vacation rentals are now creeping up along the handsome stretch of coastline. Beyond the towns, it's either west to the Pacific Missile Range Facility and enough long, broad, thick, sandy beaches to satisfy the most dedicated beach bum, or north to the cool, often misty, forested elevations of Kokee.

Although the westside is a place of many topographic contrasts, when it comes to population and lifestyle, it's still local to da max. The old ways of hunting, fishing and farming prevail here, supported by the expanses of open space running from the mountains to the sea.

THE COAST One of the first plantation towns you'll encounter driving west on Kaumualii Highway (Route 50) is Kalaheo. A detour up the hillside in Kalaheo, up Puiilima Road, will give you a broad overview of the area, as well as a taste of residential life on this part of the island. Or take a left on Papalina Road, which will lead a mile up to **Kukuiolono Park**, a lightly visited Japanese garden complete with stone bridge, ornamental pool and florid landscaping. Take a stroll through this peaceful

◀ *HIDDEN*

retreat and you'll also enjoy a stunning view that sweeps across a patchwork of fields to the sea.

Route 50 continues along to the small town of **Eleele**, another residential neighborhood. From here you can take Route 541 to the community of **Port Allen** and its small boat harbor and shopping center. If you're interested in fishing charters or tour boats, a few operate out of this area.

Back on Route 50, en route from one tinroof town to the next, you'll pass the **Hanapepe Valley Lookout**, which offers a view of native plant life dramatically set in a gorge ringed by eroded cliffs. Taro patches grow in abundance in this wet and lush valley.

HIDDEN ▶

Be sure to take the nearby fork into **Hanapepe**, a vintage village complete with wooden sidewalks and weather-beaten storefronts. During the 1924 sugar strike, 16 workers were killed here by police. Even today, the independent spirit of those martyrs pervades this proud little town. It has become a haven for artists, and galleries seem to outnumber residents.

For a sense of Hanapepe during the plantation days, drive out **Awawa Road**. Precipitous red lava cliffs rim the roadside, while rickety cottages and intricately tilled fields carpet the valley below.

On the outskirts of Hanapepe, turn right on Route 543 toward the ocean. Here you'll see ancient **salt ponds**, which are still used today. Continue to the end of the road to get to **Salt Pond Beach Park**, a spot frequented by windsurfers and locals.

A short detour off Route 50 from either Kalaheo or Hanapepe leads to the **Kauai Coffee Visitor Center**. Housed in a former plantation-worker's home, the center has pictures from the area's sugar-plantation days, as well as information about contemporary coffee production. Best of all, they have a small café and free tastings. ~ Route 540, between Kalaheo and Hanapepe; 808-335-0813, fax 808-335-3149; www.kauaicoffee.com, e-mail green sales@kauaicoffee.com.

As Kaumualii Highway winds its way past small communities, you'll see that this is still sugar country. A side trip to one of Hawaii's few remaining sugar plantations leads to the mill and to **Gay & Robinson Tours**. The road is lined with monkeypod trees and passes by former plantation-managers' homes, with their manicured gardens. Even if you don't go on a tour, it's worth seeing this street. The tour office features a mini-museum, and the tour itself takes in the cane fields and factories of a classic Hawaiian plantation. (If you take the tour, you'll need to wear closed-toe shoes and clothes you don't mind being stained red by the soil.) Reservations required. Admission. ~ Near the 19-mile marker on Kaumualii Highway, Waimea; 808-335-2824; www.gandrtours-kauai. com, e-mail info@gandrtours-kauai.com.

Just past the 22-mile marker is a road that takes you to **Russian Fort Elizabeth State Historical Park**. Now just a rubble heap, historically it represents a fruitless attempt by a maverick adventurer working for a Russian trading company to gain a foothold in the islands in 1817. Designed in the shape of a six-pointed star, the original fort bristled with guns and had walls 30 feet thick. Two other forts were built on the island—one in Princeville and another in Hanalei. Nothing is left of them.

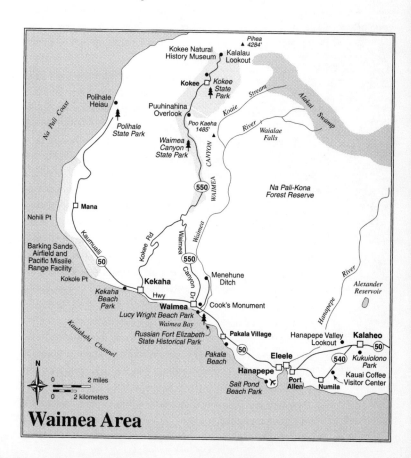

Waimea Area

An earlier event, Captain James Cook's 1778 "discovery" of Hawaii, is commemorated with a lava monolith near his landing place in Waimea. Watch for roadside markers to **Cook's Monument**. ~ Just after you cross the Waimea River, on the road to Lucy Wright Park.

Cook was not the only outsider to assume a role in Waimea's history. It seems that those industrious leprechauns who built the fishpond outside Lihue were also at work here constructing the

HIDDEN ► **Menehune Ditch**. This waterway, built with hand-hewn stones in a fashion unfamiliar to the Polynesians, has long puzzled archaeologists. ~ Outside town on Menehune Road.

In the early 20th century, **Waimea** was a thriving sugar community. Drive around town and you'll see several structures that have withstood the test of time, like the restored **Waimea Theater** and the **Yamese** and **Masuda** buildings. Those interested in getting up close and personal with the past might take the "mill camp walking tour." Plantation life and homes and gardens are highlighted. Tours are held Tuesday, Thursday and Saturday at 9 a.m. Reservations are required. Admission. ~ 808-335-2824, fax 808-335-6852.

The sand at Barking Sands Airfield is similar to that found in Egypt's Sinai Desert, the Gobi Desert of Mongolia and in Saudi Arabia.

You'll pass the town of **Kekaha**, home of a now-defunct sugar mill and a colony of plantation houses, before arriving at the next stop on this scenic itinerary—**Barking Sands Airfield**. Actually, it's not the airfield but the sands that belong on your itinerary. These lofty sand dunes, among the largest on the island, make a woofing sound when ground underfoot. This, according to scientists, is due to tiny cavities in each grain of sand that cause them to resonate when rubbed together. If you have trouble making the sound, remember what one local wag told me: The hills actually got their name from tourists becoming "dog-tired" after futilely trying to elicit a growl from the mute sand. (Since the beach here at **Major's Bay** is on a military reservation, call 808-335-4229 to make sure the facility is open to the public.) Nearby is the **Pacific Missile Range Facility** (808-335-4229), an important launch area for military and meteorological rockets and the site of periodic war games.

Having made a fool of yourself trying to get sand to bark, continue on past the deserted town of **Mana** (along a graded dirt road for the last five miles) to the endless sands of **Polihale State**

Park. This very hot, very dry, very beautiful retreat represents the last stretch of a 15-mile-long sand beach, one of the longest in the state, that begins way back in Kekaha. The sand marathon ends at the foot of the Na Pali cliffs, in an area sacred to the Hawaiians. Here the ancients built **Polihale Heiau**, a temple whose ruins remain. This sacred place is where the spirits of the dead made their leap into the spiritual world. And here the road ends, further passage made impossible by the sea cliffs that wrap around Kauai's northwest corner.

THE MOUNTAINS   Another candidate in the contest for ultimate adventure—one that is free, doesn't require a helicopter and always lies open to exploration—is **Waimea Canyon** (808-274-3433). Touring the "Grand Canyon of the Pacific" involves a side trip from either the town of Waimea or Kekaha. Waimea Canyon Drive leads from the former and Kokee Road climbs from the latter; they join about halfway up the mountain. For an overview of the entire region, go up along Waimea Canyon Drive, since it hugs the canyon rim and provides the best views, then follow Kokee Road down. See page 51 for a map of trails.

As the paved road snakes along the side of this 2857-foot-deep canyon, a staggering panorama opens. The red and orange hues of a barren southwestern landscape are splashed with tropic greens and yellows. Far below, the **Waimea River**, which carved this ten-mile-long chasm, cuts a sinuous course. Several vista points provide crow's-nest views of the territory, including **Puuhinahina Overlook** at 3500-feet elevation, which offers views of the canyon to the east and Niihau to the west.

The road continues deep into Kauai's cool interior before arriving at **Kokee State Park**, a preserve of *koa* trees, with their crescent-shape leaves, and *ohia* trees, with their gray bark and red pompon flowers. You're apt to see a variety of birds here, including the red *apapane*, the yellow-green *amakihi*, the white-tailed tropic bird and maybe the state bird, the nene. Wild boar roam the area and trout fishing is a favorite sport in the park. Hiking trails meander through the park. (See "Hiking" at the end of the chapter for more information.) Within this 4345-acre park you'll find a restaurant and cabins.

At the **Kokee Natural History Museum** is a small display space devoted to the flora, fauna and natural history of the area, as well as an exhibit about Hurricane Iniki. Collections of shells and Hawaiian artifacts are also featured. ~ 808-335-9975, fax 808-335-6131; www.kokee.org, e-mail information@kokee.org.

It's a short drive onward and upward to the **Kalalau Lookout,** where Kauai's other face is reflected in knife-edged cliffs and overgrown gorges that drop to the sea 4000 feet below. Another nearby overlook gazes out across the **Alakai Swamp** to **Mount Waialeale.** (Because of cloud cover in the valley, it's best to arrive at the overlook before 10 a.m. or after 4 p.m.) One more spectacular scene along the way, one more reason to bring you back to this magnificent island.

LODGING   Accommodations on Kauai's southwest side include beachside cottages in Waimea and ethereal facilities in Kokee State Park.

The **Kalaheo Inn** offers nine one-bedroom suites in this family-owned and -operated hostelry, and several studios and two-bedroom units, each of which has a separate kitchen and living area. There are laundry facilities on the premises. There's also a fully outfitted three-bedroom house. This is the place to stay if you want someplace clean and pleasant, but don't plan on spending much time in your room. ~ P.O. Box 584, Kalaheo, HI 96741; 808-332-6023, 888-332-6023, fax 808-332-5242; www.kalaheo inn.com, e-mail chet@aloha.net. BUDGET TO DELUXE.

Nightly, weekly or monthly, the **Kalaheo Plantation** is a good bargain. The 1926 plantation-style home, located a couple of miles from the beach, once belonged to a district judge. The management polished up the floors, added some new windows and, they won't hesitate to tell you, 500 plants, and opened for business. There are six modern suites with either a kitchenette or full kitchen; some have private lanais. You can rent the whole house but you can't wear your shoes inside. ~ 4579 Puuwai Road, Kalaheo; phone/fax 808-332-7812; www.kalaheo-plantation.com, e-mail kalaheo1@gte.net. BUDGET TO MODERATE.

HIDDEN ▶   Those seeking a neighborhood setting may prefer **Classic Vacation Cottages,** seven stand-alone vacation rentals of varying sizes at the end of a residential cul-de-sac in the quiet, hilly town of Kalaheo. They range from a modest studio to an attractive full-sized home that sleeps eight. The larger units have full kitchens, too, making them a bargain for two couples or a family. Of course, the beach isn't nearby, although Kukuiolono hilltop park and golf course aren't far. The communal hot tub is another plus.

~ P.O. Box 901, Kalaheo, HI 96741; 808-332-9201, fax 808-332-7645; www.classiccottages.com, e-mail clascot@hawaiian.net. BUDGET TO MODERATE.

Waimea Plantation Cottages is one of the most alluring and secluded facilities on the entire island. Here in a spectacular coconut grove, fronting a salt-and-pepper beach, is a cluster of charmingly rustic 1920s-era plantation cottages. Each has been carefully restored and many are furnished with rattan furniture. These one-, two- and multibedroom houses have full kitchens. Maid service is every third day. Like the rest of the complex, the swimming pool follows the style of an earlier era (most visitors swim here since the offshore waters are usually murky). A new low-key day spa adds to the relaxed atmosphere. The place is a little gem out on Kauai's remote westside. ~ 9400 Kaumualii Highway, Waimea; 808-338-1625, fax 808-338-2338; www.waimea-plantation.com, e-mail paul.schow@aston-hotels.com. ULTRA-DELUXE.

Nestled in secluded woods between Waimea Canyon and the Kalalau Lookout are the **Kokee Lodge Cabins**. Each of the 12 mountain cabins, varying in size from one large room to two-bedroom complexes, comes with a wood-burning stove, a basic kitchen and rustic furnishings. These wood cabins, 3600 feet above sea level, are a mountaineer's dream. With forest and hiking trails all around, Kokee is ideal for the adventurer. It gets chilly, so bring a jacket or sweater. Reservations are essential. ~ Kokee State Park; 808-335-6061. BUDGET.

Traveling west toward Waimea Canyon and Barking Sands, you'll find the watering places decrease as rapidly as the rainfall. Most

DINING

AUTHOR FAVORITE

You don't get to eat outside at Hanapepe's **Green Garden Restaurant**, but the tropical plants convey a genuine garden feeling. The deliciously varied dinner menu ranges from pork chow mein to rock lobster tail and includes homemade old-fashioned vegetable soup and a salad bar. I particularly enjoyed the seafood special, a platter of mahimahi, shrimp, oysters and scallops. Children's and senior portions are available. Dinner only. Closed Tuesday. ~ Kaumualii Highway, Hanapepe; 808-335-5422, fax 808-335-5528. MODERATE.

restaurants en route are cafés and takeout stands. If you're on a budget, you're in luck; if you're looking for an exclusive, elegant establishment, you'll find slim pickings out Waimea way.

At the **Kalaheo Steak House** you'll step into a comfortable wood-paneled dining room. Pull up a chair, rest your elbows on the table (it's permitted) and choose among sirloin, filet mignon, scampi, Cornish hens and several other appealing entrées. No reservations accepted. Dinner only. ~ 4444 Papalina Road, Kalaheo; 808-332-9780. MODERATE TO DELUXE.

Because Kauai is the oldest of the Hawaiian Islands, its natural world has had more time to evolve, resulting in a rich diversity of native plant and animal life. Many Kauai species are found nowhere else in Hawaii—or on earth.

Family-owned and -operated **Brick Oven Pizza** is commonly touted as having the best pies on the island. But don't expect the Americanized version of the dish. Brick Oven specializes in authentic Italian: thin crust brushed with garlic butter and minimal sauce. Red-and-white-checked tablecloths and an amiable staff complete the image. The place is often jammed, so plan ahead if you have hungry kids in tow. Closed Monday and for one week in September. ~ 2-2555 Kaumualii Highway, Kalaheo; 808-332-8561, fax 808-332-3800. BUDGET TO MODERATE.

HIDDEN ► **Kalaheo Coffee Co. and Cafe** is always bustling. Locals arrive in droves for the omelettes, hearty deli sandwiches and burgers, yummy homemade cinnamon rolls and coffee drinks. With small wooden tables and a tiny retail area, it's a cheery, clean place, with friendly service. Breakfast and lunch only. ~ 2-2436 Kaumualii Highway, Kalaheo; 808-332-5858, fax 808-332-5868; www.kalaheo.com. MODERATE.

HIDDEN ► **Camp House Grill** is a trim little café with an island-style menu. Favored by nearby residents, they serve *huli huli* chicken and pork ribs, and big, satisfying breakfasts. The homemade pies are a big draw. ~ 2-2431 Kaumualii Highway, Kalaheo; 808-332-9755, fax 808-332-7052. BUDGET TO MODERATE.

HIDDEN ► A family-run eatery, **Toi's Thai Kitchen** serves a lunch and dinner menu consisting primarily of Thai food such as yellow curry chicken and stir-fried eggplant with tofu. Fried chicken and mahimahi are also served. Recently remodeled, the decor is simple and the food is good. Closed Sunday. ~ Eleele Shopping Center, 178 Hanapepe Bay, Eleele; 808-335-3111. MODERATE.

Grinds Café & Espresso, with its low prices and large, casual menu of burgers, salads, sandwiches, pizza and coffee drinks, is another good choice. ~ Eleele Shopping Center, Kaumualii Highway, Eleele; 808-335-6027. BUDGET.

Da Imu Hut Café has Hawaiian dishes, *saimin*, fried chicken, ◀ HIDDEN
teriyaki chicken, fried noodles and hamburgers at 1950s prices. It's not much on looks, but it fills the belly. With unusual hours, always call ahead. ~ 3771 Hanapepe Road, Hanapepe; 808-335-0200. BUDGET.

Gourmet vegetarian with an Italian flair is the way they describe the food at **Hanapepe Cafe and Espresso**. Every Friday night you'll find them preparing such dinner entrées as marinated eggplant lasagna, pasta primavera with portobello mushrooms or marinara dishes made with locally grown produce. They're also open for a more casual lunch Monday through Friday. That's when you can stop by for a caesar salad, a "health-nut sandwich," pasta specials, garden burgers or baked frittata. Dinner reservations recommended. Closed Saturday and Sunday. ~ 3830 Hanapepe Road, Hanapepe; 808-335-5011. DELUXE.

Breakfast burritos, melts and deli sandwiches, fish plates and other specials are found at **Waimea Bakery & Deli**, a roadside ◀ HIDDEN
eatery that also prepares an especially good taro-teriyaki burger. Their smoothies, milk shakes, tropical fruit turnovers, Hawaiian sweetbread and other baked goodies add to the appeal. Closed Tuesday. ~ 9875 Waimea Road, Waimea; 808-338-1950. BUDGET.

Waimea Brewing Company, at Waimea Plantation Cottages, is one of those places you go to for the novelty value as much as the refreshment. Alongside the beer are served sandwiches and burgers, pasta dishes, grilled meats, chicken and fresh fish. There's relaxed, plantation-style decor inside, with a delightful, broad lanai for outdoor dining. ~ 9400 Kaumualii Highway, Waimea; 808-338-9733, fax 808-338-2338; www.waimea-planta tion.com/brew, e-mail info@kikiaola.com. MODERATE TO DELUXE.

At **Pacific Pizza and Deli** you can certainly order a typical cheese pie, but they also offer more exotic versions such as Thai or Mexican pizza. Deli sandwiches, wraps and coffee drinks are available, too. Closed Sunday. ~ Wrangler Restaurant Building, 9852 Kaumualii Road, Waimea; 808-338-1020. BUDGET TO MODERATE.

Steaks, naturally, are the order of the day at **Wranglers Steakhouse**. Here guests can choose to take their meals outside or indoors in a rustic dining room. Hardwood floors and galvanized awnings contribute to the Western feel, as do the old wagon and wooden horse. The menu features classic surf and turf dishes. You might want to take a peek at the *paniolo* artifacts in their small museum. No lunch on Saturday. Closed Sunday. ~ 9852 Kaumualii Highway, Waimea; 808-338-1218, fax 808-338-1266. MODERATE TO DELUXE.

When you're up in the heights above Waimea Canyon you'll be mighty glad to discover **Kokee Lodge** in remote Kokee State Park. From the dining room of this homey hideaway, you can gaze out at the surrounding forest. The restaurant offers a light breakfast and lunch menu. The emphasis is on fresh, healthy dishes and local specialties like *lilikoi* pie. For breakfast try the cornbread, and for lunch choose from soups, sandwiches and salads. ~ Kokee State Park; 808-335-6061, fax 808-335-5431. BUDGET.

GROCERIES   There are two **Big Save Markets** along Kaumualii Highway. Traveling west from Lihue, the first is in the Eleele Shopping Center. ~ Eleele; 808-335-3127. The second is in the center of Waimea. ~ Waimea; 808-338-1621. Both are open from 6:30 a.m. to 10 p.m., Monday to Saturday, and 6:30 a.m. to 9 p.m. on Sunday.

Also along the highway is the **Menehune Food Mart**, a convenience store. ~ Kalaheo; 808-332-7349. For groceries past Waimea, try the **Menehune Food Mart** on Kekaha Road. ~ Kekaha; 808-337-1335.

SHOPPING   Head up to Eleele off of Route 50 near Kalaheo and you'll discover **Red Dirt Hawaii**, home of the "original Red Dirt shirt." Made with stains from the iron-rich soil of Kauai, these T-shirts are a cottage industry with workers all over the island coloring them. If your shirt starts fading, don't worry—just roll it in the dirt or wash it with mud and it will look like new again! ~ 4352 Waialo Road, Eleele; 808-335-5670, fax 808-335-3478; www.dirtshirt.com, e-mail onlinesales@dirtshirt.com.

Hanapepe, which had its boom time around the turn of the 20th century, has loads of character and a relaxed feel. The wooden falsefront buildings that line its main street, which loops off Kaumualii Highway, are slowly being restored and used as artists' studios and specialty shops, creating a low-key but high-brow enclave in an otherwise country town.

This juxtaposition between old and new is highlighted at **Timespace Contemporary Art**, with its clean, sharp, modern approach to design in wall art and household furnishings. Closed Sunday. ~ 4545 Kona Road, Hanapepe; 808-335-0094.

8 Bells Gallery displays a range of mediums by local artists. They feature oil, sculpture, watercolor and limited-edition prints, and are known for their excellent framing with Hawaiian wood. Closed Sunday. ~ 4510 Hana Road, Hanapepe; 808-335-0550.

The **Dawn M. Traina Gallery** has paintings, drawings and prints of native Hawaiian people created by the store's namesake. Closed Sunday and Monday. ~ 3840-B Hanapepe Road, Hanapepe; 808-335-3993.

Kim Starr Gallery displays the owner's oil paintings, pastels and serigraphs. ~ 3878 Hanapepe Road, Hanapepe; 808-335-0381.

Well-known local watercolorist Arius Hopman is spotlighted at the eponymous **Arius Hopman Gallery**. Closed Sunday and Monday. ~ 3840-C Hanapepe Road, Hanapepe; 808-335-0227.

Hanapepe is also the home of **Kauai Fine Arts**, a singular gallery housing an outstanding collection of antique maps and prints. Open Sunday by appointment only. ~ 3905 Hanapepe Road, Hanapepe; 808-335-3778; www.brunias.com.

Consider a tropical oil painting or one of the sculptures at **Giorgio's Gallery**. Closed Sunday. ~ 3871 Hanapepe Road, Hanapepe; 808-335-3949.

Collectibles & Fine Junque has an amazing collection of glassware, aloha shirts, dolls and old bottles. It's a good place to pick up antiques or knickknacks. Closed Sunday. ~ 9821 Kaumualii Highway, Waimea; 808-338-9855.

FLYING HIGH

An unmanned, solar-powered aircraft named *Helio* has been built by NASA and AeroVironment and launched from Barking Sands, Kauai. A long, thin flying wing that researchers hope will reach 100,000 feet in altitude, more than three times higher than commercial jets fly, it is to be used as a surrogate satellite or low-cost telecommunications platform. On its first test flight from Barking Sands it soared to 76,000 feet.

NIGHTLIFE Every week Hanapepe hosts **"Friday Art Night,"** showcasing local artists in the numerous galleries in town. From 6 to 9 p.m. most galleries in this artist enclave keep their doors open, offering refreshments, a chance to talk story with the artists, and frequent musical performances. Art demonstrations, poetry readings and other performances can be found along the street.

Hanapepe Cafe and Espresso is a bit of an anomaly, with gourmet vegetarian food that would seem more at home in California than in this tiny town. On Friday night (the only evening they are open) the place is packed, with local entertainers performing Hawaiian slack-key guitar. There's no bar, but you can sit and have an espresso and dessert. ~ 3830 Hanapepe Road, Hanapepe; 808-335-5011.

You can catch live music Friday nights at **Waimea Brewing Company.** ~ Waimea Plantation Cottages, 9400 Kaumualii Highway, Waimea; 808-338-1625; www.waimea-plantation.com/brew.

BEACHES & PARKS **SALT POND BEACH PARK** A pretty, crescent-shaped beach with a protecting reef and numerous coconut trees, this park is very popular with locals and may be crowded and noisy on weekends. It's a good place to collect shells, though. The road leading to the park passes salt ponds that date back hundreds of years and are still used today to evaporate sea water and produce salt. Swimming is good in this well-protected area. Snorkeling is fair and there is diving near rocks and along the offshore reef. For surfing, there's a shore break by the mouth of the Hanapepe River nearby in Port Allen. Sandy and shallow with small waves, this area is safe for beginners. There are left and right slides. Along the outer harbor edge near Port Allen Airport runway there are summer breaks, for experienced surfers only, which involve climbing down a rocky shoreline. At Salt Pond there are occasional summer breaks (left and right slides) requiring a long paddle out. This is also a very popular windsurfing area. Rockfish and mullet are the most common catches here. Facilities include a picnic area, restrooms, showers and lifeguards. ~ Take Kaumualii Highway to Hanapepe. Turn onto Route 543 and follow it to the end.

▲ There's a grassy area near the beach for tent camping; a county permit is required.

The Forbidden
Island

There's little doubt that the most hidden place in "hidden Hawaii" is **Niihau**, Hawaii's westernmost inhabited island. About 250 native Hawaiians live on this privately owned island under conditions similar to those prevailing during the 19th century. Used as a cattle and sheep ranch and closed to the public, it is Hawaii's last unspoiled frontier.

The Robinsons, a Scottish family that came to Hawaii from New Zealand, purchased the island in the 1860s and have protected (some critics say segregated) its inhabitants from the rest of the world ever since. Residents of Niihau are free to leave the island but must ask permission to return, and while the situation does have a company-town aura about it, the Robinsons have historically shown an abiding concern for the people and ecology of Hawaii.

While Niihau measures a mere 73 square miles and rises only 1281 feet above sea level at its highest point, the island lays claim to rich fishing grounds and is famous for its Niihau shell necklaces, fashioned from rare and tiny shells that wash up on the windward shore only a few times a year.

Until the 1980s, Niihau fully deserved its nickname, "The Forbidden Island." But today outsiders with a sense of adventure (and some extra cash) can climb aboard a **Niihau Helicopter** flight and tour a part of the island. You'll fly over most of the island, avoiding the village where the population is concentrated, and land on a remote beach for a short hike along the shore. You won't meet any Niihau residents, but you will have an experience that could prove to be your ultimate encounter with "hidden Hawaii." ~ Kaumualii Highway; 808-335-3500.

If you'd rather explore the island by ground, **HoloHolo Charters** offers an interesting option. Leaving from Port Allen and including a continental breakfast, their "Supertour" first stops at the Na Pali Coast to view the natural wonders of the area. They then head to Niihau for a snorkeling visit, during which you'll receive instruction by the crew. A buffet-style lunch follows. During the meal, the crew discusses the people and history of Niihau. ~ Elele; 800-848-6130.

HIDDEN ▶ **PAKALA BEACH** 🏄 🦆 🏊 🛶 This long narrow ribbon of sand is bounded by trees and set in perfectly lush surroundings. Surfers will probably be the only other people around. They may come out of the water long enough to watch the spectacular sunsets with you and to tell you of the fabled summer waves that reach heights of 10 to 12 feet. If this book were rating beaches by the star system, Pakala Beach would deserve a constellation. When the surf is low it's a good place to swim. You can also snorkel along the reef. This is one of Hawaii's top summer surfing spots. The incredibly long walls that form along a wide shallow reef allow you to hang ten seemingly forever. Hence the nickname for these breaks—"Infinity." The one drawback: It's a long paddle out. Fishing is good from the rock outcropping off to the left. There are no facilities here. ~ Located along Kaumualii Highway near the 21-mile marker (two miles east of Waimea) you'll see a concrete bridge crossing Aakukui stream with the name "Aakukui" chiseled in the cement. Go through the gate just below the bridge and follow the well-worn path a few hundred yards to the beach.

LUCY WRIGHT BEACH PARK 🏄 🏊 🛶 This five-acre park at the Waimea River mouth is popular with locals and therefore sometimes a little crowded. Despite a sandy beach, the park is not as appealing as others nearby: The water is often murky from cane field spillage. If you're in need of a campground you might stop here, otherwise, I don't recommend the park. Swimming is fair, unless the water is muddy. Surfing varies from small breaks for beginners to extremely long walls that build four different breaks and is best near the river mouth. There's a left slide. In Waimea Bay, there are parrotfish, red goatfish, squirrelfish, *papio*, bonefish, bigeyed scad and threadfin. You can also fish from the pier a few hundred feet west of the park. Facilities include a picnic area, restrooms and showers. ~ Located in Waimea.

▲ Tent camping only. County permit required.

KEKAHA BEACH 🏊 This narrow beach parallels Kaumualii Highway for several miles along the eastern edge of Kekaha. Although close to the highway, the lovely white strand offers some marvelous picnic spots, but the rough surf and powerful currents make swimming dangerous. There are many surfing spots along here; the foremost, called "Davidson's," lies off Oomano Point.

KEKAHA BEACH PARK 🏊 🏄 🚗 Set on a beautiful ribbon of sand, this 20-acre park is a great place to kick back, picnic and catch the sun setting over the island of Niihau. Swimming is good when surf is down; otherwise it can be dangerous. For surfers, immediately west of the park are several breaks, including "Inters" (near Kaumualii Highway and Akialoa Street) and "First Ditch" and "Second Ditch," located in front of two drainage ditches. Anglers try for threadfin. There are picnic facilities and restrooms. ~ Located on Kaumualii Highway in Kekaha.

KOKOLE POINT 🏄 🚗 Out by an old landing strip/drag strip, ◄ HIDDEN
a local dump and a rifle range, there is a wide sandy beach that stretches forever and offers unofficial camping and outrageous sunsets. Fishermen, joggers and beachcombers love the place, but those who hold it nearest their hearts are surfers. The breaks here go by such names as "Rifle Range," "Targets" and "Whispering Sands." Currents and high surf usually make swimming unadvisable. However, fishing is good. There are no facilities. ~ Take the road that leads off Kaumualii Highway one mile west of Kekaha (there's a sign directing traffic to the dump). Follow any of the dirt roads in as far as possible. These will lead either to the dump or to a nearby landing strip. Walk the last three-tenths of a mile to the beach.

BARKING SANDS 🏊 🚤 🏄 🤿 🚗 The military installation at Major's Bay is bounded by very wide beaches that extend for

A FLIRTATION WITH RUSSIA

In 1815, Georg Anton Shäffer, a German-born doctor working for the Russian-American Company, arrived at Kamehameha's court under the guise of salvaging the goods from a Russian cargo ship wrecked on Kauai. He met with Kauai's Governor Kaumualii, who still harbored animosity toward his subjugator Kamehameha, and created a short-lived and loose alliance: Kaumualii promised the Russian-American Company a monopoly on the sandalwood of Kauai if the Russian government helped him defeat the king. Obviously, this plan never got off the ground. Shäffer spent much of 1816 on Kauai, building forts and renaming his land, none of this under the approval of Russia. Kaumualii was soon ordered to force Shäffer off the island. In May 1817, the renegade trader was put aboard his ship and sent from the islands in disgrace. The end of the so-called Russian alliance ended in humiliation for Dr. Shäffer.

miles. You'll see the Barking Sands dunes and magnificent sunsets and get some of the best views of Niihau anywhere on Kauai. The weather is hot and dry here: a great place to get thoroughly baked, but beware of sunburns. The **Pacific Missile Range Facility** is located here, and the area is sometimes used for war games, so these beaches are sometimes closed. Swimming is good, but exercise caution. The coral reefs make for good snorkeling. **Major's Bay** is an excellent surfing spot with both summer and winter breaks. Other breaks include "Rockets" near the rocket launch pad, "Kinkini" at the south end of the airfield runway, and "Family Housing" just offshore from the base housing facility. Windsurfers also frequent Major's Bay and "Kinkini." A particularly good fishing spot is around Nohili Point; the most common catches are bonefish, threadfin and *ulua*. There are no facilities. ~ Take Kaumualii Highway several miles past Kekaha, then watch for signs to the Pacific Missile Range Facility. Due to heightened security measures, obtaining access to the beach can be complicated. Upon arrival in Hawaii, those wishing to visit must contact the local naval center, where they will be asked to complete a clearance form. The completed form must be taken to the Lihui Police Department for a criminal background check. A photo I.D. pass will be issued, though the entire process takes a week. Call ahead for public hours; 808-335-4229.

POLIHALE STATE PARK This 300-foot-wide beach blankets the coast for over two miles along Kauai's west end. The United States' westernmost state park, Polihale is worth visiting—just to see the endless white-sand expanse. It borders the sea cliffs of the Na Pali Coast, covering 138 acres. The hot, dry weather is excellent for sunbathing and prime for burning, so load up on sunscreen. You might even want to bring an umbrella or other form of shade. The afternoons bring great sunsets. This park has magnificent mountain surroundings: Niihau looms in the distance. Swimming is for experts only. The safest swimming is at **Queen's Pond**, an area that, depending on the year's weather conditions, floods and creates a protected lagoon along the beachfront near the middle of the park. Surfing is okay; there's a shore break with left and right slides. There's good windsurfing off Queen's Pond. This beach is also especially great for shell collecting. Bonefish, threadfin and *ulua* are the most common game fish. Facilities include a picnic area, restrooms and showers. ~ Take Kaumualii Highway until it ends, then follow the signs along dirt roads for about five miles.

▲ You can pitch a tent on the beach under a star-crowded sky, or find a shady tree (though they are rare in these parts) for protection against the blazing sun. This is a wonderful place to camp for a day or two. After that, the barren landscape becomes tiresome and monotonous. Tent camping allowed. A state permit is required.

KOKEE STATE PARK 🏃🛶 This spectacular park, high in the mountains above Waimea Canyon, is a mecca for hikers, campers and other outdoor enthusiasts. Sprawling across 4345 heavily wooded acres, this rugged country offers a unique perspective on the Garden Isle. In the rivers there's excellent freshwater angling for rainbow trout during August and September; a state license is required, though. Kokee has everything but a grocery store, so come well-stocked or plan to eat at the lodge restaurant (breakfast and lunch only; 808-335-6061). There is seasonal plum picking, and pig, goat and deer hunting is allowed in the public hunting and fishing areas. The lodge (808-335-6061) also has a museum and gift shop. Nearby are cabins, restrooms, showers, a picnic area and hiking trails. ~ Take Kaumualii Highway to Waimea, then pick up Waimea Canyon Drive from Waimea or Kokee Road from Kekaha. They eventually join and lead about 15 miles up to the park. Contact the park at 808-335-9975, fax 808-335-6131; www.aloha.net/~kokee, e-mail kokee@aloha.net.

▲ An area at the north end of the park has been allocated for tent camping. There are also several wilderness camps along the hiking trails. A state permit is required for nonwilderness camping.

SEVEN

Wailua-Kapaa Area

If Lihue is the commercial center of Kauai, Wailua is the cultural heart of the island. Here along the Wailua River, the only navigable river in Hawaii, the *alii* built *heiau* and perpetuated their princely lines. There are broad surfing beaches here as well as cascades and grottos up along the Wailua River. What attracted Hawaiian royalty to Kauai's east coast was the weather along this windward shore, cooler in the summer than the baking sands of Poipu but not as moist as the tropical rainforests to the north. The Hawaiian nobility added fishponds and coconut groves to these natural features and forbade commoners from entering their domain. The oral tradition they handed down tells of a Tahitian holy man named Puna, one of the first Polynesians to arrive in Hawaii, who chose this sacred spot to live. Other legends recount the lost tribe of Mu, a pre-Polynesian people, dwarfish and cruel, who inhabited caves far up the Wailua River.

Developed as a resort destination before Poipu and Princeville, this area has nevertheless avoided the overdevelopment that plagues other parts of the island. Wailua and Kapaa, while hosting a string of oceanfront condominiums, remain working-class towns, maintaining a contemporary version of the cultural pride of the ancient *alii*.

Lydgate Park, at the confluence of the Wailua River and the ocean, is the center of sacred Kauai. The *alii* established the rocky remains of the **Hauola Place of Refuge** on this site. Here *kapu* breakers under sentence of death could flee; once inside its perimeter, their crimes were absolved. A stone retaining wall also marks the ancient **Hikina a ka la Heiau**. The **petroglyphs** etched in the rocks at the mouth of the river can be seen at low tide. Near the entrance to the marina you'll find the **Malae Heiau**. It is easy to see why this area was sacred to ancient Hawaiians—the serenity is palpable, the beauty extraordinary. ~ Kuhio Highway, Wailua.

On the other side of Route 56 you can step from the sacred to the profane. Billing itself as "Kauai's best-kept secret," **Smith's Tropical Paradise** has elements of the classic tourist trap. Covering 30 riverside acres is a series of gardens and mock Pacific villages in the form of a tropical theme park. There are hibiscus, bamboo and Japanese gardens as well as re-creations of life in Polynesia, the Philippines and elsewhere. Budding botanists will enjoy the labeled plants and trees. On Monday, Wednesday and Friday, they have a luau and show. Admission. ~ Wailua Marina State Park, Wailua; 808-821-6895, fax 808-822-4520; www.smiths kauai.com, e-mail smiths@aloha.net.

Fittingly, the adjacent marina is the departure point for boat trips up the Wailua River to **Fern Grotto**. The scenery along the way is magnificent as you pass along a tropical riverfront that is luxuriously overgrown. The grotto itself is a 40-foot cavern draped with feathery ferns, a place so beautiful and romantic that many people choose to marry here. But the boat ride is one of the most cloyingly commercial experiences in Hawaii, a 20-minute voyage during which you are crowded together with legions of tourists and led in chants by a narrator with an amplifier. Admission. ~ 808-821-6892, fax 808-822-4520; www.smithskauai.com, e-mail smiths@aloha.net.

For those not interested in joining in on this tourist institution, you can rent a kayak and paddle yourself upriver to the grotto (legally, however, you cannot dock at the grotto).

Movie buffs should take note when passing along Route 56. The large abandoned complex surrounded by a beautiful stand of palm trees is the **Coco Palms**. This resort, the first constructed on Kauai, was built around a coconut grove planted in the 1800s by a German immigrant; the area around the resort was home to Kauai's Queen Kapule in the mid-1800s. The final 20 minutes of *Blue Hawaii,* Elvis' last movie, were filmed here. Some scenes from *South Pacific* and *Miss Sadie Thompson* were also filmed here, and for "Fantasy Island" viewers, this is where Tatoo goes zipping by in his jeep. In fact, Hollywood was drawn to this location numerous times. However, it has stood empty since September 1992, when Hurricane Iniki ravaged the resort. Renovation plans are in the works.

Take a detour onto Kuamoo Road (Route 580). This road courses through Kauai's most historic region, the domain of ancient Hawaiian royalty. Watch for Hawaii Visitors Bureau signs pointing out the **Holo-Holo-Ku Heiau**, one of the oldest temples on the island, a place where human sacrifices were performed. A short distance uphill, you'll find a small but interesting **Japanese cemetery**. Ironically, this is also the site of **Pohaku-Ho-o-Hanau**, a sacred spot where royal women came to give birth.

As you continue up Route 580, the lush Wailua Valley opens to view. On the left along the hilltop rest the rocky remains of **Poliahu Heiau**, purportedly used by Kauai's King Kaumualii. A short path leads down to the **Bell Stone**, which resounded when struck with a rock, loudly signaling the birth of royal infants. All these places, vital to Hawaii's past, were located along the old King's Highway, a sacred thoroughfare used only by island rulers.

HIDDEN ▶

For vivid mountain scenery, continue on Route 580 past the 40-foot, multi-cascade **Opaekaa Falls** (a parking area along the highway brings you to a great viewpoint). The road then proceeds past **Wailua Homesteads**, what used to be a ranch and farm region filled with fruit orchards, pastures and vegetable fields but is now rapidly becoming residential.

HIDDEN ▶

A detour off of Kuamoo Road takes you to a cultural experience unique in Kauai—the **Saiva Siddhanta Church**, the Hindu monastery in Wailua. The Kadavul Hindu Temple is open mornings between 9 and 11:30 a.m., and tours are offered weekly. Currently, the Iraivan Temple—the first all-stone, hand-carved, granite Agamic temple ever built in the West—is under construction there. ~ Located about four miles up Kuamoo Road (Route 580) at 107 Kaholalele Road; 808-822-3012 (tour information); www.gurudeva.org, e-mail iraivan@hindu.org.

Route 580 ends at **Keahua Forestry Arboretum**, where hiking trails wind through groves of painted gum trees. The adjoining state forest climbs all the way to one of Kauai's tallest peaks **Mount Waialeale** (5208 feet), although no trails lead there. The mountain has an annual rainfall of more than 400 inches.

In its northerly course between Wailua and Kapaa, Kuhio Highway (Route 56) passes the **Coconut Marketplace** with its sprawling shopping mall and grove of royal palm trees.

As the road continues into **Kapaa**, you'll be passing from one Hawaiian era to another. The largest of Kauai's towns—population wise—Kapaa has a real local feel to it. At one time it was a center for rice cultivation. Later came sugar and pineapple.

Now this 19th-century town, with its falsefront stores and second-story balconies, is home to everyday folks. This is where the local plumber, carpenter and fisherman live. The population is Japanese, Hawaiian, Caucasian, Filipino and Chinese. They reside in small plantation houses and attend the local churches that dot the surrounding countryside.

From Kapaa, there's an excellent view of the **Sleeping Giant**, a recumbent figure naturally hewn out of the nearby mountain range.

Follow the highway and you'll arrive at a curving ribbon of sand known as **Kealia Beach**. Across the road are a store and post office. These clapboard buildings represent in its entirety the tiny town of **Kealia**. From Kealia, the Kuhio Highway climbs and turns slightly inland through former sugar cane fields and continues through the town of **Anahola**, a small Hawaiian homestead settlement.

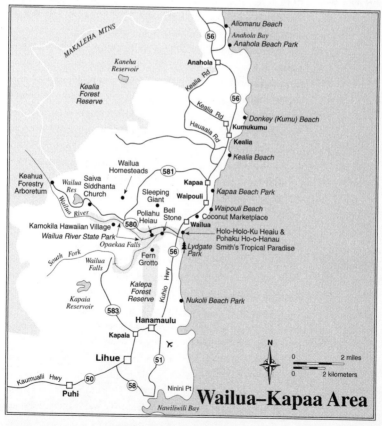

Wailua–Kapaa Area

LODGING

Rosewood exudes cheerfulness, charm and high standards, making this Wailua Homesteads bed and breakfast a reliable choice. Units include a Victorian cottage, rooms in the main house and a secluded thatched cottage. A bunkhouse, which has private sleeping lofts and shared toilets and showers, is a super budget option. Hardwood floors, color-washed walls, quality linens, nice landscaping with old shade trees and a lily pond, along with delightful outdoor showers, are just a few of the highlights. All room options come with kitchens or kitchenettes. There's also a common room with internet access. A breakfast basket comes with the more expensive units, or daily breakfast is served in the main house for an extra charge. Rosewood is set in a rural area, with mountain views and sheep grazing across the road, but there is some traffic noise. Not totally secluded, it's located three miles from the east side, beaches and restaurants. ~ 872 Kamalu Road, Wailua; 808-822-5216, fax 808-822-5478; www.rosewoodkauai. com, e-mail rosewood@aloha.net. BUDGET TO DELUXE.

The **Kauai Sands Hotel** costs a little more, but it's still a bargain. This beachfront accommodation is part of the only hotel chain in the world owned by a Hawaiian family, the Kimis. You'll find a relaxed and spacious lobby, restaurant, two pools, a well-tended lawn, carpeting, a lanai, imaginative decor and a touch of Hawaiiana. Ask about discounts. ~ 420 Papaloa Road near the Coconut Marketplace, Wailua; 808-822-4951, 800-560-5553, fax 808-822-0978; www.kauaisandshotel.com. MODERATE TO DELUXE.

HIDDEN ►

Rainbows End, a classic restored plantation cottage, has romance written all over it. Set in a secluded rural area near the hosts' home, it has special features like floors with inlaid mahogany, cozy country-decor furnishings, extra thick towels, a clawfoot whirlpool tub and an enclosed outdoor shower. It's a

sights

AUTHOR FAVORITE

The original town of Anahola was along the coast. Here a beautiful white strand curves along Anahola Bay, a prime beachcombing area. (See "Beaches & Parks" below.) On the far side of the bay is **Aliomanu Beach**, a beach shaded by ironwood trees and fringed by one of Kauai's longest reefs. (See "Beaches & Parks" below.) These are favorite local haunts.

one-bedroom place with a kitchenette, as well as a futon in the living room for extra guests. Amenities include cable TV, VCR, videos, books, beach equipment and good information about nearby trails and activities. Breakfasts include fruit grown on-site. Gay-friendly. ~ 6470 Kipapa Road, Kapaa; 808-823-0066, fax 808-823-0071; www.rainbowsendkauai.com, e-mail info@rainbowsendkauai.com. MODERATE.

To get any closer to the water than the **Hotel Coral Reef**, you'd have to pitch a tent in the sand. Located on Kuhio Highway in Kapaa, it's within strolling distance of markets and restaurants and is an excellent choice for the wanderer without wheels. A floral garden leads out to a comfortable strip of sand next to Kapaa Beach Park. In this beachfront building you can enjoy a touch of wood paneling, soft beds, refrigerator and a delightful seascape just beyond those sliding glass doors. A second building offers rooms with fans and ocean views. ~ 1516 Kuhio Highway, Kapaa; 808-822-4481, 800-843-4659, fax 808-822-7705; www.hotelcoralreef.com, e-mail hotel.coralreef@gte.net. MODERATE TO DELUXE.

Lani Keha B&B is a spacious home set amid fruit trees on three acres in Wailua Homesteads, with stunning views of the Nounou ridge. With three private guest rooms with baths, there's plenty of privacy in the house, along with a full kitchen, lanai and laundry for guests to share. Two-night minimum stay. ~ 848 Kamulu Road, Kapaa; 808-822-1605; www.lanikeha.com. MODERATE.

Funky charm and low prices make **K.K. Bed & Bath** a great ◄ HIDDEN
choice. It's just one clean, simple room, with private bathroom, fridge, TV and phone, in a historic warehouse right smack in downtown Kapaa. Three-night minimum stay. Call for address. ~ Kapaa; 808-822-7348, 800-615-6211, code 32; www.kkbedbath.com, e-mail kkbedbath@aloha.net. BUDGET.

The **Kauai International Hostel** has both dormitory and private rooms at low prices. Facilities, as you might expect, are spartan. There's a scruffy yard with two buildings; guests share a television room, a kitchen, a washer/dryer and a pool table. Like hostels everywhere, it's a good deal for the dollar. ~ 4532 Lehua Street, Kapaa; 808-823-6142. BUDGET.

GAY LODGING   There are four comfortable, airy guest rooms at the gay-friendly bed and breakfast **Mohala Ke Ola**. It's situated near the river from Opaekaa Falls and offers grand views of Mount Waialeale and Secret Falls. Amenities include a pool and jacuzzi; continental breakfast served on the deck. ~ 5663 Ohelo Road, Kapaa; 808-823-6398, 888-465-2824; www.waterfallbnb. com, e-mail kauaibb@aloha.net. MODERATE TO DELUXE.

Looking like it has been lifted straight out of the Japanese countryside, **Mahina Kai Ocean Villa** has a Japanese garden and teahouse to match. Three suites and one single guest room are fitted with kimono quilts and shoji screen doors and share a kitchen; a cottage includes a kitchenette. There's an indoor pond and a pool as well as an ocean view from this two-acre property. ~ 4933 Aliomanu Road, Anahola; 808-822-9451, 800-337-1134; www.mahinakai.com, e-mail reservations@mahinakai.com. ULTRA-DELUXE.

CONDOS   **Kaha Lani** isn't a place you'd find unless you were looking for it, making these isolated condominiums, perfect for a quiet retreat. Families will also enjoy the property's proximity to Lydgate State Park, with its child-designed Kamalani playground and protected *keiki* pools along the water. The comfy condos have well-equipped kitchens, and most are demurely decorated in a muted tropical theme. (They are individually owned, so the decor varies.) One-bedroom units start at $255; two bedrooms start at $355. ~ 4460 Nehe Road, Wailua; 808-822-9331, 800-922-7866, fax 808-822-2828.

Wailua Bay View offers one-bedroom apartments, $125 for up to four people; three-night minimum stay. Ocean view. ~ 320 Papaloa Road, Kapaa; 808-245-4711, 800-767-4707, fax 808-245-8115; www.prosserrealty.net, e-mail holiday@prosserrealty.net.

Studio apartments at **Kapaa Sands Resort** are $110 single or double, $128 for an oceanfront unit. Two-bedroom apartments, $147 (one to four people); $168 for an oceanfront location. ~ 380 Papaloa Road, Kapaa; 808-822-4901, 800-222-4901, fax 808-822-1556; www.kapaasands.com.

Along the main drag of Kapaa you'll find **Kapaa Shores**, a small resort condominium with 84 apartments; one-bedroom units start at $125 and two-bedroom units start at $140. Most are time-share, but you can reserve as long as you're staying for more than five nights. All the units have a fully equipped kitchen, a private lanai and an ocean view; some have a washer/dryer and DSL. You can request maid service. In addition, there's a pool, a spa, a tennis court and a barbecue area. ~ 4-0900 Kuhio Highway, Kapaa; 808-822-4871, 800-801-0378, fax 808-822-7984; www.kauai properties.com, e-mail aloha@kauaiproperties.com.

The **Kauai Coast Resort** is another appealing place. Located behind the Coconut Marketplace, it's popular with swimmers and shoppers alike. You'll find a pool, a spa, a fitness center and tennis courts amid the central grounds, plus a windswept lobby with adjoining restaurant. For pleasant surroundings near the center of the action, it's definitely among the area's top choices. All the condominiums are air-conditioned and include TVs, full kitchens, washer/dryers and lanais. Studios start at $195; one-bedroom units start at $255 per night; and two-bedroom units start at $330. The decor is quite tasteful, and the rates, considering the amenities, are reasonable. ~ 520 Aleka Loop, Kapaa; 808-822-3441, 877-977-4355, fax 808-822-0843; www.kauai coastresort.com.

Mokihana of Kauai has studio apartments that run $65 single or double. These units are supplied with a hotplate and small refrigerator. ~ 796 Kuhio Highway, Kapaa; 808-822-3971, fax 808-822-7387.

Kauai Kailani features two-bedroom apartments, $75 for up to four people; $7.50 for each extra person. This offers a lot of square footage for the money, but there's one catch—reservations are difficult to obtain and should be made a year in advance. Three-night minimum (loosely enforced). ~ 856 Kuhio Highway, Kapaa; 808-822-3391, fax 808-822-7387.

THE VILLAGE THAT TIME FORGOT

The **Kamokila Hawaiian Village** is so isolated, it appears to have been carved out of the surrounding tropical labyrinth. The re-created village evokes authentic early Hawaii with food- and craft-making demonstrations. Self-guided tours will take you through the paces of ancient Hawaiian life, including an assembly hall, birthing house, chief's quarters, cooking pit and athletic ground. It's also the site of a decidedly contemporary obsession: movie making. *Outbreak*, starring Dustin Hoffman and Morgan Freeman, for example, was filmed here. Closed Sunday. Admission. ~ 6060 Kuamoo Road, off Route 580, just past the Wailua Bridge across from Opaekaa Falls; 808-823-0559.

DINING

HIDDEN ▶

Never mind the stark setting of fluorescent lighting and booths with formica-topped tables, the food at **Korean BBQ** is good, plentiful and cheap. Of course, they offer a variety of Korean dishes such as fish *jun*, barbecue chicken or beef, cold noodles with mixed veggies and soups. You can substitute tofu for many of the meat dishes. Eat in or take-out. ~ 4-356 Kuhio Highway (Kinipopo Shopping Village), Wailua; 808-823-6744. BUDGET.

Antique Japanese screens set the theme at **Restaurant Kintaro**, where you can dine at the sushi bar or enjoy *teppanyaki*-style cooking. If you decide on the latter, choose between filet mignon, shrimp, scallops, steak teriyaki or oysters sautéed with olive oil. They also prepare traditional tempura and yakitori dinners as well as *yosenabe* (Japanese bouillabaisse). Closed Sunday. ~ 4-370 Kuhio Highway, Wailua; 808-822-3341, fax 808-822-2153. DELUXE.

> To ease the congestion through Kapaa, the Kapaa Bypass Road was built. Pick it up just before the Coconut Plantation in Wailua. It takes you to the north side of Kapaa, cutting through fields behind town.

There are short-order stands galore at the Coconut Marketplace. **Harley's Ribs-'n-Chicken** delivers what its name promises. ~ 808-822-2505. The **Fish Hut** lives up to its name. ~ 808-821-0033. You'll never guess what they serve at **Aloha Kauai Pizza**. ~ 808-822-4511. Any time from early morning until 8 or 9 p.m., several of these stands will be open. An interesting way to dine here is by going from one to the next, nibbling small portions along the way. ~ 4-484 Kuhio Highway, Wailua. BUDGET.

A favorite breakfast institution, **Eggbert's** is a perfect place for people watching. Try the hotcakes with coconut syrup, or the sour-cream-and-chives omelette. Lunch offerings are mainly sandwiches and salads, while dinner choices include steak, meatloaf, pork and chicken; the stir-fry is a good vegetarian option. No dinner on Sunday. ~ Coconut Marketplace, 4-484 Kuhio Highway, Wailua; 808-822-3787, fax 808-822-2012. MODERATE.

HIDDEN ▶

If cost is a consideration, stop by **Waipouli Deli & Restaurant**, located next to Blockbuster and behind McDonald's, for super-cheap and decent local-style food. The stark decor is a bit gritty and uninspired, but you can fill up on *saimin*, various fried meats, eggs and rice without running up a large tab. Closed Monday. ~ Waipouli Town Center, 4-771 Kuhio Highway, Kapaa; 808-822-9311. BUDGET.

For a light, healthful meal, you can cross the street to **Papaya's Natural Foods**. This takeout counter with outdoor tables has pasta, pizza, sandwiches, vegetable stir-fry, grilled fish and salads. Papaya's also caters to vegetarians and vegans. Closed Sunday. ~ Kauai Village Shopping Center, 4-831 Kuhio Highway, Kapaa; 808-823-0191, fax 808-823-0756. BUDGET.

Also in the Kauai Village Shopping Center is **Ba Le**. *Pho*, a fragrant Vietnamese beef broth noodle soup, is the specialty, and you'll also find a variety of tasty Asian plate lunch–style meals and excellent sandwiches on fresh-baked bread. The tapioca, including one made with taro, is a great finale. It's often busy because it's good and cheap, but you can take out if the tables are full. Closed Tuesday. ~ 4-831 Kuhio Highway, Kapaa; 808-823-6060. BUDGET.

Thai restaurants have mushroomed in Kapaa, but old-timer **King and I** is still a good bet. The small, pink dining room is decorated with ornate Thai art and cascading orchids. The food is reliably good, with lots of vegetarian choices. Try the garlic eggplant, pungent green papaya salad, *pad thai* noodles and curries. Black rice pudding is a must for dessert. ~ 4-901 Kuhio Highway (Waipouli Plaza), Kapaa; 808-822-1642. MODERATE.

It's beef, beef and beef at **The Bull Shed**. We're talking about prime rib, beef kebab, top sirloin, garlic tenderloin and teriyaki steak. All this in a casual restaurant that's so close to the surf your feet feel wet. Speaking of surf, they also serve lobster, broiled shrimp, Alaskan king crab and fresh fish. Dinner only. ~ 796 Kuhio Highway, Kapaa; 808-822-3791, fax 808-822-4041. MODERATE TO DELUXE.

Coconuts Island-Style Grill & Bar's hip attitude seems more at home in Southern California, but it does a good job with entrées like lobster ravioli, seafood paella and fresh fish. The *lilikoi* sorbet is the perfect light dessert, and the decor demonstrates the versatility and beauty of coconut wood and fiber. Dinner only. ~ 4-919 Kuhio Highway, Kapaa; 808-823-8777. DELUXE.

For quality seafood, steak and pasta, check out **Wahooo Seafood Grill & Bar**, where the emphasis is on local ingredients, tantalizing sauces and exotic flavors. The setting on Kuhio Highway is certainly nothing inspired, but the dining room manages to achieve a pleasant ambience that is best described as upscale casual. Reservations recommended for dinner. ~ 4-733 Kuhio Highway, Kapaa; 808-822-7833. DELUXE.

When nothing will do but a hearty, old-fashioned breakfast, **Kountry Kitchen** also delivers the goods. Booths line the place, which strives for an old-fashioned coffee shop look, and it's been around long enough to carry it off. Lunch is sandwiches, burgers, salads and other simple fare. Breakfast and lunch only. ~ 1485 Kuhio Highway, Kapaa; 808-822-3511. BUDGET.

In the center of Kapaa, there's a restaurant known to Mexican food aficionados for miles around. **Norberto's El Café** draws a hungry crowd of young locals for dinner. The owners raise a lot of their own vegetables, and they serve monstrous portions. If you're not hungry, order à la carte or one of the smaller dinners. If you are, choose from a solid menu ranging from enchiladas (including Hawaiian taro-leaf enchiladas) to burritos to chiles rellenos. Children's portions are available and all meals can be converted to cater to vegetarians. Definitely worth checking out. Dinner only. Closed Sunday. ~ 4-1373 Kuhio Highway, Kapaa; 808-822-3362. MODERATE.

Authenticity is the keyword at **La Playita Azul**, where they roast their own meats and make sauces from scratch. Portions are hearty and the service is friendly, although this small eatery fills up quickly at dinnertime. No lunch on Monday. ~ Kauai Village Shopping Center, 4-831 Kuhio Highway, Kapaa; 808-821-2323. BUDGET.

HIDDEN ▶   A breakfast jewel is **Ono Family Restaurant**, which offers a more exotic take on the day's main meal. Fried rice with *kim chee* omelettes are balanced by simpler selections. Lunch centers around sandwiches (cod, egg salad) and burgers (bacon, chili). Plate lunches and stir-fry are also on the menu. Their coconut syrup and

AUTHOR FAVORITE

Some of the best hamburgers on the island are found at **Duane's Ono Char-Burger**, a wood-planked burger stand next to the Anahola Post Office. Cheddar, mushrooms, bleu cheese and pineapple are some of the toppings heaped onto the thick patties. The juicy teriyaki burger is an island favorite. Don't feel like ground beef? You can also opt for a veggie burger, broiled chicken or fried fish. To round off your meal, order a fruit shake and a side of crispy fries. ~ 4-4350 Kuhio Highway, Anahola; 808-822-9181. BUDGET.

pineapple/papaya jam can be bought here, too. ~ 1292 Kuhio Highway, Kapaa; 808-822-1710, fax 808-823-8784. BUDGET.

Mema Thai Cuisine is slightly overpriced, but the food, a mix of Thai and Chinese, is pretty good. The ambience here is casual, although the silk-clad waitstaff glide around elegantly. No lunch on Saturday and Sunday. ~ 4-369 Kuhio Highway, Kapaa; 808-823-0899. MODERATE.

In north Kapaa, **The Shack** serves up burgers, sandwiches and salads, but the sports bar atmosphere, live music, big-screen TV and games seem to be a bigger draw than the rather uninspired menu. Still, it's cheap and open until midnight, making it a good choice for a simple or late meal. ~ 1394 Kuhio Highway, Kapaa; 808-823-0200. MODERATE.

Across the street you'll find **Scotty's**, home of some really great barbecue—the kind that's smoked for hours and offered with a choice of sauces on the side. The coleslaw and baked beans are great, adding up to good food in a very casual setting. Its upstairs location makes the most of a nice ocean view. Closed Sunday. ~ 4-1546 Kuhio Highway, Kapaa; 808-823-8480. MODERATE.

A far better choice is **Blossoming Lotus**, a truly inspired and delicious vegan restaurant that takes eating to new heights, without the use of any animal products. Their wonderful bakery turns out mouth-watering, wholesome sweets, and all the food is prepared with loving intent. They aspire to a more conscious way of doing business, so they use organic, local produce, eco-safe cleaning products and recycle everything. ~ 4504 Kukui Street, Kapaa; 808-822-7678; www.blossominglotus.com. BUDGET TO MODERATE.

The local crowds attest to the quality and value at **Mermaid's Café**. Serving lunch and dinner, this tiny place offers vegan and vegetarian choices as well as wraps, burritos, and chicken satay and curry plates. The menu favorite, an ahi nori wrap, contains local tuna. ~ 4-1384 Kuhio Highway, Kapaa; 808-821-2026. BUDGET TO MODERATE.

Practically next door is **Wasabi's**, an innovative Japanese restaurant that has come up with a wide range of interesting sushi rolls you won't find elsewhere. They also serve all the traditional rolls, sashimi, fresh fish, yakitori and tempura, and the small dining room is cheerful and friendly. ~ 1388 Kuhio Highway, Kapaa; 808-822-2700. BUDGET TO MODERATE.

HIDDEN ▶   Portions are hearty at the **Olympic Café**, which looks down
on the main Kapaa drag, making it a great place to people watch.
The food is high-quality and well-prepared: tasty egg dishes,
omelettes and pancakes for breakfast; a choice of big salads, sandwiches and burgers for lunch. Or try one of the Mexican entrées,
like burritos. Juices, coffee drinks and drinks from the full bar
soothe parched throats. The open-air dining room is casual and
has views of the ocean and mountains. ~ 4-1354 Kuhio Highway,
Kapaa; 808-822-5825. BUDGET.

GROCERIES   There are two major grocery stores in the Wailua–Kapaa area.
Try **Foodland** in the Waipouli Town Center. ~ Kapaa; 808-822-
7271. Or shop at **Safeway**. ~ Kauai Village Shopping Center, Kapaa; 808-822-2464. There's a **Big Save Market** at the Kapaa Shopping Center. ~ 1105-F Kuhio Highway; 808-822-4971.

          To the north is the **Handi-Pantry**. This well-stocked conven-
ience store is the largest store between Kapaa and Princeville. ~
4-4350 Kuhio Highway, Anahola; 808-822-5818.

SHOPPING   In the Kinipopo Shopping Village, **Tin Can Mailman** (808-822-
3009) specializes in new, used and rare books, particularly Pacific Island titles. It is also rich in stamps, maps, tapa cloth and
botanical prints. Closed Sunday. ~ 4-356 Kuhio Highway, Wailua.

          For campy antiques, "tropical wear" plus new and vintage
clothing, try **Bambulei**, hidden behind the Wailua Shopping Plaza.
If Hawaiiana from the 1950s appeals to you, this is the place for
a little treasure hunting. Be careful: Two cottages filled to the rim
with funky knickknacks may make you forget the beach. ~ 4-
369D Kuhio Highway, Wailua; 808-823-8641.

          The **Coconut Marketplace** is a theme mall that consists of
wooden stores designed to resemble little plantation houses. For
decor you'll find the pipes, valves, gears and waterwheels char-
acteristic of every tropical plantation. This is a good place for
clothing, curios, jewelry, toys, Asian imports and T-shirts. If you
don't want to buy, you can always browse or have a snack at the
many short-order stands here. ~ 4-484 Kuhio Highway, Wailua;
808-822-3641.

          Two galleries within the Marketplace are worthy of note.
Kahn Galleries (808-822-3636) features locally and internationally known artists. Focusing on Hawaiian seascapes and land-

scapes, the gallery offers work by Roy Tabora. Also consider **Ship Store Galleries** and its maritime theme (808-822-7758), which highlights an eclectic group of artists. **Overboard** (808-822-1777), also in the Coconut Marketplace, has aloha shirts and other Hawaiian wear. **Kauai Fine Arts** (808-821-9557) has a branch here, selling antique maps and wooden products. They also carry some pretty Niihau jewelry.

Products of Hawaii (808-821-0384; www.productsofhawaii.com) is filled with about 75 percent locally made merchandise, ranging from candles to picture frames. ~ 4-484 Kuhio Highway, Wailua.

Hawaiians use a variety of plants in herbal healing (*laau lapaau*). One of the most important plants is the *popolo* plant (Black Nightshade), used to combat fevers and respiratory infections or strengthen the body.

Kauai Village Shopping Center, a multi-store complex in the center of Kapaa, is another of Kauai's shopping destinations. Anchored by a grocery store, it features a string of small shops.

If you need to stock up on toys the kids haven't already exhausted, cajole them to **Marta's Boat**, where I guarantee they'll perk up considerably. And while they're exploring the children's merchandise, there are locally made gifts, including handmade jewelry for you to peruse, as well as clothing, shoes and lingerie. Closed Sunday. ~ 770 Kuhio Highway, Kapaa; 808-822-3926.

Hula Girl sells clothing and gifts for the entire family. Their focus is Hawaiiana, with a great selection of bowls, books and prints. ~ 4-1340 Kuhio Highway, Kapaa; 808-822-1950.

Talk about unusual. **Island Hemp & Cotton** specializes in things made from the "evil" weed. There's an attractive line of women's clothing here, not to mention soap, paper, and body lotion, all fabricated from hemp. ~ 4-1373 Kuhio Highway, Kapaa; 808-821-0225.

Some of the best shopping on the island can be found in the numerous little shops that line Kuhio Highway on the north end of Kapaa town. It's worthwhile to park and wander among the stores on both sides of the street, as you'll find items not sold elsewhere on the island.

One of my favorites is **Davison Arts**, which combines the talents of a husband-wife team. It offers beautiful custom wood furniture and smaller home furnishings, as well as original art and some unique pieces offered in an exclusive arrangement with top local artists. Closed Sunday. ~ 4-1322 Kuhio Highway, Kapaa; 808-821-8022.

Nearby you'll find **Kela's Glass Gallery**, an exquisite and colorful collection of handmade glass vases, bowls, plates and art pieces. They're happy to wrap up your fragile purchase for a safe journey home. ~ 4-1354 Kuhio Highway, Kapaa; 808-822-4527.

NIGHTLIFE If it's karaoke you want, check out **Tradewinds**, where it's offered nightly except Wednesday and Friday, when a deejay takes over the dancefloor at this South Seas–style bar. ~ Coconut Marketplace, Wailua; 808-822-1621.

If your image of the perfect paradise vacation includes tropical drinks, you're in for a treat at the **Lizard Lounge**. The place is on the funky side but the drinks are delicious and the mood festive. You can play darts, watch the game and gnaw on buffalo wings while you sip one of thirty beers. ~ Waipouli Town Center, 4-771 Kuhio Highway, Kapaa; 808-821-2205.

BEACHES & PARKS **NUKOLII BEACH PARK** Located adjacent to the Outrigger Kauai Hilton Hotel, this is a long narrow strand with a shallow bottom. From the park, the beach extends for several miles all the way to Lydgate Park in Wailua. One of the island's prettiest beaches, it provides an opportunity to use the park facilities or to escape to more secluded sections (adjacent to Wailua Golf Course). If you seek seclusion, just start hiking farther north along the shore. You'll find places galore for water sports. Swimming is good in well-protected and shallow waters. Snorkelers will be content swimming among reefs and there are good

AGED SWIMMERS

Green sea turtles are commonly seen in Hawaiian waters, popping their heads up for a breath of air or sliding along rocky reefs to feed on the seaweed, or *limu*, that gives their flesh its distinctive green tint. The Hawaiians frequently ate *honu*, which was considered a delicacy. These creatures are an amazing 150 million years old, yet in the past century they were hunted so heavily by fishing crews that their population nearly crashed. Since being federally designated as a protected, threatened species, their numbers are rising. But their newest threat is a puzzling disease that causes large tumors to grow on their flesh.

surf breaks on the shallow reef at "Graveyards." Fishing is best near the reefs. ~ Located at the end of Kauai Beach Drive. To reach the more secluded sections, go north from Lihue on Kuhio Highway and take a right onto the road that runs along the southern end of the Wailua Golf Course. This paved road rapidly becomes a dirt strip studded with potholes. Driving slowly, proceed a quarter-mile, then take the first left turn. It's another quarter-mile to the beach; when the road forks, take either branch.

LYDGATE BEACH AND LYDGATE PARK The awesome ironwood grove and long stretches of rugged coastline make this one of Kauai's loveliest parks. Near the Wailua River, it is also one of the most popular. The Hauola Place of Refuge and other sacred sites are located within the state park. (See page 132 for more information.) Two large lava pools, one perfect for kids and the other protecting swimmers and snorkelers, make it a great place to spend the day. Surfers must take a long paddle out to breaks off the mouth of Wailua River. There's a right slide. This park is also favored by windsurfers. *Ulua* is the most common catch. You'll find a picnic area, showers, restrooms, a playground and lifeguards. With kids in tow, Kamalani Playground in Lydgate Park offers a distracting alternative to making sandcastles. ~ From Kuhio Highway, turn toward the beach at Leho Drive, the road just south of the Wailua River.

▲ Although Lydgate Park is a state beach, the county will be offering camping on land it owns there. Once it begins, it will be available on a first-come, first-served basis, although reservations may be made in advance. Permits are required; $3 per nonresident adult over 18. Contact the County Division of Parks and Recreation for status. ~ 4444 Rice Street, Suite 150, Lihue; 808-241-4463.

WAILUA RIVER STATE PARK Home to the famous Fern Grotto, this small park features sacred historic sites and breathtaking views of river and mountains. It also has a marina and is the launching point for motorized and kayaking tours up the famous river, which is billed as the only truly navigable waterway on the island. In addition, waterskiing is allowed and canoe clubs practice here. There are lots of shady areas and picnic tables. Although the park is public, boat companies pay to maintain the landing at Fern Grotto upriver, which is technically off-limits to kayakers. Restrooms are available here. ~ Take Route 56 to Kuamoo Road (Route 580).

WAILUA BEACH 🏃 🛶 One of east Kauai's nicest and most accessible stretches of broad sand, Wailua Beach is perfect for sunbathing and beachwalking. Conditions can be treacherous for swimming, however, because the frequently blowing trade winds often create rough waters and the Wailua River empties into the ocean here. In rainy weather, the river often creates a strong current at the south end of the beach. Boogieboarders challenge the waves here, and a hot surf break known as "Horner's" is found at the northern end of the beach. Children gravitate toward the river area. A lifeguard is on limited duty but there are minimal facilities. The best parking is near the Wailua Bridge. ~ This beach, near the Coco Palms Resort, is easily accessed only when traveling north on Kuhio Highway.

Monk seals, one of two species of tropical seals left, sometimes snooze in the sand at Waipouli Beach; don't disturb their naps!

WAIPOULI BEACH 🏃 🚴 🏄 🛶 The longest, narrowest strip of sand on the eastside begins behind the Coconut Marketplace shopping center and ends about two miles down the road at Waikaea Canal in Kapaa. Even though many condos and resorts border this beach, it isn't that crowded and it's easy to find lots of hidden coves. The ocean in this area is usually rough, and most of the coastline is either beachrock or reef. Swimming is not recommended. Fishermen are common here, pole fishing or hunting octopus in the sand. About midway along this stretch is a protected shallow section in the reef known as "Baby Beach," because many families come here with small children. No facilities except at the boat-launching area near the canal, where you'll find restrooms and pavilions, and often some hard-drinking locals just hanging out. There's a nice trail for getting your exercise biking or walking along Waipouli Beach. ~ The beach can be accessed at a number of points behind Coconut Marketplace and along the shoreline road that runs parallel to Kuhio Highway, a few blocks *makai* (toward the ocean).

KAPAA BEACH PARK 🏄 🛶 While it sports an attractive little beach, this 15-acre facility doesn't measure up to its neighbors. Located a block from the highway as the road passes through central Kapaa, the park is flanked by ramshackle houses and a local playing field. The area has a picnic area with barbecue pits and restrooms. Swimming and fishing are only fair, but there is good squidding and torchfishing. ~ Located a block from Kuhio Highway, Kapaa.

KEALIA BEACH This strand is one of those neighbors that makes Kapaa Beach the pimply kid next door: It's a wide, magnificent beach curving for about a half-mile along Kuhio Highway. The swimming is good, but requires caution. Lifeguards are on duty daily. Surfing and bodysurfing can be found at the north end of the beach. Fish here for *papio*, threadfin and *ulua*. There are no facilities. ~ Located on Kuhio Highway, Kealia.

DONKEY BEACH OR KUMU BEACH This broad, curving beach is flanked by a grassy meadow and towering ironwoods. Favored as a hideaway and nude beach by locals, it's a gem that should not be overlooked. Also note that the two-mile stretch from here north to Anahola is lined by low sea cliffs that open onto at least four pocket beaches. This entire area is popular with beachcombers, who sometimes find hand-blown Japanese glass fishing balls. Swimmers, take care: Currents here can be treacherous and the nearest lifeguard is a world away. Surfers get their kicks at Donkey Beach, or try "14 Crack" just north of the beach. Anglers frequent this beach for pole-fishing and throw-netting. There are no facilities here. ~ Follow Kuhio Highway north from Kealia. At the 11-mile marker the road begins to climb slowly, then descends. At the end of the descent, just before 12-mile marker, there is a parking area and a path to the beach.

◄ *HIDDEN*

▲ Unofficial camping is common.

ANAHOLA BEACH PARK A slender ribbon of sand curves along windswept Anahola Bay. At the south end, guarded by ironwood trees, lies this pretty little park. Very popular with neighborhood residents, this is a prime beachcombing spot where you may find Japanese glass fishing balls. There is a protecting reef here; but as elsewhere, use caution swimming because of the strong currents. Snorkeling is good behind the reef. Surfers have a long paddle out to summer and winter breaks along the reef (left and right slides). There is a break called "Unreals" offshore from the old landing. This is also a popular bodysurf-

◄ *HIDDEN*

ing beach. There's good torchfishing for lobsters, and anglers often catch *papio*, rudderfish, *ulua*, threadfin, bonefish and big-eyed scad. Facilities include a picnic area, restrooms, showers and limited lifeguard duty. ~ Turn onto Anahola Road from Kuhio Highway in Anahola; follow it three-quarters of a mile, then turn onto a dirt road that forks left to the beach.

▲ You can pitch a tent on the grassy area near the beach; county permit required.

HIDDEN ▶   **ALIOMANU BEACH** 🏊 🐟 On the far side of Anahola Bay, separated from the park by the Anahola River, lies another sandy beach. Shady ironwood trees and roadside houses dot this area, which is a favorite among locals. What makes Aliomanu particularly popular is the offshore reef, one of Kauai's longest and widest fringing reefs. This is an excellent area for gathering edible seaweed. Swimming is fairly safe in summer, but use caution the rest of the year. Local residents spear octopus and go torch-fishing here. ~ Turn off Kuhio Highway onto Aliomanu Road just past Anahola.

EIGHT

North Shore

It is no accident that when it came time to choose a location for Bali Hai, the producers of *South Pacific* ended their search on the North Shore of Kauai. The most beautiful place in Hawaii, indeed one of the prettiest places on earth, this 30-mile stretch of lace-white surf and emerald-green mountains became Hollywood's version of paradise.

The landscape here is always green, due to the frequent showers, but the ocean changes dramatically throughout the year, from placid and lake-like in summer to tumultuous (churning up 25-foot rollers) in winter. The beaches are lovely and abundant, and suited to a variety of pastimes.

The North Shore is changing dramatically, however, and the population is booming with wealthy newcomers. Agricultural subdivisions with large homes have popped up all along the highway and coast, and vacation rentals outnumber local homes in remote Haena. Hanalei town has sacrificed much of its charm to commercial development, and the old mill town of Kilauea is struggling to retain its low-key character. The resort community of Princeville, meanwhile, continues to add new homes and condos.

But the grandeur of the landscape still dominates on the North Shore, and many residents are determined to protect it and maintain some semblance of the old way of life. That's why the bridges are rickety, the roads are narrow and the shimmering green taro fields still line the highway into Hanalei.

Backdropping this thin line of civilization is the Na Pali Coast. Here, sharp sea cliffs vault thousands of feet from the ocean, silver waterfalls streaming along their fluted surfaces. There are pocket beaches ringed by menacing rock formations and long, wide strands as inviting as a warm tub.

The North Shore is wet and tropical, drawing enough precipitation to dampen the enthusiasm of many tourists. It is suited for travelers who don't mind a little rain on their parade if it carries with it rainbows and seabirds and a touch of magic in the air.

You might want to begin your introduction to the North Shore at the **Guava Kai Plantation**, which offers 480 acres that produce more than half of Hawaii's guava crop, making them the largest producer in the country. The guava was introduced to Hawaii in the late 1700s and now grows wild throughout the islands. The fruit at Guava Kai Plantation is hand-picked. The visitors center, which also sports a snack shop, will give you a taste of guava products. There's a self-guided tour of the guava-juicing process. Bring a picnic and follow the short path leading past tropical plants and a pond to a pretty picnic area. ~ 4900 Kuawa Road, Kilauea; 808-828-6121, fax 808-828-1880; e-mail info@ guavakai.com.

Kilauea itself is a former sugar town with a cluster of stores and a couple of noteworthy churches. The cottages that once housed plantation workers are freshly painted and decorated with flowering gardens and the place possesses an air of humble well-being.

The **Christ Memorial Episcopal Church** is an ideal spot for reflection. The beautiful building was consecrated in 1941. It's built out of lava stone and has stained-glass windows imported from England. ~ Kilauea Road, Kilauea; 808-826-4510.

Another chance for history cum meditation is **St. Sylvester's Roman Catholic Church,** an octagonal building containing works by Jean Charlot, a local artist. The church was constructed, in part, to illustrate the importance of art to the Catholic religion. ~ Kilauea Road, Kilauea; 808-822-7900, fax 808-822-3014.

Along the North Shore, humankind is a bit player in the natural drama being presented here. To take in that scene, you need

HIDDEN ▶ venture no farther than **Kilauea Point National Wildlife Refuge**. Here on Kilauea Point, a lofty peninsula that falls away into precipitous rockfaces, you'll have the same bird's-eye view of the spectacular coastline as the boobies, tropicbirds, albatross and frigate birds. As you stand along this lonely point, gazing upon the ocean and along the cliffs, birds—graceful, sleek, exotic ones— swarm like bees. A vital rookery, the refuge is also frequented by Hawaiian monk seals and green turtles, as well as occasional

North Shore

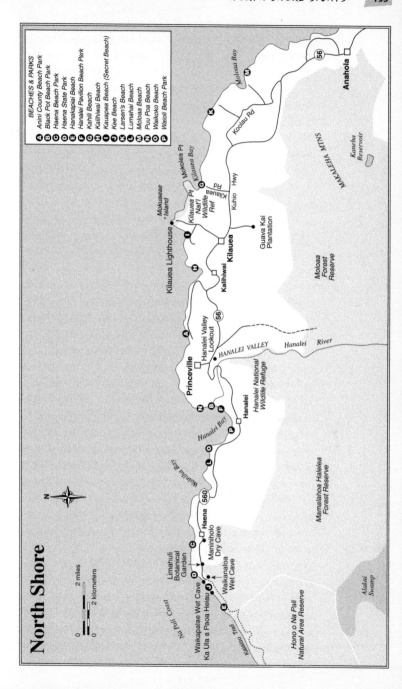

N

0 ____ 2 miles
0 ____ 2 kilometers

BEACHES & PARKS
Ⓐ Anini County Beach Park
Ⓑ Black Pot Beach Park
Ⓒ Haena Beach Park
Ⓓ Haena State Park
Ⓔ Hanakapiai Beach
Ⓕ Hanalei Pavilion Beach Park
Ⓖ Kahili Beach
Ⓗ Kalihiwai Beach
Ⓘ Kauapea Beach (Secret Beach)
Ⓙ Kee Beach
Ⓚ Larsen's Beach
Ⓛ Lumahai Beach
Ⓜ Moloaa Beach
Ⓝ Puu Poa Beach
Ⓞ Waikoko Beach
Ⓟ Waioli Beach Park

Na Pali Coast

Kalalau Trail

Limahuli Botanical Garden
Wakapalae Wet Cave
Ka Ula a Paoa Heiau
Maniniholo Dry Cave
Waikanaloa Wet Cave

Hono o Na Pali Natural Area Reserve

Alakai Swamp

Haena

560

Wainiha Bay

Hanalei Bay

Hanalei

Hanalei National Wildlife Refuge

Princeville

Hanalei Valley Lookout

56

HANALEI VALLEY

Hanalei River

Mamalahoa Halelea Forest Reserve

Kilauea Lighthouse
Mokuaeae Island
Kilauea Pt
Mokolea Pt
Kilauea Bay
Kilauea Nat'l Wildlife Ref

Kilauea Rd

Kuhio Hwy

Kilauea

Kalihiwai

Guava Kai Plantation

Moloaa Forest Reserve

Koolau Rd

MAKALEHA MTNS

Kaneha Reservoir

Moloaa Bay

56

Anahola

whales and dolphins. Offshore is **Mokuaeae Island**, a state bird preserve. Admission. ~ End of Kilauea Road, Kilauea; 808-828-1413, fax 808-828-6634.

Counterpoint to this natural pageant is the **Kilauea Lighthouse**, a 52-foot-high beacon built in 1913 that bears the world's largest clamshell-shaped lens. Capable of casting its light almost 100 miles, it is the first sign of land seen by mariners venturing east from Asia. This old lighthouse, now replaced by a more modern beacon, sits on the northernmost point of Kauai. People gather at the point for interpretive talks of the bird life and natural history of the region.

HIDDEN ▶ But before you get to the lighthouse, take a detour to **Kahili Beach**, nestled in Kilauea Bay. The lagoon here is one of the island's most pristine estuaries. (See "Beaches & Parks" below for more information.) Then, just past the town of Kilauea, is the road

HIDDEN ▶ to **Secret Beach** or, as the Hawaiians call it, Kauapea Beach. It may not exactly be a secret anymore, but if seclusion is what you are looking for, give it a try by heading down Kalihiwai Road. If the beach is not exactly secluded, you can still birdwatch, or people-watch if that species has gathered. (See "Beaches & Parks" below for specific directions.)

Along Route 56 you'll see **Kalihiwai Bay**. There's another (ho-hum) beautiful beach here, surrounded by ironwood trees. A sweeping but shallow lagoon has been formed by the Kalihiwai River. (See "Beaches & Parks" below for directions to Kalihiwai Beach.)

Continuing along Route 56 is a turnoff for Kalihiwai Road (take the second one, the one farthest from Lihue—the bridge that connected the road was washed out by a tsunami). Here you'll discover a beach setting ideal for families. **Anini County Beach Park** provides great swimming and picnicking, and you'll probably be sharing the beach with local families. In ancient times, this was a prime fishing spot for the *alii*. Now windsurfers scale the water and snorkelers swim among the reef fish. (See "Beaches & Parks" below for more information.)

Civilization stakes its claim once again at **Princeville**, a one-time plantation named by R. C. Wyllie in honor of the son of Ka-mehameha IV and Queen Emma. This 11,000-acre planned resort community combines private homes, condominiums and the elegant Princeville Resort. Set along a luxurious plateau with scintillating views of the Na Pali Coast, it is a tastefully designed complex complete with golf courses and acres of open space.

The adventurous might want to make the trek down to **Queen's Bath**, a large lava tidepool at the end of a slippery trail. ~ In Princeville, near the Pali Ke Kua condominium parking lot. There is a sign pointing to the trail.

These taro patches and surrounding wetlands comprise the 917-acre **Hanalei National Wildlife Refuge**, home to the Hawaiian duck, Hawaiian stilt, the Hawaiian coot and the Hawaiian moorhen, all of which are endangered. For a close-up version of this panorama, turn left onto Ohiki Road near the old bridge at the bottom of the hill. It will lead you back several eras to a region of terraced fields and simple homesteads. There is no parking or facilities.

In town, a combination of plantation-style buildings, dramatic mountain views and curving beaches creates a mystique that can only be described in a single word—**Hanalei**. It makes you wonder if heaven, in fact, is built of clapboard. The town is little more than a string of woodframe bungalows and falsefront stores lining the main road. On one side a half-moon bay, rimmed with white sand, curves out in two directions. Behind the town the *pali*, those awesome cliffs that fluctuate between dream and reality in the focus of the mind, form a frontier between Hanalei and the rest of the world.

◄ HIDDEN

The **Hanalei Pier**, on the National Register of Historic Places, was constructed in 1892. Although the pier has since been reinforced with concrete, it still adds a touch more romance to the already unreal seascape.

That little green-and-white church along the highway is the **Waioli Hulia Church**, part of the Waioli Mission, built in 1912.

AUTHOR FAVORITE

Past Princeville, the road opens onto the **Hanalei Valley Lookout**, a vista point that transcends prose with its beauty. Below you spreads a patchwork of tropical vegetation, fields of broad-leafed taro that have been cultivated for over 1200 years. This green carpet, swaying and shimmering along the valley floor, is cut by the thin silver band of the Hanalei River. Framing this scene, as though a higher power had painted the entire tableau, are deep-green cliffs, fluted and sharp, that rise 3500 feet from the tilled fields.

If you get a chance to go in, take a look at the beautiful stained-glass windows. ~ Kuhio Highway, Hanalei; 808-826-6253, fax 808-826-9625.

It's almost superfluous that the **Waioli Mission House**, built in 1836, provides glimpses of a bygone era: The entire town seems a reflection of its former self. But this one-time home of Abner and Lucy Wilcox, missionaries from New England, extends a special invitation to step back into the 19th century. A small but stately house, shiplap in design with a second-story lanai, it sits amid palm and *hala* trees on a broad lawn. The rooms look undisturbed since the days when the Wilcoxes prayed and proselytized. The china rests in the cupboard and an old rocker sits in one room while the canopied bed and cradle still occupy a bedroom. The walls are decorated with photos of Abner and Lucy Wilcox and knickknacks from their era are scattered about the entire house. Guided tours are led Tuesday, Thursday and Saturday between 9 a.m. and 3 p.m. ~ 808-245-3202, fax 808-245-7988.

History buffs also will enjoy touring the **Haraguchi Rice Mill**, which tells the story of Kauai's Chinese and Japanese immigrants. Tours include a visit to the taro fields in a national wildlife refuge with endangered birds. Guided tours held on Thursday mornings, by reservation only. ~ 808-651-3399; e-mail haraguchiricemill@yahoo.com.

The road winds on from Hanalei past single-lane bridges and overgrown villages. The air seems moister and the real world more distant as you pass **Lumahai Beach**, a sandy scimitar where Mitzi

---

BEEN HERE BEFORE?

Does this place seem familiar? Are you on the set of *Jurassic Park*? Isn't that Bali Hai from *South Pacific*? Kauai's beauty and tropical ambience have provided numerous backdrops for blockbuster movies and television shows. The Huleia River still sports the rope swing used in *Raiders of the Lost Ark*, and the Coco Palms Resort, abandoned after Hurricane Iniki in 1992, awaits Elvis' return to *Blue Hawaii*. **Hawaii Movie Tours** will take you to some of these sites while you watch the featured scenes in your "theater on wheels." If you want to take home the scenes, purchase *The Kauai Movie Book* by Chris Cook. ~ Kapaa; 808-822-1192, 800-628-8432, fax 808-822-1608; www.hawaiimovietour.com, e-mail tourguy@hawaiian.net.

Gaynor vowed to "wash that man right out of my hair" in the 1957 movie *South Pacific.* ~ Off Kuhio Highway about five miles west of Hanalei.

Several caves along this route were created eons ago when this entire area was underwater. The first is **Maniniholo Dry Cave**, which geologists claim is a lava tube but which legend insists was created by *Menehune*. The **Waikapalae** and **Waikanaloa Wet Caves** nearby are said to be the work of Pele, the Hawaiian goddess of volcanos, who sought fire in the earth but discovered only water.

A loop trail three-quarters of a mile long winds through the **Limahuli Botanical Garden**. Devoted to conservation of native and Polynesian-introduced plants, the valley is rich in history and contains several archeological sites. A path winds through ancient terraces with Hawaiian taro, into a forest being restored with many endangered Hawaiian plants, and out to ocean and mountain views. Self-guided and guided tours are available; reservations required for guided tours. Closed Monday and Saturday. Admission. ~ 808-826-1053; www.ntbg.org.

The cinematic appears once more at **Kee Beach**, a lovely strand with protecting reef that was used to film some of the torrid love scenes in "The Thorn Birds." It was just east of Kee Beach that the 1960s encampment, dubbed Taylor Camp after actress Elizabeth Taylor's brother, who owned a piece of the land, was located. Now it's over-"occupied" by daytrippers who flock to the beach park. This is the end of the road, beyond which the fabled Kalalau Trail winds along the Na Pali Coast.

Just above Kee Beach at the far west end of the strand rises **Ka Ulu a Paoa Heiau**. This grass-covered terrace was also the site ◄ HIDDEN of a hula platform and ceremonial hall; Hawaii's greatest hula masters once taught here. According to legend, the volcano goddess Pele departed Kauai from here, settling on the Big Island, where she still lives. ~ Follow the path on the top of the stone wall just above Kee Beach. About ten yards past the end of the beach, take the left fork in the path. Another 20 yards and you will be on the platform.

Kee Beach is the end of the road. But what awaits the adventurer lies beyond—the **Na Pali Coast**. With sea cliffs sculpted by wind and rain that seem to reach to the stars, towering over lush mountain valleys—this is hidden Kauai. There are various ways to explore this misty and mystical region. Numerous out-fitters offer catamaran, sailboat or zodiac rafting trips along the coast. Kayakers can cruise the coastline in a group tour or on their own. Helicopters fly deep into the valleys, swooping like birds, brushing up against waterfalls and adze-like cliffs. Or you can hike along an ancient Hawaiian trail 12 miles to Kalalau Valley. (See "Hiking Kalalau" later in this chapter) Anyway you can, do it. This is truly one of the most magnificent spots on earth.

For those wanting just a taste of the coastline, there's a two-mile hike to **Hanakapiai Beach**. It's an arduous trek climbing up some 800 feet, hugging cliffs along a narrow trail, crossing streams, and walking in mud. But the reward at the end is a spectacular valley with a picture-perfect white-sand beach. (The current can be tricky here; use caution when swimming.) Two more miles inland on a rough and often slippery trail are **Hanakapiai Falls**, which feed a large swimming pond.

Tucked into this verdant area is the **Hono o Na Pali Natural Area Reserve**. This was a major taro-growing region in ancient times, with remnants of terraced hills still clearly visible. Wild fruit and coffee plants thrive in the rain-soaked valleys and on surrounding cliffs.

If you're on foot, it's another five and a half miles to **Kalalau Beach** and the once-thriving **Kalalau Valley**. Two miles wide and three miles deep, studded with guava and mango trees, it was not so very long ago, in the early 1900s, that a community populated this area. Now, hikers and kayakers, who need permits to visit, seek out the freshwater pools and pristine beach. For the less adventurous, the valley can be viewed from the Kalalau Lookout at Waimea Canyon. (See Chapter Six).

A note of caution: If you do venture along the coast in a kayak or on foot, remember that this coastline is wild and unpredictable. Even experienced adventurers have needed to be rescued here.

LODGING

HIDDEN ►

Jade Lily Pad is a true adventure experience. You need a four-wheel-drive vehicle to reach this heavenly, two-bedroom cottage in Moloaa that sits right on a stream. Two kayaks await to take you a short way to the lovely white-sand beach of Moloaa Bay. High-quality furnishings, a large, well-equipped kitchen, cathedral ceilings and hardwood floors make for a casual elegance and bright openness; the sound of the surf will lull you to sleep. An outside garden shower and jacuzzi add to the tropical delights, as do front and back lanais. There's even a gas grill for barbecuing. Though the setting is private, other houses are nearby. ~ Moloaa Road, Moloaa; 808-822-5216, fax 808-822-5478; www.rosewoodkauai. com, e-mail rosewood@aloha.net. DELUXE.

Farm life, North Shore Kauai–style, is the experience at **North** ◄ *HIDDEN* **Country Farms**, a small organic family farm with two separate cottages (one of which can accommodate up to six people) that are run like a bed and breakfast. The setting is pleasant and quiet, amid fields and orchards, with mountain views, and owner Lee Roversi strives to use and serve natural products. The cottages are clean, simple and comfortable, with an instant homey feel that families, couples or those planning a longer stay would appreciate. Each sleeps at least four comfortably, with no cleaning fee, making this a real bargain for the $120 per night price. Both have a TV/VCR (one with cable), but plenty of books, puzzles, games and toys will keep you occupied, if that's what you prefer. ~ Kahili Makai Street, Kilauea; 808-828-1513, fax 808-828-0805; www.northcountryfarms.com, e-mail ncfarms@aloha.net. BUDGET TO MODERATE.

The North Shore's premier resting place is a clifftop roost called the **Princeville Resort**. Situated on a point and sporting one of the best views this side of paradise, it's a 252-room complex decorated in European style with a large touch of Hawaiiana. The hotel rises above a white-sand beach and features several restau-

AUTHOR FAVORITE

The **Hanalei Colony Resort** is the only beachfront condominium complex on the North Shore. It's a five-acre lowrise complex with the ocean as your only distraction (no TVs or phones). You can choose one of 48 two-bedroom condos, most with two bathrooms, all with fully equipped kitchens and private lanais. Each unit is stylishly furnished with Hawaiian-style decor. In summer they run a special program for families. The Hanalei Day Spa (treatments, yoga classes), Tunnels Bar and Grill (lunch and dinner) and Napili Art Gallery and Coffee House are recent additions. Check their website for more information. Two-bedroom apartments run $195 to $385. ~ Kuhio Highway, Hanalei; 808-826-6235, 800-628-3004, fax 808-826-9893; www.hcr.com, e-mail aloha@hcr.com.

rants as well as a pool and jacuzzi. Trimmed in gold plating and marble, this is a concierge-and-doorman resort long on service. ~ Princeville; 808-826-9644, 800-325-3589, fax 808-826-1166; www.luxurycollection.com. ULTRA-DELUXE.

Hanalei Bay Resort, spectacularly perched on a hillside overlooking the coastline, provides full vacation facilities. The 22-acre property, which descends to a beach, contains a restaurant, lounge, tennis courts and two spacious swimming pools. The guest rooms are located in three-story buildings dotted around the grounds; some include kitchens. Be forewarned: We have had complaints that the facilities do not warrant the price tag. ~ 5380 Honoiki Road, Princeville; 808-826-6522, 800-827-4427, fax 808-826-6680; www.hanaleibaykauai.com. ULTRA-DELUXE.

HIDDEN ► **Mana Yoga** is a great little vacation hideaway in a rural North Shore area that has stunning mountain views. It's on a five-acre farm, and is the downstairs portion of the Edwards' family home. But not to worry—there's plenty of privacy, with your own lanai, entrance, kitchen and bath. It has two bedrooms and easily sleeps four people. Yoga classes, private and public, are provided by the owner, who is also a masseuse. Three-night minimum stay. ~ Ahonui Place, Princeville; 808-826-9230; www.manayoga.com, e-mail michaelle@manayoga.com. MODERATE.

The North Shore is short on bargains, but at **Hanalei Inn** there are eight studio units (five with kitchens). They are attractive rooms with outdoor barbecues, hardwood floors, local art on the walls and fresh flowers. There's also a tiny budget-priced room for unfinicky backpackers looking for a place to crash for the night; it barely sleeps two. This intimate inn sits amid a garden 100 yards from the beach. ~ 55468 Kuhio Highway, Hanalei; 808-826-9333; www.hanaleiinn.com. BUDGET TO MODERATE.

At the YMCA's beachfront **Camp Naue,** there are dormitory accommodations in bunkhouses. Bring your own bedding. There is also an adjacent area for camping. Reservations can only be made for large groups; otherwise, it is on a first-come, first-served basis. Calls will only be returned if they're local or if the campsite can call collect. ~ The camp is located off Kuhio Highway, Haena; 808-246-9090. BUDGET.

CONDOS   In the Princeville Resort complex, a few miles east of Hanalei, are several condos: **The Cliffs at Princeville** has condominiums

from $200. ~ 808-826-6219, 800-367-8024, fax 808-826-2140.
The **Pali Ke Kua** offers one- and two-bedroom apartments for
$131 and up. ~ 808-826-9394, fax 808-826-4159. **Pahio at Kaeo
Kai** has studios from $108. These are modern units with wet
bars, but no kitchens. There is a swimming pool on each property. ~ 808-826-6549, fax 808-826-6715.

Although the Princeville Resort area is awash with condos,
they're generally pretty bland. **Sealodge**, tucked away on a quiet
side street, is the exception. The privacy and setting make these
condos distinct. One-bedroom units are $120 per night, with a
$75 one-time cleaning fee. Two-bedroom apartments run $145,
with a $85 one-time cleaning fee. A pool, barbecue area, and
plenty of parking round out the special features. ~ Princeville;
808-826-6751.

For information on other condominiums, as well as cottages
and houses, and to learn where the best deals are available during
any particular time, check with **Hanalei Vacations**. You can also
browse (virtually) through every one of their properties at their
website. ~ P.O. Box 223206, Princeville, HI 96722; 808-826-
7288, 800-487-9833, fax 808-826-7280; www.800hawaii.com,
e-mail rentals@aloha.net.

DINING

If you'd simply like a pizza, the little town of Kilauea offers up **Pau
Hana Pizza**, a combination kitchen and bakery that cooks up some
delicious pies. ~ Kong Lung Center, Lighthouse Road, Kilauea;
808-828-2020. MODERATE TO DELUXE.

In the Princeville market you'll find the informal **Paradise Bar
& Grill**. It serves sandwiches at lunch and steak and seafood

AUTHOR FAVORITE

The romantic **Lighthouse Bistro**, in the historic Kong Lung
Center in Kilauea, offers bistro-style fare with European and Asian influences
in an open-air setting. This translates into shrimp parmesan; blackened,
broiled or sautéed fresh fish with various sauces, like Thai mango sesame;
chicken and steak. Lunch is sandwiches, pasta and salads. Full bar and
good wine list. ~ Kong Lung Center, Lighthouse Road, Kilauea; 808-828-
0480, fax 808-828-0481; www.lighthousebistro.com, e-mail finedining@
lighthousebistro.com. MODERATE TO DELUXE.

every evening. ~ Princeville Market, Princeville; 808-826-1775. MODERATE.

The prize for prettiest dining room on the North Shore goes to **La Cascata**, the Princeville Resort's signature restaurant. That is not even taking into account the edenic views of the Na Pali Coast or the soft breezes wafting in from the ocean. All we're counting is the tilework, the murals and the Mediterranean pastel colors. The bill of fare is mostly Italian-influenced Mediterranean. Dinner only. ~ Princeville; 808-826-9644, fax 808-826-1166. ULTRA-DELUXE.

Any restaurant critic in the world would immediately award five stars to the view at **Bali Hai Restaurant**. Perched on a deck high above Hanalei Bay, it overlooks a broad sweep of mountains and sea. The menu features classic island fare, ranging from fresh catches to steak to pasta. Reservations are recommended. ~ Hanalei Bay Resort, 5380 Honoiki Road, Princeville; 808-826-6522, fax 808-826-6680. MODERATE TO ULTRA-DELUXE.

Another winner in the Princeville community is newcomer **Sabella's**, of the California Sabella clan. Euro-Asian entrées emphasize local seafood with a twist; the knockout apple brandy lobster is a deservedly popular choice. Tucked into the Pali Ke Kua condominiums, the dining room isn't especially noteworthy, but the live dinner music—light jazz or classical guitar—adds greatly to the experience. Dinner only. Closed Monday. ~ 5300 Haku Road, Princeville; 808-826-6225. DELUXE TO ULTRA-DELUXE.

AIRBORNE ATHLETES

Seabirds are amazing creatures, flying thousands of miles to their seasonal feeding and nesting grounds and even spending years at sea. Boobies, Laysan albatrosses, wedgetail and Newell's shearwaters, tropic birds and frigate birds are commonly seen on Kauai's north and east shores, soaring on the currents and dipping into the sea to pluck out fish or squid. Albatrosses often nest on the golf courses and expansive lawns at Princeville and elsewhere from February through June, and their elaborate courtship rituals are an entertaining sight. With wing spans reaching five feet or more, these big, beautiful birds are awkward on land, giving rise to their nickname "goonie birds," but very graceful in flight. The Kilauea National Wildlife Refuge is the best place to see all these seabirds, as well as Hawaii's state bird, the endangered nene goose.

As beautiful and popular as Hanalei happens to be, the area possesses only a few low-priced facilities. If you've ever tried to find a place to stay here, you know how tight things can be. And the budget restaurant situation is not a whole lot better.

The **Hanalei Wake-Up Café** is a low-key eatery with omelettes and other egg dishes in the morning. There's a small dining room with a deck. Breakfast only. ~ Aku Road, Hanalei; 808-826-5551. BUDGET.

Postcards is a fun, gourmet semi-vegetarian restaurant tucked into an old plantation cottage on the outskirts of town. The dinner menu features lots of organic produce and is short and simple: fresh fish specials, pasta with veggies or seafood, Cajun crusted ahi with chipotle sauce, phyllo wraps with veggies and taro fritters. Smoothies, juices and salads, too. Service can be sketchy, but then, it *is* Hanalei. Dinner only. ~ 5075-A Kuhio Highway, Hanalei; 808-826-1191. MODERATE TO DELUXE.

Hanalei Taro & Juice Co., owned by a couple who farm taro   ◄ HIDDEN
just down the road, lays to rest the notion that taro equals sour poi. The roadside cart, with a couple of covered picnic tables out front, sells fruit smoothies, sandwiches and dessert treats, all made from the wholesome, starchy vegetable that was a mainstay of Hawaiian diets. They bake their own taro *mochi*. Lunch only. Closed Sunday. ~ 5-5070 Kuhio Highway, Hanalei; 808-826-1059. BUDGET.

The atmosphere of **Hanalei Gourmet** is laidback and local. To fit this feeling, the menu is solid but unpretentious. There are numerous salads, including a chicken salad boat and an ahi pasta salad. The sandwich selection features a shrimp sandwich and a special concoction with eggplant and red peppers. Following this seafood and vegetable theme are the dinner entrées, which change nightly. The bar scene is lively, there's live entertainment at least three nights a week and the kitchen prepares good food at favorable prices. ~ 5-5161 Kuhio Highway, Hanalei; 808-826-2524, fax 808-826-6007; www.hanaleigourmet.com. MODERATE TO DELUXE.

Hanalei Mixed Plate, a takeout stand, serves everything from buffalo burgers to veggie burgers as well as stir-fry, tofu, ginger chicken and *kalua* pig. ~ Located next to Ching Young Village, Kuhio Highway, Hanalei; 808-826-7888. BUDGET.

There are several luncheonettes, including **Village Snack and Bakery**, which serves standard lunch fare. ~ Ching Young Village, Kuhio Highway, Hanalei; 808-826-6841. BUDGET.

Sushi Blues Grill, a Hanalei hotspot, combines industrial decor with live entertainment every night. The menu at this second-floor restaurant/club includes sizzling seafood stir-fry, coconut shrimp, linguine and scallops, and of course a host of sushi selections. Dinner only. ~ Ching Young Village, Kuhio Highway, Hanalei; 808-826-9701; www.sushiandblues.com. DELUXE.

Hearty Mexican meals like fajitas and enchiladas, as well as quiche, veggie burgers, salads, wraps and more, are prepared well at the **Polynesia Café**. Coffee drinks, ice cream smoothies and yummy baked goods baked on-site add to the appeal, along with a cheerful staff. ~ Ching Young Village, Kuhio Highway, Hanalei; 808-826-1999. BUDGET TO MODERATE.

HIDDEN ▶

Forget all this nonsense about good health and low cholesterol, step up to the window at **Bubba's** and order a hot dog or a "Big Bubba" (a half-pound hamburger with three patties). ~ 5-5161 Kuhio Highway, Hanalei; 808-826-7839. BUDGET.

Mount Kawaikini, at 5243 feet, is Kauai's tallest peak.

On the road since 1978 was the **Tropical Taco**, a van cum taco stand that is now dispensing its mouth-watering fish tacos from a permanent location. Dine inside or on the deck, where you can do some serious people watching. Closed Sunday. ~ 5088 Kuhio Highway, Hanalei; 808-635-8226. BUDGET.

HIDDEN ▶

The **Tahiti Nui Restaurant** is a refreshing alternative to the commercialized luaus of big hotels—this is a family affair. If you miss it, try offerings from the menu, which features steak, fresh fish, calamari, scampi, pasta and chicken dishes. And check out the bamboo-fringed lanai, or the lounge decorated with Pacific Island carvings and overhung with a thatch canopy. ~ 5-5134 Kuhio Highway, in the center of Hanalei; 808-826-6277. MODERATE.

With woven *lauhala* walls, bamboo bar and outrigger canoe, **Zelo's Beach House** certainly looks the part. It's airy and informal—a great spot to relax. When you're ready to order, you'll find an eclectic menu. The central focus is pasta: linguine and clams with toasted pine nuts, Cajun chicken pasta and an all-you-can-eat spaghetti dish. But they also have steak, baby back ribs and fresh seafood. ~ 5-5256 Kuhio Highway, Hanalei; 808-

826-9700; www.sushiandblues.com, e-mail sushi.blues@verizon. net. DELUXE.

From the porthole windows to the Japanese fishing balls, the **Hanalei Dolphin Restaurant and Fish Market** presents an interesting aquatic decor. Built smack on the bank of the Hanalei River, this eatery offers a turf-and-surf menu that includes fresh fish, shrimp dishes and New York steak. The restaurant, which is highly recommended, does not take reservations. The fish market at the back of the restaurant offers many of the same fish found on the menu to take home and cook yourself. ~ 5-5016 Kuhio Highway, Hanalei; 808-826-6113, fax 808-826-6699. ULTRA-DELUXE.

The best place on the North Shore is **Foodland**. It's very well **GROCERIES** stocked and open from 6 a.m. to 11 p.m. ~ Princeville Shopping Center, off Kuhio Highway; 808-826-9880.

Hanalei supports one large grocery store on Kuhio Highway, **Big Save Market**. ~ Ching Young Village, Hanalei; 808-826-6652.

Hanalei Health Foods carries organic and health-related items. Open 9 a.m. to 6 p.m. ~ Ching Young Village, Kuhio Highway, Hanalei; 808-826-6990.

Papaya's Natural Food offers a broad selection of organic foods, health supplements and produce. Open 9 a.m. to 8 p.m. Monday to Saturday, 9 a.m. to 3 p.m. Sunday. ~ Hanalei Center, Kuhio Highway, Hanalei; 808-826-0089.

Healthy Hut Natural Foods Store offers the widest choice of wholesome groceries (and the best prices) on the North Shore, with an excellent produce section supplied by local farmers. Open 8:30 a.m. to 9 p.m. ~ 4270 Kilauea Lighthouse Road, Kilauea; 808-828-6626.

Banana Joe's Tropical Fruit Farm has ripe, delicious fruits as well as smoothies and dried fruit. ~ 5-2719 Kuhio Highway, Kilauea; 808-828-1092.

Kong Lung Co. carries a marvelous assortment of Pacific and **SHOPPING** Asian treasures in addition to a good selection of Hawaiian books. Don't miss this one. ~ Kilauea Lighthouse Road, Kilauea; 808-828-1822.

Princeville is the closest you will come to a shopping center on the North Shore. The **Princeville Shopping Center** features a cluster of shops that represents the area's prime spot for window browsers. Kids define heaven as **Magic Dragon Toyland and Supply,** (808-826-9144), which specializes in unique toys and games and a variety of fine art supplies—fun for the whole family. ~ Off Kuhio Highway, Princeville; 808-826-3040.

Hanalei's **Ching Young Village** is a small shopping mall that contains a variety store, clothing shops and several other outlets. There's a **Hot Rocket** here for beachwear (808-826-7776) and **On the Road to Hanalei** (808-826-7360) for tapa cloth, woodcarvings, jewelry, quilts and other locally and globally fashioned craft items. **Pedal 'N Paddle** (808-826-9069) provides any equipment you may need for a variety of outdoor activities, from kayaking to camping. The shopping center also has **Blue Kauai Tattoos** (808-826-0114), for obvious reasons. ~ Kuhio Highway, Hanalei; www.chingyoungvillage.com.

Across the street you'll find the **Hanalei Center**, made up of seven buildings, six of which are restored historical structures including the Old Hanalei School Building. There are shops, restaurants, a health clinic, a yoga studio, and more. ~ Kuhio Highway, Hanalei; 808-826-7677; www.hanaleicenter.com.

Ola's showcases the work of over 100 craftspeople from Hawaii and the mainland. ~ Off Kuhio Highway, next to Hanalei Dolphin Restaurant, Hanalei; 808-826-6937.

Kai Kane is an attractively decorated shop featuring fashions of their own design. It's a great place to shop for alohawear. ~ 5-5088 Kuhio Highway, Hanalei; 808-826-5594.

Yellowfish Trading Company has a marvelous collection of antiques and Hawaiian collectibles. ~ Hanalei Center, Kuhio Highway, Hanalei; 808-826-1227.

You can't get away with visiting the Garden Isle and only bringing back pictures of the tropical vegetation. **Kauai Exotix** is on a local farm and cuts flowers the same day you order them, shipping the hand-picked blossoms within 48 hours. The arrangements are classic Kauai. Closed Saturday. ~ 5-5949 Kuhio Highway, Hanalei; 808-826-7133; www.besttropicals.com.

If you're interested in homemade goods, you'll find a few more stores in other small towns along the North Shore.

NIGHTLIFE In all the world there are few entertainment spots with a view as grand as the Princeville Resort's **Living Room Bar.** Overlooking Hanalei Bay, it also features a singer and pianist playing standards and contemporary music nightly. ~ Princeville Resort, Princeville; 808-826-9644.

At nearby Hanalei Bay Resort's **Happy Talk Lounge**, you can enjoy the views of Hanalei Bay and relax with contemporary Hawaiian music daily and jazz on Sunday. ~ 5380 Honoiki Road, Princeville; 808-826-6522.

Amelia's, located out at the Princeville Airport, has live music Wednesday, Friday and Saturday nights. ~ 5-3541 Kuhio Highway, Princeville; 808-826-9561.

For a tropical drink amid a tropical setting, place your order at **Tahiti Nui Restaurant**, which has live entertainment nightly as well as karaoke and a satellite feed. ~ 5-5134 Kuhio Highway, Hanalei; 808-826-6277. Or try the **Hanalei Dolphin Restaurant**. ~ Kuhio Highway, Hanalei; 808-826-6113.

The **Hanalei Gourmet** has live performances by local artists Wednesday and Friday evenings and Sunday afternoons. Call to see if any extra shows have been scheduled. ~ 5-5161 Kuhio Highway, Hanalei; 808-826-2524.

There's music seven nights a week at the **Sushi Blues Grill**. One night there's karaoke, another night there's dancing, and the rest of the time they have jazz and blues. Occasional cover on Friday and Saturday. ~ Ching Young Village, Hanalei; 808-826-9701.

MOLOAA BEACH 🏊 🐟 ⚓ Nestled in Moloaa Bay, a small inlet surrounded by rolling hills, Moloaa Beach is relatively secluded, though there are homes nearby. A meandering stream di-

BEACHES & PARKS

ADVENTURE AFOOT AND AFLOAT

Combine an education about the history, flora and fauna of Kauai's interior with a hiking/kayaking adventure. **Princeville Ranch Hike & Kayak Adventures** offers a number of options. Tours include the "waterfall excursion" (which takes you first to a spectacular 360° view of ocean and mountain and then on to a five tiered waterfall), the "Jungle Waterfall Kayak Adventure" (a combination kayaking/hiking/inner-tubing experience), and the "Zip 'n' Dip Expedition" (which includes jumping with a zipline from a suspension bridge into a very deep swimming hole). There is also a range of private excursions available, with length and destinations tailored to your interests. Children over five are welcome (over 12 for the "Zip 'n' Dip). ~ Princeville; 808-826-7669, 888-955-7669; www.kauai-hiking.com.

vides the beach into two strands. You'll see a coral reef shadowing the shore. There is good beachcombing at the west end of the strand. Swim with caution. Snorkeling and fishing are good, as is lobster diving. There are no facilities. ~ Take Koolau Road where it branches off Kuhio Highway near the 16-mile marker. Go one and three tenths miles, then turn onto Moloaa Road. Follow this to the end. All roads are paved.

HIDDEN ► **LARSEN'S BEACH** 🏖️ 🦟 🛶 This narrow, sandy beach extends seemingly forever through a very secluded area. Rolling hills, covered with small trees and scrub, rim the strand. Glass fishing balls and other collectibles wash ashore regularly, making this a prime beachcombing spot. A protecting reef provides excellent swimming and snorkeling. It is also very popular for seaweed gathering and throw-netting. There are also good fishing spots. Surf is sometimes dangerous here, so exercise caution. There are no facilities. ~ It's hard to get to, but more than worth it when you arrive. Take Koolau Road as it branches off Kuhio Highway near the 16-mile marker. Go two and a half miles to a cane road on the right, which switches back in the opposite direction. Get on this road, then take an immediate left onto another dirt road (lined on either side with barbed wire). Don't let the fences scare you—this is a public right of way. Follow it a mile to the end. Hike through the gate and down the road. This leads a half-mile down to the beach, which is on your left. (There is also an access road from Koolau Road that is located one and a fifth miles from the intersection of Koolau Road and Kuhio Highway.)

HIDDEN ► **KAHILI BEACH** 🏖️ 🛶 🛶 Tucked away in Kilauea Bay, this beach is bordered by tree-covered hills and a rock quarry. It's a lovely, semi-secluded spot with a lagoon that represents one of Hawaii's most pristine estuaries. Kahili is also a prime beach-

FROM THE MOUNTAINS TO THE SEA

Designated one of fourteen American Heritage Rivers, the **Hanalei River** receives federal monies to help preserve the 15-mile waterway. The river is one of the largest in the state, and considered among the most pristine in Hawaii. Together with its estuarine bay it is considered "outstanding in Hawaii and in the Pacific for the abundance and quality of natural, cultural and scenic resources."

combing spot. For a spectacular view of windswept cliffs, follow the short quarry road that climbs steeply from the parking area. Swimming is good when the sea is calm. The favorite surf break is "Rock Quarry," located offshore from the stream. Fishing is rewarding, and the reef at the east end of the beach is also a favored net-throwing spot. There are no facilities. ~ From Kuhio Highway, about two miles south of Kilauea town, head east on Wailapa Road for about three-quarters of a mile. Look to your left for the white post that marks the dirt beach access road. Take this road about one mile to the beach; it's rough, but passable, although it can be very muddy during wet weather.

▲ Unofficial camping. *Note:* The U.S. Fish and Wildlife Service recently acquired ownership of the wetlands around the Kilauea River; an enforcement officer patrols the entire beach for campers and illegal fishing activities.

KAUAPEA BEACH OR SECRET BEACH 🏊 Inaccessibility means ◄ HIDDEN
seclusion along this hidden strand. Ideal for birdwatching, swimming and unofficial camping, this half-mile-long beach lies just below Kilauea Lighthouse. Very wide and extremely beautiful, it is popular with nudists and adventurers alike. No facilities spoil this hideaway. Note that this place is notorious for car break-ins, so leave nothing in your vehicle. ~ The beach can be seen from Kilauea Lighthouse, but getting there is another matter. From Kuhio Highway just west of Kilauea, turn onto Kalihiwai Road (be sure to get on the eastern section of Kalihiwai Road, near Banana Joe's Tropical Fruit Farm). The road immediately curves to the left; go right onto the first dirt road; proceed three-tenths mile to a parking lot; from here follow the fenceline down into a ravine to Kauapea Beach.

▲ Unofficial camping.

KALIHIWAI BEACH 🏄 🛶 Bounded by sheer rock wall on one ◄ HIDDEN
side and a rolling green hill on the other, this semi-secluded beach is crowded with ironwood trees. Behind the ironwoods, the Kalihiwai River has created a large, shallow lagoon across which stretches the skeleton of a bridge, a last grim relic of the devastating 1946 tidal wave. "Kalihiwai" is one of the top expert winter surfing breaks on the North Shore. It's also popular for bodysurfing. Swimmers should exercise caution. Bonefish and threadfin are the most common catches. This is also a great spot

for surround-netting of akule. No facilities. ~ Take heed—there are two Kalihiwai Roads branching off Kuhio Highway between Kilauea and Kalihiwai. (The washed-out bridge once connected them.) Take the one closest to Lihue. This paved road leads a short distance directly to the beach.

ANINI COUNTY BEACH PARK Here a grass-covered park fronts a narrow ribbon of sand, while a protecting reef parallels the beach 200 yards offshore. I thought this an ideal place for kids: The ocean is glass smooth and the beachcombing is excellent. As a result, it's very popular and some-times crowded. Swimming is excellent and very safe. Snorkeling is also topnotch. Surfers' note: There are winter breaks on very shallow reef (left and right slides). This is also a very popular windsurfing site. The beach has the only boat launch on this side of the island, and anglers take advantage of it to catch bonefish, *papio* and *ulua*. People also torchfish, throw-net, spear octopus and harvest seaweed at Anini. Facilities include a picnic area, rest-rooms and a shower. ~ Between Kilauea and Hanalei, turn off Kuhio Highway onto the second Kalihiwai Road (the one farthest from Lihue, on the Hanalei side of the Kalihiwai River). Then take Anini Road to the beach.

▲ Pleasant, but lacks privacy. A county permit is required. Tent camping only.

PRINCEVILLE BEACHES There are three beaches directly below the plateau on which the Princeville Resort com-plex rests. The most popular is **Puu Poa Beach**, a long and wide strand located next to the Princeville Resort and reached through the hotel. It offers good swimming and easy access to the hotel's (expensive) facilities but is often crowded. The other two are pocket beaches. **Sealodge Beach**, reached via a right of way behind Unit A of the Sealodge condominium, is a white-sand beach back-dropped by cliffs. Offshore is a surfing break called "Little Grass Shacks." **Hideaways** consists of two mirror-image beaches, one below Pali Ke Kua condos and the other below Puu Poa condos. They are both good spots for swimming and snorkeling and feature a well-known surf break. ~ To reach Sealodge Beach, turn right from Kuhio Highway onto Kahaku Road and into the Princeville complex. Turn right on Kamehameha Road and follow it to the Sealodge condos. Access to Hideaways is located between Puu Poa condos and the Princeville Resort near the end of Kahaku Road.

Hidden Beaches
and Cane Roads

Strung like jewels along Kauai's shore lies a series of hidden beaches that are known only to local people. Among these are some of the loveliest beaches on the entire island, removed from tourist areas, uninhabited, some lacking so much as a footprint. For the wanderer, they are an uncharted domain, and to the camper they can be a secret retreat.

Over a dozen of these hideaways are described in the accompanying sections on Kauai's beaches. Some are located right alongside public thoroughfares; others require long hikes down little-used footpaths. Most can be reached only by private cane roads that were once owned by the plantations. Some still are, but many others are now privately owned. All require a permit and a liability waiver.

Local people use them with the greatest courtesy and discretion, realizing that they are treading on private property. Most important, they respect the awesome beauty of these areas by leaving the beaches as they found them. As one Hawaiian explained to me, the golden rule for visitors is this: "If you want to go native, act like one!"

HANALEI BAY BEACHES ⚓ ⛵ 🏄 🏊 ⛱ 🎣 A sandy, horseshoe-shaped strip of sand curves the full length of Hanalei Bay. Along this two-mile strand there are four beach parks. **Black Pot Beach Park**, a local gathering place, lies at the eastern end of the bay and is bounded on one side by the Hanalei River and on the other by a 300-foot-long pier (Hanalei Landing). With showers and lifeguard facilities available to beachgoers, it is very popular with watersport enthusiasts of all stripes—swimmers, surfers, bodysurfers, windsurfers, kayakers and anglers. It is located at the eastern end of Weke Road. **Hanalei Pavilion Beach Park**, located along Weke Road between Pilikoa and Aku roads, is a favorite picnic spot. **Waioli Beach Park**, a small facility set in an ironwood grove, is situated near the center of the half-moon-shaped bay. It can be reached from the end of either Hee Road or Amaama Road. Black Pot Beach Park, Hanalei Pavilion Beach Park and Waioli Beach Park all have lifeguards on duty. **Waikoko Beach** is a slender strand paralleled by a shallow reef. Popular with families who come here to swim and snorkel, it lies along Kuhio Highway on the western side of the bay.

There are three major surf breaks here. "Impossible" breaks require a long paddle out from the pier; right slide. "Pine Tree" breaks, off Waioli Beach Park, are in the center of the bay. "Waikoko" breaks are on the shallow reef along the western side of the bay. All are winter breaks. Surfing in Hanalei is serious business, so be careful. Early morning and late afternoon are the best surfing times. The bay is also a popular bodysurfing area. Fish for squirrelfish, rockfish, red bigeye, *oama*, big-eyed scad, *ulua* and *papio*. There is crabbing off Hanalei Landing pier. All beaches

BEACHGOERS TAKE NOTE

All along the North Shore, the numerous side roads that led from Kuhio Highway to hidden beaches have been fenced off and closed with alarming regularity, greatly restricting vehicular access to the coastline. Things have changed on Kauai, and it's unwise to travel down any private or unmarked roads. **Anini Road**, however, snakes along the shorelines for several miles on the east side of Anini County Beach Park, offering a number of pedestrian accessways leading to more secluded coves. Just make sure you're not parking, or walking, in someone's driveway.

have picnic areas, restrooms and marvelous ocean and mountain views. ~ Located in Hanalei just off Kuhio Highway.

▲ Tent camping permitted on weekends and holidays at Black Pot Beach Park only. A county permit is required.

LUMAHAI BEACH ⌐ Many people know this strand as the Nurse's Beach in the movie *South Pacific*. Snuggled in a cove and surrounded by lush green hills, Lumahai extends for three-fourths of a mile. With white sand against black lava, it's a particularly pretty spot. Swim only when the sea is very calm and exercise extreme caution. During the winter months, it's one of the most treacherous spots on the island. You can try for *papio* and *ulua*. There are no facilities. ~ Watch for a vista point near the 5-mile marker on Kuhio Highway. From here, a crooked footpath leads to the beach. The beach can more easily be accessed about a mile down the road, at the Lumahai River bridge. Do not swim at the river mouth because of strong currents.

TUNNELS (MAKUA) BEACH AND OTHER HAENA BEACHES ⌐ There are beach access roads all along Kuhio Highway near Haena. Taking any of these dirt roads will shortly lead you to secluded strands. Most popular of all is "Tunnels," a sandy beach with a great offshore reef. According to divers, the name "Tunnels" derives from the underwater arches and tunnels in the reef; but surfers claim it's from the perfect tunnel-shaped waves. Windsurfers consider this one of the best sites on Kauai. You'll also find swimmers, snorkelers, sunbathers and beach-combers here. **Kepuhi Point** is one of the best fishing spots on the North Shore; Tunnels attracts fishermen with nets and poles. There are no facilities here. ~ These beaches are located along Kuhio Highway near Wainiha Bay and Kepuhi Point. Tunnels is two-fifths mile east of Maniniholo Dry Cave.

HAENA BEACH PARK ⌐ This grassy park, bounded by the sea on one side and a sheer lava cliff on the other, is right across the street from Maniniholo Dry Cave. It's very popular with young folks and provides good opportunities for beachcombing. There are very strong ocean currents here, which make swimming impossible in winter but fine in summer. Surfing "Cannon's" breaks on a shallow reef in front of Maniniholo Dry Cave is for experts only (right slide). There is excellent surfcasting and torch-fishing for red bigeye, squirrelfish, *papio* and *ulua*. Cardinal fish are sometimes caught on the reef at low tide during the full moon. A picnic area, restrooms and a shower are the facilities here. ~ Located on Kuhio Highway five miles west of Hanalei.

▲ It's an attractive campground, sometimes crowded, open to both tents and trailers, and requiring a county permit. There is also camping nearby at the YMCA's **Camp Naue** (808-246-9090).

HAENA STATE PARK AND KEE BEACH 🏊 🚣 🎣 🚻 💧 At the end of Kuhio Highway, where the Kalalau trail begins, 65.7-acre Haena State Park encompasses a long stretch of white sand, with Kee Beach at its western end. This reef-shrouded beach is one of the most popular on the North Shore. When the surf is gentle, swimming is superb. At such times, this is one of the best snorkeling beaches for beginners, with its protective coral reef brilliantly colored and crowded with tropical fish. In addition, there are 4000-year-old sea caves to explore. The Haena shoreline is also one of the island's best shelling beaches. Surfing is good at "Cannons" and "Bobo's" breaks. This is also a prime windsurfing area. There is good fishing along the reef. There are restrooms and showers. ~ Located at the end of Kuhio Highway.

Recommended Reading

Beaches of Kauai and Niihau, by John Clark. University of Hawaii Press, 1990.

Hawaii, by James Michener. Fawcett Books, 1986.

Hawaiian Antiquities, by David Malo. Bishop Museum Press, 1987.

Hawaiian Hiking Trails, by Craig Chisholm. Fernglen Press, 1999.

The Kauai Movie Book, by Chris Cook. Mutual Publishing Company, 1996.

Kauai Trailblazer: Where to Hike, Snorkel, Bike, Paddle, Surf, by Jerry Sprout. Diamond Valley Company, 2004.

The Legends and Myths of Hawaii, by David Kalakaua. Mutual Publishing Company, 1990.

Shoal of Time, by Gavan Daws. University Press of Hawaii, 1974.

Index

Lodging Index

Dining Index

HIDDEN GUIDES

Adventure travel or a relaxing vacation?—"Hidden" guidebooks are the only travel books in the business to provide detailed information on both. Aimed at environmentally aware travelers, our motto is "Where Vacations Meet Adventures." These books combine details on unique hotels, restaurants and sightseeing with information on camping, sports and hiking for the outdoor enthusiast.

PARADISE FAMILY GUIDES

Ideal for families traveling with kids of any age—toddlers to teenagers—Paradise Family Guides offer a blend of travel information unlike any other guides to the Hawaiian islands. With vacation ideas and tropical adventures that are sure to satisfy both action-hungry youngsters and relaxation-seeking parents, these guides meet the specific needs of each and every family member.

HIDDEN GUIDEBOOKS

____ Hidden Arizona, $16.95
____ Hidden Bahamas, $14.95
____ Hidden Baja, $14.95
____ Hidden Belize, $15.95
____ Hidden Big Island of Hawaii, $13.95
____ Hidden Boston & Cape Cod, $14.95
____ Hidden British Columbia, $18.95
____ Hidden Cancún & the Yucatán, $16.95
____ Hidden Carolinas, $17.95
____ Hidden Coast of California, $18.95
____ Hidden Colorado, $15.95
____ Hidden Disneyland, $13.95
____ Hidden Florida, $18.95
____ Hidden Florida Keys & Everglades, $13.95
____ Hidden Georgia, $16.95
____ Hidden Guatemala, $16.95
____ Hidden Hawaii, $18.95
____ Hidden Idaho, $14.95
____ Hidden Kauai, $13.95
____ Hidden Los Angeles, $14.95
____ Hidden Maine, $15.95
____ Hidden Maui, $13.95
____ Hidden Miami, $14.95
____ Hidden Montana, $15.95
____ Hidden New England, $18.95
____ Hidden New Mexico, $15.95
____ Hidden New Orleans, $14.95
____ Hidden Oahu, $13.95
____ Hidden Oregon, $15.95
____ Hidden Pacific Northwest, $18.95
____ Hidden San Diego, $14.95
____ Hidden Salt Lake City, $14.95
____ Hidden San Francisco & Northern California, $18.95
____ Hidden Seattle, $13.95
____ Hidden Southern California, $18.95
____ Hidden Southwest, $19.95
____ Hidden Tahiti, $17.95
____ Hidden Tennessee, $16.95
____ Hidden Utah, $16.95
____ Hidden Walt Disney World, $13.95
____ Hidden Washington, $15.95
____ Hidden Wine Country, $13.95
____ Hidden Wyoming, $15.95

PARADISE FAMILY GUIDES

____ Paradise Family Guides: Kaua'i, $17.95
____ Paradise Family Guides: Maui, $17.95
____ Paradise Family Guides: Big Island of Hawai'i, $17.95

Mark the book(s) you're ordering and enter the total cost here ⇨ [   ]

California residents add 8.75% sales tax here ⇨ [   ]

Shipping, check box for your preferred method and enter cost here ⇨ [   ]

❑ Book Rate   FREE! FREE! FREE!

❑ Priority Mail/UPS Ground   cost of postage

❑ UPS Overnight or 2-Day Air   cost of postage

Billing, enter total amount due here and check method of payment ⇨ [   ]

❑ Check   ❑ Money Order

❑ VISA/MasterCard _____Exp. Date_____

Name _____Phone_____

Address _____

City_____ State _____ Zip_____

Money-back guarantee on direct orders placed through Ulysses Press.

ABOUT THE AUTHOR

RAY RIEGERT is the author of eight travel books, including *Hidden San Francisco & Northern California*. His most popular work, *Hidden Hawaii*, won the coveted Lowell Thomas Travel Journalism Award for Best Guidebook as well as a similar award from the Hawaii Visitors Bureau. In addition to his role as publisher of Ulysses Press, he has written for the *Chicago Tribune, Saturday Evening Post, San Francisco Examiner & Chronicle* and *Travel & Leisure*. A member of the Society of American Travel Writers, he lives in the San Francisco Bay area with his wife, co-publisher Leslie Henriques, and their son Keith and daughter Alice.

ABOUT THE UPDATE AUTHOR

JOAN CONROW is a freelance journalist who writes frequently about Hawaii and its natural world. Her work appears regularly in national and regional magazines, and on Reuters news service, and she has contributed to several Hawaii guidebooks. She has lived on Kauai since 1987.